At David C Cook, we equip the local church around the corner and around the globe to make disciples. Come see how we are working together—go to **www.davidccook.com**. Thank you!

transforming lives together

What people are saying about …

THE WURMBRANDS' STORY

When I broke my neck in 1967 and became confined to a wheelchair, little did I realize that I would soon be reading a just-released Christian book that would impact my views about suffering for Christ. The book was *Tortured for Christ*, and my college-bound friends insisted I read it. They said it would help me come to grips with my own struggles to trust God in the midst of deep suffering and loss.

Up until the diving accident that caused my paralysis, I assumed God wanted His children to live happy, healthy lives that were free from trouble. But in reading *Tortured for Christ*, I realized that God's purpose in redeeming us is not to make life a soft bed of roses but to make us more like Jesus. Loss, grief, pain, and suffering are His choicest tools in accomplishing that goal.

Now, having lived fifty years in a wheelchair as a quadriplegic—as many years as *Tortured for Christ* has been used of the Lord—I can truthfully say that deep affliction in a Christian's life is what provides the most powerful platform for the success of the gospel. That is why I thank God for this remarkable book and its timeless message.

Joni Eareckson Tada, founder, Joni and Friends

I praise the Lord for the constant mercy and grace demonstrated through the lives of Richard and Sabina Wurmbrand. Their message greatly challenged my own heart. In the early years of Operation Mobilization, we carried many of Richard's books and prayed they would be greatly used by God, especially Sabina's book, *The Pastor's Wife*, as we felt a need to have more books appealing to women. We also praise God for *Tortured for Christ*, of which we distributed thousands of copies around the world.

In all the ways God used him, Richard continued to walk humbly and meekly, always ready to learn new lessons at Jesus's feet. Richard's testimony cut to the heart of sleeping Christians unaware of the suffering of other Christians. To this day, his testimony and legacy through The Voice of the Martyrs are still opening the eyes of Christians to their persecuted family. I believe God gave Richard a vision for the far reaches of the world, and that vision has not changed in fifty years.

George Verwer, founder, Operation Mobilization

Our dear Brother Wurmbrand hit us right in the heart with his example. Because of him, YWAM started smuggling Bibles into countries behind the Iron Curtain. It has been a great thing to partner with VOM in the kingdom, and we want to keep this ministry close to our hearts because the unity we are seeing is a wonderful love thing God has put within His family. Our focus at YWAM is keeping the Word of the Lord clearly before us, and we have been inspired by leaders such as Richard and Sabina.

Loren Cunningham, founder, Youth With A Mission (YWAM)

As a twelve-year-old pastor's daughter, my heart moved with pity as I read *Tortured for Christ*. I remember wondering if I would have Wurmbrand-type courage to endure hardship for the sake of the gospel. Although I do have my own captivity story, I have never shared in the sufferings of Christ as the Wurmbrands did through imprisonment and torture, stripped of all earthly possessions. All these years later, I am reminded there is no pity in the heart of the Enemy of our souls. Now as then, he stalks around like a wild beast seeking someone to devour. But the Enemy has not gained a victory in these stories! These brave redeemed ones—detested on earth— now join in a wondrous chant on high: "Unto Him that loved us and washed us from our sins, to Him be glory and dominion forever and ever. Amen." May we find courage within these pages to live heroically as Richard and Sabina did, until we join them in their magnificent song!

Gracia Burnham, New Tribes Mission,
author, *In the Presence of My Enemies*

Although Richard and Sabina Wurmbrand were born more than a hundred years ago, their timeless story has a freshness and timeliness that comes through clearly in these pages. Yes, they were heroes for the gospel during the Cold War days, when the West was fighting Communist expansion. But they are heroes for our day too, demonstrating with their lives a love and commitment to Christ that would not be swayed or diminished by pressure, persecution, or pain. The first time Richard's and Sabina's stories are both contained within one cover, this book contains a wealth of insight into the lives of these two heroes of the faith. Their story challenges all of us to "go and do likewise" as we boldly live out our own walk of faith with Jesus.

Todd Nettleton, host, VOM
Radio (VOMRadio.net)

In my close association with persecuted Christians—serving them and serving with them on the world's most difficult and dangerous missions frontiers in more than fifty nations—I have witnessed the power of Richard and Sabina's testimony. Few stories outside the canon of Scripture have inspired so many to serve so faithfully. And when we consider how the Wurmbrands' story has challenged Western Christians to a deeper commitment to Christ, His church, and His Great Commission, it is easy for us to see that this is one of the most important Christian biographies in history. *Wurmbrand* is much more than a historical record detailing the lives of two Christians who experienced atrocities at the hands of Romanian communists. This story is a testimony of God's faithfulness and the exemplary service of His saints in the face of imprisonment, torture, and death, and God has used it to transform millions of people worldwide. Every Christian should read this book.

Cole Richards, president,
The Voice of the Martyrs

WURMBRAND

WURMBRAND

TORTURED FOR CHRIST
THE COMPLETE STORY

the voice of the martyrs

DAVID C COOK

transforming lives together

WURMBRAND
Published by David C Cook
4050 Lee Vance Drive
Colorado Springs, CO 80918 U.S.A.

David C Cook U.K., Kingsway Communications
Eastbourne, East Sussex BN23 6NT, England

The graphic circle C logo is a registered trademark of David C Cook.

LCCN 2017952211
ISBN 978-1-4347-1117-5
eISBN 978-1-4347-1233-2

The David C Cook Team: Abby DeBenedittis, Keith Wall, Nick Lee,
Rachael Stevenson, Jennifer Lonas, Kayla Fenstermaker, Susan Murdock
The Voice of the Martyrs Team: Merv Knight, Cole Richards,
Cheryl Odden, Todd Nettleton, Olive Swan
Cover Design: Amy Konyndyk
Cover Photo: The Voice of the Martyrs, Inc.
Lead Writer and Researcher: Rebecca P. George

Printed in the United States of America
First Edition 2018

1 2 3 4 5 6 7 8 9 10

121517

Note to Readers

In our present era, readers and movie viewers are accustomed to tales based on a true story, which often makes them wonder how much has been exaggerated or fabricated. The account that follows is factually accurate and faithfully rendered according to actual documents, writings, and historical records.

So readers can trust the historicity of the book, and to be faithful to the legacy of the Wurmbrands, we have not created any dialogue in this book. When dialogue is in quotation marks, we have used Richard's and Sabina's own words, modernizing them where necessary.

PROLOGUE

February 29, 1948
Bucharest, Romania

A black van raced through the snowy streets of Bucharest. Its tires screeched to a halt, breaking the Sunday-morning silence. Richard Wurmbrand knew that government-ordered kidnappings were common in his Communist city. He'd been arrested before, and like so many others, he lived in constant fear it would happen again. But he didn't expect to be a victim that morning, especially not on his way to church.

As he mulled over the points of his sermon, his thoughts were interrupted when the van clipped the curb beside him. Two men wearing dark suits leaped from the vehicle. Their eyes, cold and intimidating, locked on to the thirty-nine-year-old pastor as he stumbled in shock.

Even at a towering six foot three, Richard was unable to resist his captors, his lanky frame ill suited to fending off an attack. They lunged at him. One man grabbed his arms while the other landed a gut-wrenching blow to his ribs. Any hope of screaming for help was lost as Richard crumbled to the ground, unable to catch his breath in the frozen air.

As the men wrestled him into the back seat of the hearse-shaped Ford, a profound thought entered Richard's mind. Two days earlier, while reading the book of Joshua, he had noticed an endless repetition of the message "Do not fear." Richard had been curious. Why was that command repeated so many times in Scripture? How many *more* times did it appear? He decided to count each instance and discovered that it occurs 366 times in the Bible.

For every possible day of the year, including an extra leap-year day, Richard realized the Christian didn't have to be afraid. God's promise even covered February 29, the day Richard was abducted.

The driver accelerated even before the door slammed shut, but Richard smiled. He and his wife, Sabina, had known this moment was coming. They knew the high cost of their Christian activities and had counted that cost for years. Even now, as Richard was being kidnapped, he had a reminder from God's Word not to fear.

A third man in the passenger seat aimed a pistol at Richard as the men flanking him chained his foot to his wrist.

Richard's smile widened, and his captors exchanged worried glances. Their prisoner was under arrest, yet he smiled. Had he already lost his mind? They needed information from him, and an insane man wouldn't be of much use.

"Why are you smiling?" one man asked.

"Because it's written 366 times," Richard said.

Now the men were sure he'd gone mad.

"Sir, what's written 366 times?"

"Just what I need."

The man sighed in exasperation. "What is it you need?"

"Man doesn't live only on bread," Richard replied. "He lives on the Word of God, and I have words from God that I don't have to be afraid."

Even though Richard was in the custody of the secret police, he knew he was in the hands of the almighty God, and this quieted his heart.

As the van disappeared down the quiet street, Richard closed his eyes. God had prepared him for what was to come, and he prayed he would be found faithful.

1

By his second glass of plum brandy, Richard had lost the sharpness of his senses. The long day at his brokerage firm in Bucharest, Romania, had come to an end, and now he could turn his attention to something more pleasing: the cabaret dancer in the feathered red dress. She seemed to recognize Richard, winking at him from the stage all evening.

The dancer's set ended, and as she sauntered toward him, Richard smiled. His good looks and tall build drew the gaze of many women, and his eyes—blue as ice—complemented the suits he could finally afford.

Richard knew what this woman wanted. It's what all women wanted: escape. Richard wanted to escape too. The early 1930s had been good to him, and in 1934, at the age of twenty-five, Richard no longer had to worry about finances. Yet with each promotion came more opportunities to indulge his fleshly desires. He had rightfully earned his playboy reputation, but all the wealth and women he accumulated ultimately failed to numb the bitter memories of his childhood. Inebriation promised relief, and with each burning swig of his brandy, Richard's painful past grew blurry and strangely tolerable.

In search of a better life, his father, a dentist, had transplanted the family from Bucharest to Istanbul, Turkey, in the midst of the First World War. The move seemed profitable at first but soon fell to pieces. The life he envisioned for his children ended when, like so many others, he succumbed to the ravages of the global flu pandemic of 1918–19. Richard was only nine years old when his father drew his final breath.

Some memories were easier for Richard to erase than others. A year after losing her husband, Richard's grieving mother moved her four children back to Bucharest. World War I had deprived their family not only of food but of clothes as well. Richard's wardrobe consisted of little more than threadbare hand-me-downs that often left him susceptible to the cruel Romanian winters.

Once a man offered to buy Richard a new suit. He had walked with Richard to a men's clothing shop, and the tailor sorted through the available options, choosing a pricey outfit—the best he had in stock. But when he held up the clothes next to the young man, the tailor's brow had furrowed. Richard would never forget his words: "Much too good for a boy like this."

If the tailor could only see him now.

Now a successful stockbroker, Richard was consumed by worldly pleasures. When he wasn't at the office, he passed his time in noisy places with half-naked women, loud music, and flowing alcohol. Yet somehow these distractions never filled the hollowness within. When the cabaret closed its doors each night, Richard always found himself longing for something more, something substantial.

Tonight as he blinked at the bright lights on the cabaret stage, he thought back to his early struggles about God. The Wurmbrands were Jewish, but their faith rarely permeated their daily lives. His family avoided the synagogue and didn't observe the Sabbath. Richard's transition from childhood to adolescence even lacked the defining mark of Jewish manhood, a bar mitzvah. As a young teen, he struggled to reconcile religion with the suffering around him and, years later, found himself searching for answers at a synagogue service. There he saw a man praying for his sick daughter, pleading with God to heal her. The following day the daughter died.

"What kind of God could refuse such a desperate prayer?" Richard asked the rabbi, who had no answer. With so many people starving in this world, Richard couldn't believe in a silent God, much less worship or serve Him.

A gentle touch brought Richard back to the present moment. The dancer in the red dress brushed her hand across the folds of his suit lapel, obviously admiring its quality. Her eyes smoldered and her rosy lips parted in a seductive smile. Richard smiled back and downed one final swig of his drink. Tonight this woman offered all the midnight pleasure he desired.

Richard stood, took the dancer's arm, and guided her out of the cabaret into the crisp night air of Little Paris.

2

In the early 1930s, Sabina Oster tilted her head toward the warm Parisian sun, its rays highlighting her delicate features and heating her thick, dark hair. Sabina's last class of the day had finally ended, and she'd been lucky to find a seat at the crowded café. The giddiness of her newfound independence had begun to sink in.

Sabina was not the only woman to find freedom studying chemistry, physics, and math at Paris's famed Sorbonne. Forty years earlier, a woman named Marie Sklodowska had also studied at this university before meeting and marrying scientist Pierre Curie and eventually joining the school's elite faculty. Maybe Sabina, like Marie Curie, would also win a Nobel Prize for her work. These hallowed halls had spawned countless brilliant men ... so both scholarship and courtship were possible for the seventeen-year-old.

Sabina's childhood in the Romanian university town of Czernowitz was modest but happy and full. Surrounded by older brothers, younger siblings, and a rich Jewish culture, she rarely lacked the necessities of life. But her Orthodox Jewish upbringing had been strict, and she stifled under the stiff prohibitions that surrounded her like a hedge.

For the first time in her life, Sabina was on her own, unconstrained and free. She sank back into her chair, daydreaming about the big event scheduled for that evening.

• • • •

Sabina slipped her small feet into a narrow pair of black high heels. The clock on the wall counted down the seconds before the bell would ring and the caller would escort Sabina on her very first date.

She giggled at the thought of how her older brothers would react if they were here to meet her handsome beau at the door. Where would the young gentleman take her? What would they talk about? Catching her breath, she hadn't considered the alarming thought that forced its way into her mind. *What if he tried to hold her hand?* Heat spread up her chest to her neck and across her cheeks.

Sabina's suitor arrived right on time, a proper gentleman indeed. Sabina hugged her roommate and stepped outside to greet her date. For the first time in her life, she didn't have to abide by the stringent rules of her parents.

After dinner, the young man guided Sabina from the bustling restaurant onto the moonlit cobblestone street. Dinner had been delicious, and Sabina marveled at how easily the conversation had flowed. So far the night had more than met what she had anticipated.

Sabina's date brushed his hand across her palm and intertwined his fingers with hers. Through the Paris streets they strolled, past the Jardin du Luxembourg and the newly constructed Institut d'Art et d'Archéologie, a Mesopotamian-style monstrosity where art-history and archaeology students attended lectures. The couple made their way toward the recently opened international students' residence where Sabina lived, marveling at how the university town bustled with the activity of a student population that had tripled in size since the end of World War I.

As the evening came to a close, Sabina turned to thank her date. But as her eyes reached his, she froze suddenly and jerked her head back in surprise. He was leaning in for a kiss.

Sabina stumbled against the stone wall and raised her arms in protest. Her parents would never approve. She scrambled to explain her upbringing and the moral limitations of her childhood.

Her date laughed. "If you believe in God," he proposed, "wouldn't you say that the same God made the hands and the lips?"

Sabina blushed, unable to answer.

"If I can hold your hand," the fellow continued, "why is it wrong to touch your lips?"

He moved in closer, sliding his arms around the small of her waist and pulling her body toward his. Sabina struggled to respond.

"And shouldn't it be okay for me to hold you?" he persisted.

She was aware of his body only inches from hers.

In a classroom setting, Sabina might have countered his logic with rational answers. But with her head clouded and attraction welling up inside her, she couldn't conjure up an appropriate response. And who was going to judge her? Thirteen hundred miles separated her from her parents; maybe this was what freedom felt like.

Sabina succumbed to his argument and then to his advances. Her eyes widened as he cupped her chin with his hand and pressed his lips against hers.

• • • •

In the weeks and months that followed, Sabina enjoyed the carefree lifestyle of Paris. Gone were the days of morality, purity, and parental judgment. Gone were the constraints and restraints of Romania. Sabina happily sacrificed her former convictions on the altar of Parisian pleasure. Her body was her own, and she freely offered it to her boyfriend.

After all, she reasoned, an atheist is free to do whatever she wants.

3

After two blithe years, Sabina departed Paris for a vacation back home in Bucharest. She spent the break with family and other relatives but concealed her newfound open lifestyle.

One day her uncle, whose company she always enjoyed, invited her for a drive to his friend's house. As the car approached the residence, Sabina looked up and saw a young man on the balcony of the house. Upon further inspection, she noticed how irritated he looked, his face scowling in her direction. She could almost feel his anger as she debated the wisdom of exiting the vehicle.

When the man shifted his gaze to Sabina's uncle, his features softened, and he waved to them. Moments later he was at the front door greeting them. Her uncle introduced his young niece to Richard Wurmbrand, a man as handsome as any she had known in Paris. Admiring his height and countenance, she felt a faint flutter of enthusiasm.

Richard ushered them into the front room and politely invited them to sit. Looking embarrassed for giving his beautiful guest a negative first impression, he explained, "My mom's nagging me to get married. She's even picked out the girl, an heiress with a family business, two homes, and a million in dowry."

"That sounds really nice," Sabina said.

"It does," he replied while laughing, "and I definitely don't mind having the business and the inheritance. It's the girl I don't like. My mother thinks this is the best way for us all to be rich." Richard looked at Sabina and smirked. "But then I came out on the balcony and saw you."

Sabina wasn't expecting his honesty, but she was intrigued.

"The thought occurred to me that if I could have a girl like you, I wouldn't care about the cash," he concluded.

• • • •

Following their initial conversation, Richard and Sabina entered a whirlwind courtship and spent every available moment of her vacation together. She was pleased to hear that Richard was an up-and-coming stockbroker and was making good money. He certainly didn't seem to mind spending it on Sabina. Every night they went to nightclubs and theaters, parties and bars, casinos and cabarets.

The more they dated, the less the boys of Paris meant to Sabina, especially when she discovered that she and Richard not only shared a host of common interests and experiences but were also Jews who had abandoned their religion for the prospect of wealth, luxury, and indulgence.

One night, though, Richard surprised Sabina with a sobering comment.

"I'm not an easy person," he said, sipping a dark elixir. "You'd suffer a lot with me."

Perhaps. But Sabina had fallen in love with him. And if suffering was in their future, she was certain there would be enough pleasure to compensate.

4

Sabina never returned to Paris. She had found a better life with Richard in Bucharest and was soon employed with a local insurance agency. Their courtship continued until October 23, 1936, when the two were married in the home of a rabbi. The newly wedded couple stood beneath a traditional Jewish covering, or *chuppah*, and crushed a wineglass beneath their feet as a reminder of the Babylonian sacking of Jerusalem in 586 BC. The religious symbolism meant little to the atheist couple, but they were happy to appease their parents.

Having children was out of the question for Richard and Sabina. They couldn't allow anything—especially little ones—to encumber their untroubled life. Their goal was simple and achievable: they would chase pleasure wherever it could be found.

Richard's womanizing habits died hard, even after his marriage. Without a moral code they could rely on, Sabina looked the other way when her husband's eyes and heart strayed toward other women. Lying and indulging became routine vices for both of them. Yet despite his indiscretions, Richard and his young bride spent the early days of their marriage in carefree revelry.

• • • •

For the better part of a year, the newlyweds enjoyed happiness. All that changed, however, when Richard's indulgent lifestyle caught up with him. It started as an annoying, persistent cough that he was able to ignore for a while, but he eventually surrendered to his wife's insistent pleas and made an appointment with his doctor.

A ghastly pallor masked his usually stalwart features the day he returned home from the appointment.

In the 1930s, tuberculosis was a death sentence. One of the world's most critical health crises, it spread through Europe with frightening speed. Doctors were scrambling to find a cure, but it would take nearly a decade before a newly developed TB vaccine was routinely administered.

Excessive drinking had so weakened Richard's immune system that he became susceptible to mycobacterium tuberculosis, which invaded his respiratory system. The threatening patch of bacteria on his lung soon spread, causing night sweats and feverish chills that wreaked havoc on his feeble body. His lungs, which were filling with liquid, struggled to deliver oxygen to his brain and caused Richard to cough up blood. In short, Sabina's twenty-seven-year-old husband would soon drown in his own fluids.

Richard's only option was to relocate to an isolated sanatorium deep in the Carpathian Mountains, where he could breathe fresh air and sit under ultraviolet lamps. With enough bed rest, he might recover. But the prognosis wasn't good. He had a fifty-fifty chance of survival.

Sabina grieved her new husband's death sentence. Their marriage had proved happy, but Richard's diagnosis became an unbearable burden. For the first time in their relationship, their thoughts turned toward the future and the haunting likelihood that Sabina would be widowed.

As Richard boarded a train and traveled over the rolling green hills of the Romanian countryside to the sanatorium, Sabina went to live with his mother. Every two weeks, Sabina made the long journey to visit her ailing husband, but being with him didn't keep her from crying herself to sleep. Other women wept over Richard as well, including his mother and even some of the ladies he had seduced.

For Richard, however, the serenity of the sanatorium offered the respite he had lacked in Bucharest. "For the first time in my life," he told his wife, "I'm resting."

But the silence of the mountains also forced him to confront his past, from the immeasurable hours he had squandered in bars, theaters, and nightclubs to the many people he had hurt.

Waves of painful memories ambushed him, each one plaguing him as much as his tuberculosis. He could see the faces of business associates he had cheated and hear the lies he'd told as clearly as when he had first uttered them. The mountain air brought to the surface every thought, word, deed, and sin. *It's coming back to me like scenes from an agonizing play*, he thought. Richard had invested his youth in defaming, mocking, and deceiving others—and for what? The landscape of his life was before him, a wasteland of foolishness. He had lived for himself, and now he would die by himself.

The irony of his isolation felt deserved in these secluded surroundings. Soon the stubborn atheist's first prayer to God emerged
when he least expected it. Though his body had betrayed him, his
soul was preparing to breathe out a prayer to the God he didn't
believe in.

5

Richard's youth had been difficult, and he had turned to books to alleviate his childhood agonies. By his tenth birthday, he had consumed every piece of literature in his house. He especially identified with Voltaire, a French religious skeptic he came to admire. In spite of his age, Richard was also becoming a skeptic. If the all-powerful God was supposed to be loving and good, he ruminated, why had He allowed Richard's father to die?

Once while attending a Catholic service, Richard approached an ornate statue of the Virgin Mary and decided to join the people surrounding him who were praying to her.

"Hail, Mary, full of grace," he began to pray, but the words couldn't fill the emptiness inside. Truncating his prayer, he looked up at Mary's statue and said, "Really, you *are* like stone. So many plead, and you have nothing for them." If the Virgin Mary couldn't inspire Richard's faith in God, neither could the Catholic Mass, conducted entirely in Latin. He struggled to understand the readings and prayers and stumbled over the words of the doxology:

Domine Deus, Rex caelestis,
Deus Pater Omnipotens.

Domine Fili unigenite Jesu Christe.
Domine Deus, Agnus Dei,
Filius Patris.

Entirely disenchanted with the Roman Catholic Church, Richard was equally unimpressed with the Eastern Orthodox tradition. By the time he was a teenager, Richard Wurmbrand was a confirmed atheist. He wanted nothing to do with the church. For a Jew, the anti-Semitism of the Orthodox Church was impossible to justify. Religion seemed too concerned with tradition and make-believe to have any relevance to his own life.

In the Old Testament, Yahweh had delivered the Israelites from their imprisonment in Egypt and even provided manna, a wafer-like bread, for them to eat in the wilderness. But bread was in short supply in Romania. Richard knew what hunger felt like, that gnawing ache beneath his ribs. Money was scarce for the Wurmbrands, and survival itself depleted the few resources his family could muster.

Richard's rejection of an all-powerful, all-loving God drove him into meaningless materialism, in which nothing existed beyond the natural world. He shunned all ideas of the supernatural and constantly pondered the mysteries he couldn't explain. Were humans anything more than atoms and minerals? What happened after death? Was there such a thing as a soul? Richard didn't think so anymore. Yet his father's death haunted him, and even though his mind had abandoned the idea of God, his heart still hoped He existed.

In winter, Richard often wandered among the frozen dead in the cemeteries of Bucharest. He admired the glistening gravestones and mused that one day he'd be dead too. The snow would fall on his tomb while the living would laugh, embrace, and enjoy life without him. He wouldn't exist anymore, and after a short time, nobody would remember him. *So what use is anything?* he wondered. Even though he was convinced there was no life after death—and no God either—Richard often wished it was otherwise. Shouldn't there be a reason for his existence in the universe?

Atheism appealed to Richard, and the fourteen-year-old devoured any literature that denied the existence of God. He was particularly enthralled with the writings of the nineteenth-century philosopher Karl Marx, who convinced him the very idea of God was toxic to the human mind. After all, Richard sought facts, not fiction. He longed for truth about the world, not mythological inventions cloaked in religious garb. Karl Marx once said, "[Religion] is the *opium* of the people,"[1] and Richard agreed.

With his sharp intellect, quick wit, and keen knack for learning languages, Richard soon became active in the Communist Youth Movement. Seeking to enhance his education, he traveled to Moscow to study Marxism. Fluent in nine languages, Richard had no trouble navigating Russian culture, and by the time he returned to Romania, he was already a Comintern agent determined to overthrow the bourgeoisie class and establish an international Soviet republic.

Communism promised answers for the poverty Richard had experienced during his childhood and witnessed throughout

Romania. The idea of common ownership of property and possessions attracted the young atheist. He also craved the camaraderie of like-minded followers—a companionship he had never experienced in church. At long last, Richard had found a cause worth fighting for and a *communion* worth celebrating. He directed all his energy into overthrowing the corrupt, upper-class Romanian government with the hope that one day a Communist party would restore fairness in his country.

But soon Richard discovered a problem. Though he found the agenda of his leftist politics exciting, he was still drawn to the idea of God. Richard rarely walked past a church without stopping to listen to a sermon. The absence of his earthly father created a deep yearning in Richard's soul for a heavenly Father whose heart could beat for him as well. Not even Marxism, with its strong emphasis on community, could satisfy this longing.

• • • •

Now, in an isolated sanatorium, Richard prayed his first hesitant prayer. "God, I'm absolutely sure You don't exist," he whispered. "But if, by some chance, You *do* exist, it isn't *my* job to believe in *You*. It's *Your* job to reveal Yourself to *me*."

As it turned out, Richard wasn't the only man praying to God in the rural hills of Romania. High up in the mountains, in a village as isolated as the sanatorium, an aged German carpenter named Christian Wölfkes had spent the entire night on his knees praying to God. For years he and his wife pleaded for the chance to lead a single Jew to a saving knowledge of Jesus Christ. For hours at a time, the couple poured out their hearts before their Creator, praying over their Bible and interceding with tears for the salvation of the Jew they had never met.

"My God," Christian prayed aloud, "I've served You on earth, and I want to have my reward on earth as well as in heaven. And my reward should be that I shouldn't die before I bring a Jew to Christ, because Jesus was from the Jewish people." He sighed. "But I'm poor, old, and sick. I can't go around and find a Jew. In my village, there aren't any. Bring a Jew into my village, and I'll do my best to lead him to Christ."

• • • •

Richard was in a reflective mood when Sabina visited his sanatorium.

"I've been thinking about the past," he said to her. "All the people I've hurt.... My mother. All the girls you don't even know about." He drew in a sharp breath and confessed, "For my entire life, I've thought only about myself."

"Don't worry about it," Sabina said dismissively. "My life hasn't been much different. We're young; that's what people do."

Sabina tried to cheer him with stories of the good times they would have when he returned to Bucharest. But deep within, Richard questioned if he would return the way he had departed. His intense soul searching had produced an unexpected outcome his wife would not understand. The sins of his former life seemed less appetizing than he remembered them. Somehow his lust had lost its luster. There was less value, he reasoned, in meaningless womanizing and frequenting nightclubs.

• • • •

As Richard's health improved, his soul was becoming healthier as well. Sabina's enticements failed to elicit the reaction she had anticipated. But when she saw the peculiar new book Richard was reading, she was horrified. The Christian Bible! Her atheist Jewish husband was actually reading the New Testament, which a fellow patient had loaned him.

Growing up in a traditionally Jewish home, Sabina hadn't been allowed to even speak the name of Jesus Christ under her father's roof. When passing by a Christian church, she and her siblings were instructed to look the other way. And why not? After all the persecutions and humiliations Christians had inflicted on the Jewish people, the resentment of Sabina's family was understandable. Jewish history was bathed in blood spilled at the hands of Christ's followers, not to mention the forced baptisms and Catholic masses. She even remembered studying about Jews who chose to murder their children and then commit suicide to avoid converting to Christianity and being tarnished.

Sabina couldn't forget walking home from school as a child, dreading the corner of the street where two older girls often stood. "Dirty little Jewess!" they shouted. The girls laughed as they yanked Sabina's hair and grabbed her tiny arms.

The most forceful anti-Semitic organizations were Christian: the Orthodox Church, the Lutheran Church, and the National Christian Defense League, whose primary purpose seemed to be beating Jewish students and destroying Jewish businesses. If that was Christianity, Sabina wanted nothing to do with it.

And now as she listened to her husband describe the Jesus he encountered in the New Testament, Sabina couldn't disguise the shock and dismay she felt. Christianity tarnished history, and now it was threatening her marriage. Before, they agreed not to have children. But now her husband went on and on about how to raise children with morals. He was ruining everything.

Richard had immersed himself in other strange books too. He handed Sabina a book from a fellow patient about Christians who loved Jews so much they gave their lives to help them. "It's about the brothers Ratisbonne," he said. "They founded an order of monks to convert Jews."

She looked away in disappointment as she listened to Richard describe these Christians from the past who had been serving Jews.

"People have been praying for me while I wasted my life," he said.

• • • •

As weeks of convalescence evolved into months, Richard's lungs improved enough for him to leave the tuberculosis sanatorium and retreat to a quiet village in the nearby mountains to continue his recovery.

One afternoon as he and Sabina wandered through the cobblestone streets, Richard encountered a feeble old man who invited them into his home. His name was Christian Wölfkes. When Christian discovered Richard was Jewish, his eyes filled with tears. "I asked God to grant me one favor at the end of my life," he said, gripping Richard's arm with a calloused hand. "Because Christ was a Jew, I wanted to bring a Jew to Him. But since there aren't any here, and since I can't leave the village, I knew God had to send me one. And here you are! An answer to my prayer!"

Richard thought about the brothers Ratisbonne, and as they parted ways, Christian handed him a tattered Bible, worn out from years of use. As Richard flipped through its tear-stained pages, Christian added, "My wife and I have prayed for hours over this, asking for your conversion."

Richard's heart was strangely warmed by the generosity of his new friend, but he could tell that Sabina was crushed. The look in her eyes conveyed the betrayal she felt.

6

In the following days and weeks, Richard pored over Christian's Bible. Every day was spent on the sofa in his small cottage, buried in the stories of the New Testament. When he was younger, he had read the Bible casually, mainly out of curiosity. He read about Paul, who had been imprisoned for his faith but declared, "I am not ashamed of the gospel, for it is the power of God for salvation to everyone who believes, to the Jew first and also to the Greek" (Rom. 1:16). Richard wondered if that could be true. Jesus Christ offered salvation *first for the Jew*?

Each word of the New Testament awakened within him a desire to keep reading. Even the punctuation between the words seemed to glow with truth he had never noticed before. Christianity had intrigued him as a child, but now it ruined him for the pleasures of the past. Richard examined the parables of Jesus and pondered His astonishing words: "But I say to you, Love your enemies and pray for those who persecute you, so that you may be sons of your Father who is in heaven" (Matt. 5:44–45). The Jews had been persecuted for centuries. Could he really forgive those who harmed and hated him? Richard continued reading as though his very life depended on it.

Soon Jesus became as real to Richard as the woman who brought him his meals. Each night he drifted to sleep wanting to know more about Him. A civil war was raging inside him. His heart was drawn to God, but his mind mustered up arguments against Him. "You'll never have me as a disciple," he prayed. "I want money. Travel. Pleasure. I've suffered enough." Richard clenched his fists. "Your way is the way of the cross, and even if it's also the way of truth, I won't follow it."

An answer came into his head, like a plea, interrupting his thoughts. *Come My way! Don't fear the cross! You'll find that it's the greatest joy possible.*

Richard wept at the notion of finding joy. Lust he knew, but joy was a new and unfamiliar sensation. Could Jesus forgive his former life, so tarnished with sin and selfishness? Could Christ exchange Richard's guilt for grace? The words of Jesus spoke to his heart: "Come to me, all who labor and are heavy laden, and I will give you rest" (Matt. 11:28). Richard needed rest. That's why he had fled to the sanatorium. But the rest Jesus promised was more than physical; it was spiritual.

Richard remembered the ancient Chinese story about the exhausted man trudging under the insufferable heat of the sun. He rested beneath the shade of a towering oak tree and said, "What a happy coincidence that I found you!"

The oak replied, "It's not chance. I've been waiting for you for four hundred years."

Suddenly Richard's eyes were opened. The path to salvation was clear. Jesus Christ had been waiting for him—waiting to teach

Richard how to rest in His love. Perhaps even tuberculosis was part of God's plan to pull him out of the heat of the world and cover him with the shade of the cross.

Right there in a quaint cottage nestled in the Carpathian Mountains, Richard embraced the love of Jesus Christ, a love that refused to let him go.

"God," Richard prayed, "I was an atheist. Now let me go to Russia to work as a missionary among atheists, and I won't complain if, afterward, I have to spend all the rest of my life in prison."

• • • •

The sound of Jesus's forbidden name infuriated Sabina. The change that had rapidly overtaken Richard's life was unacceptable. She had married an atheist not a Christian.

"I don't need Him!" Sabina insisted. "*You* don't need Him. It isn't natural." She stomped her foot on the wooden planks of the cottage floor. "We're *Jewish*! It's a totally different way of life." But she couldn't deny the change that had come over her husband. His new faith in Jesus Christ had transformed him. "I'd rather die than see you become a Christian!" Sabina blurted out.

She offered Richard an ultimatum. If he had to have religion, he could practice his own Jewish faith. But when he mentioned his desire to be baptized, Sabina nearly lost her mind. Baptism was absolutely out of the question.

For a while, this arrangement seemed to work. Richard attended synagogue and went through the motions. But even there, he spoke mainly of Jesus. On one occasion back home in Bucharest, Richard convinced Sabina to peek inside a church. Afraid but curious, she followed her husband through the heavy wooden front doors and across the threshold. Sabina held tightly to the back of his coat and surveyed the colorful walls decorated with images of saints. They were Christian saints. Richard drew her attention to each of them, reminding her that half of them were Jews, including Jesus and His mother.

Sabina's eyes adjusted to the dimly lit nave, and she examined the vaulted ceiling as Richard explained the meaning behind the Ten Commandments. She remembered how her father cherished those commandments inscribed in the Jewish book of Moses. Richard explained how Christians embraced the writings of the Old Testament, like the Jewish collection of King David's psalms. In fact, the entire Old Testament—the Jewish holy book—contained numerous prophecies about the coming Messiah, Jesus Christ.

"The fact is," Richard said, "the Christian religion is simply our Jewish faith opened to all the nations of the earth." Turning to face Sabina, he asked, "Who made it possible for Jewish values, morals, and wisdom to spread throughout the world? And who made it possible to reach so many hundreds of millions of people over two thousand years?"

Sabina listened as her husband's speech quickened.

"Only Christ could have done it," he continued. "Because of His work, the holy book of the Jews has been translated from Hebrew into a thousand languages." His voice rose with excitement.

"And now the Bible can be read by ignorant peasants and the most brilliant scientists like Pasteur and Einstein."

But what about all the evil that Christians had inflicted on Jews? Weren't Jesus's followers the strongest evidence against Christianity? For weeks Sabina pondered these questions. She sympathized with Gandhi, who once said, "I like your Christ. I do not like your Christians."[1] Perhaps she could accept Christ without Christianity?

Richard shook his head. "You can't accept Jesus without accepting His disciples. He wouldn't leave them to come to you. And you can't accept the disciples without calling even Judas a friend, as Jesus did."

Sabina knew Richard desired his wife to share in the enthusiasm of his newfound faith. He patiently explained the beauty of the gospel and the call to forgive others in the same way God forgave him. When Sabina finally agreed to read the New Testament, a look of joy spread across Richard's face. A new day had dawned for the Wurmbrands. Sabina even found herself admiring and beginning to love her husband's Savior.

• • • •

Sabina's intellectual objections to the Christian faith were overcome, but her emotional ties to Judaism, ingrained by thousands of years of Jewish persecution, were still deeply rooted in her soul.

He's right, her mind whispered. But fiery hatred for Christians continued to rage within her.

One night Richard returned home from a prayer meeting at the Anglican Mission to the Jews. He hurried to his wife, clasped her hands, and announced with great excitement that he had publicly surrendered his heart to Christ. The next step was to be baptized.

The news was more than Sabina could bear. She imagined the disappointment on her parents' faces when they found out. She hadn't been allowed to even look at a Christian church, much less give her husband her blessing to be baptized in one. Usually strong and resilient, Sabina could take no more. She began to weep in the kitchen, threw her dish towel on the counter, and shut herself in her room. For hours she remained in bed sobbing. If Richard could make a horrible decision, so could she.

She made up her mind: on the day of Richard's baptism, she would kill herself.

7

In 1938 the day of Richard's baptism arrived, and he departed for the train station, since the service would take place in a neighboring town. Sabina expected him to be gone for hours, long enough for her to follow through with her plans. In desperation she bolted the door of her home and threw herself onto the floor. Her body, weary from wailing, would not have to suffer much longer.

"Jesus, I can't come to You!" she lamented. "And I don't want Richard to be Yours. I can't take it anymore!"

Suicide would be her final argument. Sabina reflected on the life she and Richard could have had—one of status, opportunity, and wealth. Christianity, as she understood it, was a call to die, not live. And if she couldn't have the life she wanted, then death would be preferable. When Richard came home, he would find her body and finally realize how destructive his faith was. He would remember the day of his baptism with sadness in his heart. Sabina curled herself into the corner of her room and considered her options.

For hours she contemplated what it would be like to die. She hoped in the reality atheism and Communism promised: death was the ultimate end of life and the afterlife was only a myth propagated by the poor, who hoped for a better existence.

Sabina was, after all, made only of minerals and atoms. When she took her final breath, she would be buried and would simply decompose.

But what if Richard was right? What if, after she closed her eyes for the final time, she opened them in a new reality, one worse than she was currently experiencing. Her husband believed in the concept of hell, an eternal separation from God prepared for those who did not embrace Christ's love. The thought of suffering in the eternal fires of torment unsettled her as much as the thought of Richard's heartache at discovering her body. Would he find a new wife, a Christian wife who always went to church with him? Would they raise their children in the Christian faith?

The more she pondered, the calmer she became. The risk of dying seemed too great a gamble at the moment. Perhaps there was another way. A reluctant but gradual shift began to unfold in her heart. The life she had been so willing to end that morning began to flow back into her. If God really did exist, perhaps He loved her too.

Sabina composed herself, got up from the floor, and smoothed her dress. Through puffy eyes, she stole a glance at the clock. If she hurried, she could make it to the train station to greet her newly baptized husband.

Baptism in the Christian tradition, she knew, was the point of no return. It was a symbol of salvation—dying to the old life and rising from the dead to live anew. She remembered Richard's excitement as he left the house that morning, so she snatched a handful of flowers and greeted him at the station.

The Wurmbrands stayed up until the early morning hours discussing the day's events. Richard looked heartbroken when he learned about his wife's despair. Yet as she talked, she could tell he noticed a difference in her he had not seen before. It was the same difference she had seen in him just before he had opened his heart to God at his rural retreat in the Carpathian Mountains.

• • • •

Over the following months, the whisper of hope in Sabina's heart had not yet fully matured. She still wasn't willing to own the name *Christian*. She expressed an increasing interest in God but struggled to change her habits. At night, when she closed her eyes, Sabina thought about dying to herself. But in the daytime, the pleasures of her past were still alive and fresh. She continued spending time in bars and nightclubs, and the theater still held her attention more than the sermons she heard in church. She'd been so restricted in her early life and wasn't ready to give up the future she dreamed of. Young and beautiful, she would still find a way to make up for lost time.

Richard went along with her old habits for a while, but she knew he did it mainly to humor her. One Sunday evening he suggested they go to a church service. In frustration, Sabina burst into tears and demanded they see a movie instead.

"All right," he said. "We'll go … because I love you."

They walked from theater to theater searching for the perfect movie. Then, oddly, Richard purchased tickets to the most vulgar, decadent film he could find. Sabina was astonished. Perhaps his faith had been a passing fad.

When the movie concluded, they strolled to a nearby café for dessert. Finishing her bite of cake, Sabina couldn't believe the words that came out of her husband's mouth.

"Now, go home and go to bed," he said. "I want to find a girl to take to a hotel."

Her head jerked up, her eyes ablaze. "What did you say?"

Richard met his wife's stare. "It's pretty simple," he stated. "You go home. I want to find a girl to take to a hotel."

"How can you even say that?" she hissed, throwing down her fork.

"But you made me go to the movie," Richard said, "and you saw what the hero did. Why shouldn't I do the same thing?"

Sabina frowned, but her husband continued. "If we go tomorrow and the next day to movies like those …" His words drifted off.

Sabina understood what he was getting at: Shouldn't he try to become just like the men in the movies they watched?

"Every man becomes what he looks at," Richard observed. "If you want me to be a good husband, come to church with me sometimes."

Richard had proved his point. Sabina did want him to be a good husband, and even she knew she could be a better wife. Before Richard's conversion, he had cheated on her numerous times and broken their marriage covenant. But his newfound faithfulness to God had resulted in an unexpected faithfulness to her as well.

Richard would never sleep with other women again, and she wondered if she could also break her attachment to selfish living. There was still so much of the world she wanted to experience.

One Sunday evening Sabina convinced Richard to visit a nightclub in Bucharest. Instead of going to church, which was the usual routine, he acquiesced to her desires. Clouds of smoke enveloped the couple as they surveyed the room. Brandy and vodka flowed as freely as the lewd conversations in the crowded room. Couples made love openly, and Richard followed his wife through the maze of sweaty bodies. An inebriated man sloshed his drink onto Sabina's shoes, and she staggered backward into another couple.

Richard led Sabina over to a small table where their friends were sitting. As they talked and laughed, Sabina nursed her drink. The conversation devolved quickly, and she suddenly realized she wasn't enjoying the party as much as she expected to. In fact, she wasn't enjoying herself at all.

"Let's go," she shouted into Richard's ear. "Can we leave?"

"Why?" Richard said. "We've just gotten here." He insisted it would be rude to leave so soon. There was still so much of the night to enjoy.

Around midnight Sabina again asked to leave, but Richard again refused. An hour later, she inquired once more, but like the last time, he found an excuse to stay.

For the first time in her life, Sabina felt truly sick and disgusted. The whole evening hadn't satisfied her in the slightest. Richard finally yielded to her request and guided his wife through the crowded room. They opened the door and breathed in the clean evening air. The moon was high and bright in the sky, its light piercing the night in a way Sabina had never noticed before.

"Richard," she said, "I'm going straight to the pastor's house, and I'm going to make him baptize me. It'll be like taking a bath after all this filth!"

Richard laughed. "You've waited this long; you can wait until tomorrow morning. Let the poor pastor sleep."

He squeezed Sabina's hand and gently led her homeward, the club disappearing behind them.

• • • •

The next morning Richard took his wife to the Anglican Mission in Bucharest to introduce her to Pastor Adency and Pastor Ellison. The two men seemed otherworldly to Sabina. Both had surrendered everything to follow Jesus and shared the same zeal for Christianity she saw in Richard. She wondered how they were able to part ways with their former lives.

As Sabina listened to their stories, her heart warmed once again. They opened the Bible and spoke to her about the fullness God offered those willing to step out in faith. Christ did not want *part* of her; He wanted *all* of her. He wanted to redeem her past, with all its regrets and grievances. Sabina knew how close she had come to killing herself, and as the two men spoke, she felt the hollow places in her life fill with truth.

They explained that knowing Jesus intimately could allay the unresolved tension within her. God could give her a new heart—a renewed heart—and a new set of desires. Christ offered to absorb her filthiness and exchange it for His righteousness. He could unclench her death grip on the things of this world and inject lasting meaning into her marriage.

Sabina wanted to believe in a God who could accomplish that, a Christ who could transform and release her. She wanted to finally put her trust in the only One who would love her perfectly and unfailingly. The gospel had often grated against her sensibilities, but now she couldn't ignore the unsettledness she felt at the night-club. She could finally see the lewdness for what it was—hollow. Sin was losing its seductive power and couldn't possess her any longer. Once and for all, Sabina was prepared to commit herself to Jesus Christ. No more meaningless indulgences. No more evenings of drunkenness. No more thoughts of suicide. Sabina professed Christ and was baptized the next day.

Over the following months, Sabina couldn't conceal her budding happiness. She told everyone she could about her discovery of faith. Life—and death—finally made sense. A clean break with her past was next on the agenda, and she renounced her former life, never to walk in its ways again.

Richard explained that following Christ would be costly, even dangerous. But Sabina was willing to take the risk. At work in Bucharest, she pulled her best friend aside, a Jewish girl, and shared the gospel with her. Sabina's eyes sparkled as she rushed to explain her change of heart. Yet the more she spoke, the less her friend listened.

She backed away from Sabina and shook her head. "So now I've completely lost you!" she cried.

The words stung, but Sabina understood her friend's objections. She had once been there, suspended between the impossible rules of Judaism and the life-giving reality of the cross. But she couldn't be dissuaded from sharing her faith. She attended church every week with Richard, enjoying new friendships forged from similar experiences. The sermons touched her and subdued the restlessness she used to feel. Richard was progressing in his faith too. His relationship with Christ was becoming deeper and more active. She admired his passion and wondered where it might lead them.

One day Richard came home from work with an enthusiastic glow on his face. She inquired about his excitement but was unprepared for its cause.

He wanted to be a pastor.

8

The dark clouds of a Nazi invasion had been gathering above Romania for some time, but by 1939, the political climate became unbearable as the country came into the iron sights of Adolf Hitler. The Jews resented the German dictator's advances, and fear—tangible enough to touch—swept the nation. Rumors of persecution became the centerpiece at every Jewish dinner table, including the Wurmbrands'.

It was a difficult year to bring a child into the world, but God had answered Richard and Sabina's prayers. Though once shunning the idea of having children, the couple welcomed their firstborn son with arms wide open and named him Mihai.

"He's dark like you," Richard told Sabina, "and so beautiful." A mischievous smirk stretched across his face. "But he only cries. When will he say something clever?"

Richard kissed his son and wrapped his arms around his wife. The Wurmbrands, who once feared that children would only interfere with their pleasure-seeking lifestyle, were now gloriously happy. Before his conversion, Richard would have divorced Sabina without a second thought if she had impeded his philandering lifestyle. But now the arrival of his newborn son accentuated the great spiritual change that had occurred in his life, and Richard embraced his responsibilities as a father.

• • • •

Several months later, in another part of the city, nine men lay prostrate on the floor of an Orthodox church building, their bodies forming the shape of a cross as they prepared for the murderous morning ahead. The assassins—a Gestapo-trained lawyer, several young fanatics, and a draftsman whose strategy would guide the attack—had been carefully selected by fascists from Germany, Italy, and Romania. In the death squad's sights was Armand Calinescu, Romania's new prime minister, who had been in office only six months but whose leadership proved problematic for the Iron Guard.[1] Now, on the evening of September 20, 1939, they readied themselves for the assassination.

• • • •

Throughout the Nazi occupation of Romania, the Iron Guard used members of the Orthodox Church as pawns in their political schemes. On the morning of September 21, 1939, the assassins succeeded in murdering Premier Calinescu as he was chauffeured through the streets of Bucharest on his way back to Cotroceni Palace. His bodyguard and driver were also killed, and twenty bullets were later removed from Calinescu's lifeless body. In time the Iron Guard maneuvered Hitler's protégé, General Ion Antonescu, into power. The Iron Gurard also forced the abdication of King Carol, the controversial head of Romania, in favor of his son, Michael, behind whom Antonescu ruled Romania as dictator. The Iron Guard had moved their final puzzle piece into place.

The green-uniformed militants could deal freely with those they deemed threats to their power. Jews, Communists, and Protestants all fell into their snare, and murder stalked the streets of Romania. The Iron Guard accused the Wurmbrands' mission in Bucharest of treachery, and Richard fell victim to daily threats.

One Sunday he looked out across his congregation and saw a group of men in green uniforms file quietly into the sanctuary. The congregation, facing the altar, was unaware of the intrusion, but Richard saw the revolvers in their hands. If this was going to be his last sermon, he'd better make it a good one.

Richard preached about the hands of Jesus. He painted pictures of Jesus's hands wiping away tears, lifting children, and feeding the hungry. He told of the Savior's hands healing the sick, being nailed to the cross, and blessing the disciples before Jesus ascended into heaven. Then Richard paused and looked up from his Bible. Looking out at his congregation, he thundered, "But you! What have you done with your hands?" Church members blinked in amazement. In their hands they held prayer books. What could the pastor mean?

Richard steeled himself and continued his tirade. "You're killing and beating and torturing innocent people! Do you call yourself Christian? Clean your hands, you sinners!" In the back of the church, the soldiers of the Iron Guard seethed. But reacting would draw attention to their presence, so they stood with weapons drawn as Richard concluded the service.

When nearly all his congregants had exited the building, Richard slipped from the pulpit and slid behind a curtain. Behind him shouts filled the air: "Where's Wurmbrand? After him!"

Richard glided through a small door, locking it behind him. The secret passageway had been constructed years earlier, awaiting the day it would save Richard's life. From there he made his way to a side street and disappeared into the bustling boulevards of Bucharest.

As the war advanced, many members of minority Christian denominations were massacred or forced into concentration camps along with the Jews. During the wartime years, the Nazis arrested Richard three times. The trials, interrogations, beatings, and imprisonments foreshadowed the cruelty to come under the Communist regime.

• • • •

Before their marriage, Richard had warned Sabina, "You'd suffer a lot with me." And in the white-hot conflict of World War II, his warning became a reality. After joining the Anglican Mission to the Jews in Bucharest, the Wurmbrands began ministering to war-torn families. They smuggled Jewish orphans from ghettos, preached daily in bomb shelters, organized relief programs for Hungarian gypsies, and participated in clandestine Christian activities—all of which was illegal.

Under the leadership of Hitler's puppet General Antonescu, Romanian fascists unleashed fresh waves of persecution on the Jews. The Wurmbrands were forced to move to a much smaller apartment to endure jeers and scorn from violently anti-Semitic neighbors. In their apartment courtyard, anti-Jewish posters and propaganda were displayed. There was no escaping their identity, as the word *JEW* was stamped on Richard's and Sabina's identity cards. Hatred for Jews metastasized throughout Europe and even spread among Christians who did not resist the nationally endorsed phobia. Out of a population of nine million Jews living in Europe, the Nazis would exterminate between five million and six million.

Even still, Richard went door-to-door building relationships with anti-Semites and sharing the love of Christ with his neighbors. He strategically befriended the new landlord first and then those living near his apartment. Richard's use of language, his natural charisma, and his quick wit opened as many hearts as they did doors.

Mr. Parvalescu, who lived on the third floor, once told Richard, "You Jews have never done anything that's any good!"

Richard replied, "That's a fine sewing machine. What's its make? A Singer! Hold on … Wasn't that invented by a Jew? Mr. Parvalescu, if you really think the Jews are so useless, you'd better get rid of it!"

Mrs. Georgescu, a middle-aged anti-Semite, often spoke hatefully about "those Jews." Richard listened to her struggles, and before long, she poured out her heart to him. She described her sorrow when her husband abandoned their family and the anxiety she felt over her son, who was living a wild and promiscuous life. She worried he would catch a venereal disease.

"But even if he were to catch something," Richard assured her, "these things can be cured now. Although the remedy was invented by a Jew."

Richard's neighbors were charmed by the new blue-eyed, well-spoken pastor who could make them laugh. Even the roughest of neighbors, like the alcoholic policeman who physically abused his wife, could not escape the kindness and friendship of Richard. Richard's relationship with the man resulted in a change of heart and his eventual conversion. Afterward, Richard allowed him to take Mihai for long rides on his motorcycle, an extremely rare privilege for Jewish boys during the war. During the dreaded air raids, when it was illegal for Jews to travel outside the city, the policeman drove Mihai deep into the country to keep him out of harm's way. If caught, the policeman instructed Mihai to say his name was Jon M. Vlad.

Richard's amiable and empathetic personality gradually won the trust of others in his apartment block. Day by day he worked tirelessly to dismantle his neighbors' prejudices and share his faith. Once a target for hatred, the Wurmbrands' living quarters became an environment of friendship, encouragement, and peace. Inside the courtyard, posters of Bible verses replaced the anti-Jewish propaganda. Though hell raged outside, Mihai was surrounded with love, new friends, and as much happiness as could be mustered. Richard never allowed his busy schedule to keep him from playing with Mihai and telling him adventure stories.

· · · ·

Many Romanians underplayed or ignored the persecution of the Jews, resulting in the massacre of thousands who could have been saved. But Richard and Sabina could not look away. They personally felt the sufferings of their people and wept for those experiencing the horrors of the Holocaust. They even risked their lives to save Jews, like seven young girls who survived a massacre in the village of Tassy. The Wurmbrands negotiated to have the girls arrested and brought by rail to Bucharest. As the children were being transported, Richard and Sabina intercepted the train and smuggled the orphans to safety.

Other dangerous missions followed, resulting in the Wurmbrands' arrest and imprisonment. They were frequently charged with conducting unauthorized religious gatherings, and guards often beat them before they had to defend themselves in front of Nazi judges.

On one occasion, a Romanian woman stormed into the police station where Richard and Sabina were being held. "You have detained my Jewish brethren," she said. "It would be a privilege for me to suffer with them."

The policemen granted her wish, along with the wishes of many others who supported the young couple. Court testimonies were plentiful, like that of Pastor Fleischer, a German Baptist, who risked his life to provide evidence to secure Richard and Sabina's release.

In 1940 the relationship between Romania and Britain disintegrated, and the Anglicans ministering in Bucharest were forced to leave the city. Richard, who worked as the secretary to Rev. George Stevens, head of the Church of England Mission, was forced to continue ministering alone. By the end of the war nearly five years later, Richard decided to adopt a new Christian tradition. He had considered becoming Orthodox, the tradition to which most of the population belonged, but he resented their outward formalities, rituals, and meaningless pomp. He refused to become a Roman Catholic for similar reasons and especially detested the use of Latin, which, in his view, only disguised the Bible.

On the other hand, Richard admired the simplicity and directness of Protestant worship, with its emphasis on the plain preaching of the Bible. He was fascinated by the life and legacy of the sixteenth-century Protestant Reformer Martin Luther and decided to be ordained as a Lutheran pastor. He admired Luther's direct, passionate preaching and his immovable commitment to making Jesus Christ known to the common person.

Both men believed in the power of the gospel to transcend denominational barriers. In resisting the religious establishment of his day, Luther could be belligerent and quarrelsome. Yet Luther's stubbornness, like Richard's, was born out of a spiritual vitality held captive to the Word of God. For Luther, salvation was by grace, not works. Knowing full well the depths of his own depravity, Richard understood that no one could be good or holy enough to merit salvation. Richard also yearned deeply for the same spiritual awakening Luther witnessed in Europe during the Protestant Reformation. Could revival sweep over Europe again? Romania was not beyond the reach of a reformation. And if, like Luther, Richard also had to endure being hunted by opponents, persecuted by goverments, and kidnapped and imprisoned in isolation, so be it.

Richard's popularity as a preacher soon spread throughout the country, and his Lutheran congregation—mainly composed of Jewish converts—reached one thousand persons. He ministered in prisons, brothels, and pubs; worked for Norwegian, Swedish, and British missions; participated in the World Council of Churches; and played a central role in the formation of the Romanian underground movement. By the end of World War II, Richard had printed more than one hundred thousand copies of Russian New Testaments and distributed them to Communist troops living in Romania.

He expressed gratitude to God for these opportunities, praying, "Oh, Lord, how can I thank You that I'm among the beaten and mocked ones and, through Your grace, not among those who beat and mock?"

• • • •

For five years, the Wurmbrands resisted the Nazis' aggressive persecutions. Always in and out of prison, Richard and Sabina were almost sentenced to death. During their trial at the Romanian military tribunal—and only hours from their executions—the chief editor of Romania's most popular newspaper marshaled enough interest from prominent religious leaders to pressure the courts to release the Wurmbrands. Other citizens and even politicians risked their reputations to help. The repeated interventions of Swedish diplomat Reuterswärd ensured that Richard wouldn't spend the Nazi era behind bars. The diplomat's significant influence over General Antonescu resulted in Richard's release after he was arrested and forced to work in a labor gang.

On August 23, 1944, a group of political militants working under the guise of the child-king Michael's leadership courageously deposed General Antonescu, effectively ending his allegiance to Nazi Germany.

In Moscow, a meeting convened to determine the shape of the postwar world. Allies Winston Churchill and Joseph Stalin sat across from each other in Stalin's Kremlin office.

"So far as Britain and Russia are concerned," Churchill began, "how would it do for you to have 90 percent dominance in Romania,[2] for us to have ninety percent of the say in Greece, and go fifty-fifty about Yugoslavia?"[3]

Churchill scribbled his proposal on a single sheet of paper, and after a moment's consideration, Stalin added a blue check mark of agreement.

Soon one million Russians poured into Romania, and the country found itself with a new set of "allies."

• • • •

The Soviets swept into Berlin with unprecedented fury, exacting vengeance on the Nazis, who had raped, tortured, and pillaged their people. World War II had claimed 3 percent of the world's population. The United States lost almost half a million lives; the Germans lost approximately seven million lives. But the Soviet loss of life was much higher than both of these combined—more than twenty million people.

Sabina was thirty-one years old when Adolf Hitler committed suicide in his bunker after losing the battle for Berlin. Mihai was only six. The beatings Richard and Sabina had endured under the Nazis were severe, but they paled in comparison with the cruelties the Communists would inflict. The Communists would introduce the greatest carnage the world had ever witnessed, claiming nearly one hundred million lives. Moreover, compared with Hitler, who tolerated state-sponsored Christianity and even claimed to be religious himself, there was no place for religion in Communist-controlled Romania. Joseph Stalin's Marxist convictions interpreted Christianity as a threat to the government—a threat to be eradicated. As such, Christians were targeted, tortured, and executed to an extent they had never been under the Nazis.

The Lord had prepared Richard and Sabina for the horror ahead. Living in Nazi-controlled Romania prepared them to carry out their Christian work in secret. They learned to identify people who could be trusted with confidential information and how to overcome ethnic prejudice with love.

The Wurmbrands learned that with the help of the Holy Spirit, they could withstand any amount of torture and they could forgive their enemies. No matter how excruciating, humiliating, or degrading, the physical and psychological abuse Communism inflicted on them could be endured, and they could love those who inflicted it. Christ had been tortured for them, and He would assist them when they were tortured for Him.

9

The war offered ample opportunities to forgive those who harm. When Romania first entered the war, tens of thousands of Jews had been killed or deported. In the city of Iasi alone, eleven thousand people were slaughtered in a single day. Because Richard and Sabina lived in Bucharest in 1939, their lives were spared, but Sabina's Jewish parents, three sisters, young brother, and other relatives who lived in Bukovina were rounded up and sent to Transnistria, a desolate border province annexed from Russia.[1] The journey to Transnistria was treacherous and claimed the lives of many. Starvation, humiliation, and brutal execution awaited those who arrived. In a sweeping genocide, every member of Sabina's family was murdered in Transnistria.

When Richard broke the news to his wife, Sabina crumbled. Memories of her childhood rushed back into view. She would never see her mother and father again. She would never again embrace her sisters and her younger brother. How did they die? Who took their lives? She clutched her chest as guttural sobs flowed out.

If Sabina ever wept for her family again, Richard never saw it. "I'm not going to cry," she said, straightening her shoulders and slowing her breath. "You should have a happy wife, and Mihai should have a happy mother. Our church deserves a servant with courage."

Not long after, the Wurmbrands' landlord, a devout Christian, told Richard there was a soldier staying at his house. "I knew him before the war," he said, wringing his hands, "but he's changed completely. He's become an absolute brute who boasts about how he volunteered to exterminate Jews in Transnistria. He brags about killing hundreds with his own hands."

Transnistria? Richard felt a chill run down his spine. *Can it be?*

During dinner with Sabina and Mihai, Richard kept the news of the soldier to himself, turning it over in his mind and contemplating what he should do. After Sabina tucked her son into bed, she drifted to sleep. But Richard remained awake, his thoughts racing. God would not let him sleep. He crawled out of bed and went upstairs to the landlord's apartment for an all-night prayer vigil. Richard knocked on his landlord's door. As it opened, he saw the silhouette of a soldier lounging in the living room.

As the landlord made introductions, the soldier stood to his feet, towering over Richard. His name was Borila, a battle-seasoned veteran who filled the room with an intimidating aura. Richard could almost smell the metallic waft of blood still lingering on his clothes. He joined the two men, and Borila began recounting his wartime experiences, bragging about slaughtering countless Jews. He even boasted of killing infants still in their parents' arms.

Richard listened to his stories, wavering between feelings of rage and sorrow. Borila stopped to sip from his glass. "It's a frightening story," Richard interjected, "but I'm not scared for the Jews.

God will compensate them for what they've suffered." He looked squarely at the soldier. "I'm anguished thinking about what will happen to their murderers when they stand before God's judgment seat."

Borila leaped from his chair, a large vein pulsing in his thick neck. The landlord leaped up as well, fearing what he might do. Richard and Borila were guests in his house, and he wouldn't allow a brawl. Borila eyed Richard suspiciously as he regained composure and then returned to his lounge chair.

Over the course of the evening, the conversation drifted to more neutral topics. Richard noticed that Borila became a pleasant conversationalist. He loved music and described how, while stationed in Ukraine, he'd fallen in love with the local songs. "I wish I could hear them again," Borila mused nostalgically.

Richard knew some of those old songs as well and saw an opportunity. *The fish has entered my net!* he thought. "If you'd like to hear some of them," he told Borila, "come down to my flat. I'm definitely no pianist, but I can play a few Ukrainian melodies."

Though his family was asleep, Richard welcomed the two men into his home and softly played the songs Borila loved. The soldier's eyes welled up, and his face turned red. Like David, the Jewish shepherd boy who played the harp before King Saul, Richard knew the music was having a profound effect.

It didn't take long for Richard to exhaust his repertoire. He slid his hands from the piano keys and faced the murderer. "I have something very important to tell you."

Borila wiped his eyes. "Go on."

"If you were to look through that curtain," Richard said, gesturing toward the wall, "you'd see that someone's asleep in the next room. It's my wife, Sabina. Her parents, her sisters, and her twelve-year-old brother were killed with the rest of her family." The soldier glanced at the curtained room. "You told me that you killed hundreds of Jews near Golta."

Borila nodded.

"That's where they were taken. You yourself don't know who you've shot, so we can assume you're the man who murdered her family."

Borila jumped up from his chair.

Richard held up his hand. "Wait. I want to try something. Let's do an experiment. I'm going to wake up my wife and tell her who you are and what you've done. And I can tell you exactly what will happen."

Borila looked at the pastor in bewilderment.

"My wife won't speak one word of reproach to you," Richard assured him. "In fact, she'll hug you like you're her brother, and she'll bring you the best supper she can find in this house."

Borila clearly didn't believe him. If he had murdered her family, she would most certainly demand his blood.

Richard continued, "So if Sabina, who's a sinner like all of us, can forgive and love like this, imagine how Jesus, who is perfect love, can forgive and love you. If you turn to Him, everything you've done will be forgiven."

Borila's hardened exterior crumbled. Confronted with guilt and forgiveness, the killer clutched his shirt with both hands and ripped it apart. "Oh, God, what do I do? What do I do?" Borila cradled his head in his hands and sobbed. "I'm a murderer. I'm soaked in blood. *What do I do?*"

Richard declared, "In the name of the Lord Jesus Christ, I command the devil of hatred to leave your soul!"

Borila began to tremble as the two men prayed together aloud. Over and over, Borila asked God to forgive him, to relieve his conscience of his crimes.

When Borila had exhausted himself in prayer, Richard said to him, "I promised you an experiment, and I'm going to keep my word."

He drew back the doorway curtain and slipped into Sabina's room. "There's a man here you have to meet," he whispered, patting Sabina's shoulder. She rubbed her eyes and sat up. "I believe he's the man who murdered your family," he added, "but he's repented, and now he's our brother."

Sabina wrapped herself in a robe, sat in silence for a few minutes, and then went to greet her family's murderer.

Borila was surprised when Sabina embraced him. The two held each other and wept together, kissing each other's cheeks again and again. Richard knew his wife's heart. If God could forgive her for the crimes in her own past, she could forgive Borila. If God could cleanse her conscience of all the people she hurt, all the strangers she cheated, all the damage she inflicted, then God surely could do the same for Borila. Then, just as Richard predicted, Sabina went into the kitchen to prepare the soldier a meal.

As Sabina worked in the kitchen, Richard went into the next room to retrieve their two-year-old son. He brought Mihai, still asleep in his arms, into the living room to show his guest. It had been only a few hours since Borila had boasted of killing Jewish children in their parents' arms.

"Do you see how quietly he sleeps?" Richard asked. "You're also like a newborn child who can rest in your Father's arms. The blood that Jesus shed has cleansed you."

• • • •

Borila remained with the Wurmbrands that night and awoke refreshed. "It's been a long time since I slept like that," he confessed. After breakfast he went with Richard to the homes of other Jewish Christians, each time recounting his story and being welcomed like the returning prodigal son.

Richard gave Borila a copy of the New Testament and shared with him stories about how Jesus Christ can change even murderers. He explained how Saul of Tarsus also murdered God's people and how after he met Christ on the road to Damascus, he became known as Paul and became a great missionary.

But soon the time came for Borila to rejoin his regiment in a neighboring town. His unit had been ordered back to the front lines, and he was forced to make a decision.

"What do I do?" he asked Richard. "I'll have to start killing again."

"No," Richard said, "you've killed more than a soldier needs to." He wrapped his arms around his new brother and said, "Better allow others to kill you instead. The Bible doesn't forbid that."

Borila nodded, put on his military cap, and departed.

Over time he became one of the Wurmbrands' closest friends. As Richard later reflected, the only two men Sabina ever kissed after her marriage were her husband and the man who murdered her family.

10

"They're coming!" the boy shrieked as he frantically pedaled his bicycle toward Richard and Sabina. "The Russians are coming!"

As the first columns of Russians neared Bucharest on August 31, 1944, the Wurmbrands had braved the heat and sweltering sun to take the number-seven tram to meet them. "We have to," Richard said. "To talk to Russians about Christ is heaven on earth."

A wartime pastor, Richard had known many Russians in Romanian prison camps. Despite twenty-five years of atheist brainwashing, the Russians remained instinctively religious, and with thirsty souls, they drank in the gospel.

A cluster of red flags dotted the skyline above a group of local Communists who had emerged from hiding to greet the "glorious Red Army." The Communists looked at Richard and Sabina with interest as a nearby pair of Romanian officials nervously rehearsed their Russian greeting. In their hands they held the traditional gifts of a loaf of bread and a handful of salt.

The war was over, and Richard and Sabina felt the welcome relief of new possibilities. Richard stood tall, his broad shoulders echoing the confidence he had in his faith. His petite wife stood by his side, smiling. In the distance bells tolled, and there was no more gunfire. Perhaps everyone could now be friends again.

Richard and Sabina looked up the empty road and wondered what to expect. The Russians were allies now, but they were also a conquering army with well-known appetites for robbery and rape. How long would they stay in Bucharest? Richard and Sabina heard the approaching roar of motorcycles. Enormous tanks followed, red-starred helmets sprouting from their turrets and the ground shaking under their weight.

The Romanian Communists stood at attention as their comrades entered the city. They quivered out the lyrics to the Socialist anthem "The Internationale," their voices drifting off as the treads of the first tank slowed to a stop. Sabina looked up at the dusty gray steel of the tank, her eyes moving skyward toward the enormous gun mounted on top.

As the Romanian officials finished their welcome speech, they raised their offering of bread and salt to the tank commander. The young sergeant beside him glanced at thirty-one-year-old Sabina, one of the few women on the street that afternoon. "Well, sweetheart," he said, leaning over the edge of the tank and grinning. "What do you have to offer?"

Sabina stretched up on her tiptoes and handed him a book. "I've brought you the Holy Bible."

"Bread, salt, and Bibles, when all we want is a drink!" He chuckled and pushed back his helmet, his light hair glittering in the sun. "Thanks anyway!"

The tank rumbled to life again, its metal treads biting into the road. Richard and Sabina choked on the black clouds of exhaust bellowing from the engines as the column thundered past.

On their way home, Richard and Sabina watched from the tram window as the soldiers looted the meager shops that lined the street. They rolled wine casks onto the sidewalk and filled sacks with hams, chickens, and sausage. Bucharest had been ravaged by the Nazi occupation, but to the young Russian soldiers, it was rich beyond belief.

When the Wurmbrands exited the tram, Richard tried to start a conversation with one of the Russians, but the soldier's only response was, "Where can we find vodka?"

Richard and Sabina returned home to formulate a new plan. God had been stolen from the Russians in exchange for the promise of an earthly paradise that could never be fulfilled by human means alone. The Nazi terror was over, and the people of Romania hoped the Russians would soon leave in peace. Few guessed that Romania had set out on a road that led to prison and would be marked by the graves of countless friends.

A new and more horrifying tyranny had just begun.

11

The population of Romania totaled twenty-four million when the Russians invaded the country, and the Communist Party was a paltry ten thousand strong—hardly enough to fill a stadium. But the country was now run from Moscow, though the local Communists still played at democracy.

"We want friendship with everybody!" they claimed. "Freedom of worship? Absolutely! An all-party cabinet with King Michael as constitutional monarch? Why not?"

The Communists fooled the West with their promises for Romania, and for a short period of time, the country enjoyed religious freedom. The Orthodox leaders who had exercised tyranny over Jews and Protestants had lost their absolute power, and the dictator Antonescu had been executed. Finally Romania seemed to have a democratic government. But the mask soon dropped.

"You have to appoint Communists to the government!" The Soviet Union's foreign secretary, Andrey Vyshinsky, bellowed at the young King Michael and pounded his fist on the table in the king's office. The Romanian army and police were disarmed and dismantled, and the Communists seized power. In Russia, the Orthodox

Church had been made a pawn of the state. How long before that happened in Romania?

• • • •

The new Russian occupiers had one vision for their life: to drink, steal, and ravage. Men were robbed on the street of their bicycles and watches. Russian soldiers burst into homes and raped thousands of women, from the young to the infirm. The Red Army restored a vestige of order among their ranks with their guns, but the plundering continued on a large scale.

The Russians stripped Romania of its entire navy, most of its merchant fleet, half of its trains and railway cars, and every automobile. They pillaged farm produce, livestock, and petroleum and carted them back to Russia. Romania, which had been known as the granary of Europe, became a starving nation as famine struck the country.

One day Anutza, a sprightly Romanian woman from Norway and one of Sabina's closest friends, visited the Wurmbrand flat for coffee. "Oh, these Russians! Have you heard about our new deal with Moscow?" Her eyes sparkled with mischief. "They take all our wheat, and in return we give them all our oil. Yesterday I saw a Red Army man with three watches on each arm. They take them from people like they're collecting bus tickets!"

Anutza laughed, but for Romania, it was no laughing matter. The Soviet army looted goods worth billions of dollars. The stores were empty, and people waited in endless lines for the most basic necessities. The Romanians had hope, though, that Stalin would keep his word and the Red Army would leave when Germany was finally beaten. It would all be over soon.

• • • •

Throughout the Nazi occupation, the Wurmbrands had worked tirelessly to help the fascists' minority victims. But now a new minority had been created, and the hunter became the hunted. German troops were abandoned after the Nazis' retreat, and they were left to fend for themselves against the Russian troops, who chased them through the streets. The Germans were starving and terrified, and many died. The men whose ranks had killed millions, devastated countries, and murdered the Wurmbrands' family and friends were now just like them—victims of war. Richard and Sabina couldn't refuse to help them.

"God is always on the side of the persecuted," Richard answered those who derided him for risking his own safety for the sake of murderers. God had given the Wurmbrands the ability to return good for evil.

A constant stream of former German soldiers passed through Richard and Sabina's home. Once, a tiny outhouse in their yard hid three officers. Trudging through the knee-deep snow, Richard and Sabina brought them food and emptied their latrine buckets at night. They hated the atrocities they had committed but now welcomed the soldiers, trying to make them feel less like caged animals.

One night a German captain stopped Sabina. "I have to tell you something that's been on my mind. You know it's a death sentence to shelter a German soldier, and yet you do it—and you're a Jew!"

Even in the dark, Sabina saw him shake his head.

"When the German army recaptures Bucharest, which it will definitely do," he said, "I'd never do for you what you've done for us."

Sabina sat on an overturned box and tried to explain. "I'm your host. My family was killed by the Nazis, but even so, as long as you're under my roof, I owe you not only protection but also the respect due a guest." She saw the strange look on his face and continued. "The Bible says, 'Whoever sheds the blood of man, by man shall his blood be shed' [Gen. 9:6]. I'll protect you as much as I can from the police, but I can't protect you from the wrath of God."

"That's ridiculous," the captain said, patting Sabina on the shoulder.

She recoiled from the hand that had shed innocent blood.

"I'm sorry," he replied. "I didn't mean that badly. I just wondered why a Jewess would risk her life for a German soldier. I don't like Jews, and I don't fear God."

Sabina described to him God's command to love strangers and forgive others in the same way God had forgiven His children, but her words fell on deaf ears.

"Wait a minute," interrupted the officer. "Jews have committed crimes against the German people and all humankind. Honesty requires that I say that to your face. But from your perspective, you look on us as men who've committed crimes against the Jews. And you forgive them all?"

Sabina leaned in and tried once more to explain. "Even the worst crimes are forgiven by faith in Jesus Christ. I don't have authority to forgive, but Jesus will, if you repent."

The man lit a cigarette Richard had scrounged up for him. He took a deep draft and passed the butt to his friend. "Madam," the captain said, "I won't pretend to understand you. But perhaps if no one had this gift of returning good for evil, then there would never be an end to killing."

These soldiers eventually crossed the border safely into Germany, but thousands like them were captured and sentenced to years of hard labor in Soviet camps together with Russian Christians who might have taught them further. German soldiers, along with other groups of people, were the recipients of the Wurmbrands' Christian charity.

12

In 1945 on a train between Bucharest and Budapest, Sabina—the only woman on a train full of Russian soldiers—sat in a cargo car among the packages. She braced her legs against food and goods strewn around her.

"You can't go!" Anutza had begged. "The Russian soldiers are hungry for women. You walk through the streets and find girls with their throats sliced, and no one does anything!"

But Sabina knew that without supplies, the relief workers in Hungary wouldn't be able to feed the starving Jews and Christians of Budapest. The Russians had ransacked the Hungarian city, and Richard couldn't leave Bucharest. No one else would volunteer to make the delivery, so Sabina had to go.

After a long search, she found a corner in one of the few available train cars. The Russians had commandeered all the others.

The journey that should have been quick and easy took days. As the train pulled into Budapest, Sabina's eyes widened. Soldiers were still fighting, and everything was in ruins. The city's public transportation had been destroyed, and buildings spewed smoke from smoldering ashes.

With her packages in tow, Sabina stumbled through the streets of the war-torn Hungarian city. The people she sought were nowhere to be found. Some had been killed in the last days of fighting, and the Germans had deported the rest. At last she found two Christian leaders—Pastor Johnson of the Norwegian Mission and Pastor Ungar, a Jewish Christian who led the church where Jews and other nationalities worshipped. To them, Sabina was an angel sent from God.

The famine in Budapest was at its worst. As people emerged from the cellars, food had grown scarce. Hundreds were homeless, church buildings had been razed, and the people had resorted to eating a horse killed in the fighting. Sabina's help arrived just in time.

From Budapest, Sabina planned to go to Vienna. The Austrian city was also in ruins, and its people were starving. She arrived at the Budapest station for a train to Vienna, but people already hung from the doors and spilled over the roof of the available car. Suddenly Sabina heard her name and a round of cheerful laughter.

"There's no room, but we'll make room!" called out a girl who was with a group crowded together on the top of the train car. They were Auschwitz refugees who had stayed with the Wurmbrand family in Bucharest. Sabina climbed to the top of the car and joined the girls. The four-hour journey from Budapest to Vienna now took six days. For weeks Sabina had no contact with Richard, but she stayed in Austria until the work was finished. Although her work in Vienna may have been complete, the task in Bucharest was unending.

• • • •

"Strange news," Pastor Solheim said, interrupting Richard's work arranging the sanctuary for the Sunday service. "The government is summoning what it calls a Congress of the Cults. Every confession—every religion, in fact—is asked to send a big delegation." Solheim snorted. "And the conference is to be held in the parliament building! Whoever heard of such a thing? What can they be planning now?"

The mix of amazement and apprehension on his friend's face concerned Richard.

Everyone shared guesses and rumors about the meaning of the upcoming congress. Many believed the government's promise of full religious freedom, but Richard saw a larger, darker picture. *Isn't it happening here just as it happened in Russia?* he mused. *Lenin defended the persecuted sects ... until he came to power. Then tens of thousands died in concentration camps. First the church is lulled into acceptance. Then the blow falls.* Richard shuddered as horrific scenes flooded his memory.

Richard and his colleagues met with Pastor Solheim to discuss their involvement in the impending assembly. With Solheim, the head of the mission, lay the final judgment, and Richard saw the determination shining in his dark eyes.

"We'll go, and we'll speak out," he said. The decision was made.

• • • •

In Romania, the Christian church had begun a dangerous dance with Communism. Orthodox and Protestant leaders seemed to compete with one another in submitting to Communism. An Orthodox bishop stitched the hammer and sickle on his clerical robes and asked to be referred to as "Comrade Bishop" not "Your Grace."

Other priests became officers of the secret police, and seminary leaders added dangerous new theology to their curriculum. The deputy bishop of the Lutheran Church in Romania explained to his ministerial students that God actually had given three revelations not two: one through Moses, one through Jesus, and one through Stalin. It was under Stalin's revelation that the church now lived.

The Communists had "elected" the church leaders, and the church had little choice but to accept them. One group of Baptists in the town of Resita flew the Red flag over their annual meeting and sang the anthem of the Soviet Union as if it were a hymn of the Christian faith. The president of the Baptists praised Stalin as a great Bible teacher and proclaimed his fulfillment of God's commandments. Ministers who refused to dance with the Communists suffered greatly. Now all these ministers gathered at the Congress of the Cults.

· · · ·

On the morning of the gathering, Richard and Sabina joined their fellow clergy members climbing Parliament Hill. Crowded into the galleries and on the great hall's floor were four thousand religious leaders. Orthodox bishops and Catholic priests joined Protestant pastors and ministers. Jewish rabbis and Muslim mullahs sat side by side. The crowd cheered as Comrade Stalin, whose enormous portrait ominously stood guard over the hall, was named patron of the congress. No one seemed concerned that Stalin was an atheist and a mass murderer of Christians.

Red flags filled the auditorium, and top Communist leaders (the Romanian prime minister and minister of the interior) joined a grouping of top religious leaders on the platform. The assembly convened, blessed by the trembling old Orthodox patriarch Nicodim, whose hand the Communist leaders kissed while crossing themselves and paying homage to the Orthodox icons. Prime Minister Groza opened the congress with assurances of the Romanian government's support of faith—any faith—and the guarantee that the government would continue to pay the clergy. In fact, there would be raises. Those gathered welcomed the lavish promises of religious support from the government, and cheers and applause shadowed every speech.

Following the Communist assurances were responses from the priests and pastors. One by one they praised the government leaders for their support of religion and declared their loyalty to the new Romanian government. The state could count on the church if the church could count on the state. Communism and Christianity were fundamentally the same, the leaders said, and could certainly coexist. Throughout history, streams of all political colors had joined the great river of his church, one bishop said. He welcomed the prospect of a red one now entering as well. Over the airwaves, the glee and fervor of the religious leaders and Communist puppets were broadcast to the entire country.

Richard's blood began to boil. He tugged at his tightening shirt collar and seethed at the cowardice of the religious leaders. Communism hated religion! The ministers spoke out of fear for their families, their jobs, and their salaries, but why couldn't they just have stayed silent?

· · · ·

Next to Richard, Sabina shifted and sighed in exasperation, her anger growing with every fawning lie. Communism was dedicated to religion's *destruction*, not defense. The religious leaders had seen what happened in Russia. Why would they be so foolish as to think it would be any different here? The church had been seduced by the empty deceptions of Communism. This congress was spitting in the face of Christ.

Finally Sabina couldn't take it any longer. She exhaled slowly and wiped her sweaty palms on her lap. Her heart racing, she leaned toward her husband and grabbed his hand. Under her breath, she whispered in Richard's ear, "Richard, stand up and wash this shame from the face of Christ!"

Richard slowly turned toward Sabina and stared into her angry eyes. It was clear he knew she was right, but she could also tell he understood the consequences.

"If I do," he warned, "you'll lose your husband."

Sabina's eyes bored into Richard's, and she squeezed his hand harder. Her nails dug into his palm. With courage only from the Holy Spirit, she spoke again.

"I don't want a coward for a husband."

13

Richard sent his identification card forward and requested a chance to speak. The leaders of the congress were delighted to usher him to the podium. They glanced at one another and smiled, imagining the next day's news release: "Pastor Wurmbrand of the Swedish Church Mission and the World Council of Churches congratulates the Communist government on its support of religion in Romania!" They could almost see the headline and were already congratulating themselves on the propaganda win. But Pastor Wurmbrand had something else in store for the Congress of the Cults.

He took the podium, and a great hush fell on the hall. Sabina could feel the Spirit of the Lord drawing near. As Richard began his speech, the room sat in rapt silence. The object of Richard's praise wasn't Communism but Jesus Christ.

With faith-fueled courage, Richard reminded his colleagues that their duty as priests was to glorify God the Creator and Christ the Savior who died on the cross, not temporal earthly powers. He extolled the church's calling to support Christ's everlasting kingdom of love against the vanities of the day and ignored the party line, speaking biblical truth instead.

As he went on, the atmosphere of the entire room began to change. Ministers who had sat motionless for hours, passively absorbing the flattering fabrications of the Communist Party, seemed to wake up. Their glazed eyes refocused, and they shook themselves as if from sleep. Sabina's heart filled with joy as she realized her husband's gospel message was being broadcast to the entire country.

Suddenly someone began to clap. The tension snapped, and waves of applause washed over the room. Delegates stood and cheered. The Romanian church had awoken again.

From the platform, the minister of cults, a former Orthodox priest named Burducea, leaped to his feet. "Your right to speak is withdrawn!" he called out. With veins pulsing in his reddened neck, he barked orders to his minions on the floor below. "Cut that microphone!"

The audience shouted him down. "*Pastorul! Pastorul!*" they chanted rhythmically. From "a pastor," Richard had become "the pastor."

Richard ignored Burducea's order, reminding him that his right to speak came from God. As Richard verbalized the message all the Christian leaders wanted to speak, the crowd supported him with robust applause.

The uproar continued for minutes, with Communist lackeys scampering across the parliament hall in a frantic effort to silence Pastor Wurmbrand and calm the delegates. They severed the microphone wires, but it did little to quell the exhilaration in the room. Christian leaders shouted and clapped long after Richard left the stage.

The congress was now over for the day, and Richard and Sabina wound their way through the clamor and chaos back onto the streets of Bucharest. The risk Richard took would be worth it, but he would pay dearly.

• • • •

Richard's mother fiddled with the dial on her radio. She'd been listening to the broadcast of the congress, but when the radio went silent, she feared the worst.

When her son and his wife walked through the door later that afternoon, she gasped. "I thought they'd arrested you both! What will happen now?" Her white-faced concern betrayed the terror she'd experienced that afternoon.

"Mother," Richard said, enveloping her in a warm hug, "I have a powerful Savior. He'll do what's best for me."

Richard soon learned that the ministry of cults planned to cancel his license as a pastor, and he was advised to seek help from Justinian, the powerful Orthodox patriarch elect. Richard tried to reach him several times, but each time he failed to secure a meeting. At long last, he succeeded.

Justinian was newly responsible for the Orthodox Church—80 percent of Romania's churchgoing population. In a moment of inspiration, Richard decided to forgo arguing his own case before the patriarch; instead, he would use his precious time to encourage the man in his new role. At that fateful meeting, Richard began a relationship of influence with the head of Orthodoxy at a time when Communism was wreaking havoc all around him. He taught Justinian the Bible, prayed for him, and encouraged him to lead using scriptural examples. But even as Justinian grew in his knowledge of God and his faith deepened, the Communist Party launched a full-scale campaign against religion in Romania.

Until this point, Richard's life as a pastor had been full of satisfaction. His salary could support Sabina and Mihai, and his church family loved and trusted him. But Richard wasn't at peace. Why had God allowed him to live as usual while a tyrannical dictatorship was destroying everything around him and while other Christians were suffering for their faith? Many nights Richard and Sabina prayed for God to give them a cross to bear. Soon their prayers would be answered.

14

Soon after the ill-fated Congress of the Cults, Communists targeted the Wurmbrands' church. The growing congregation had recently moved to a new and bigger church building, and Communist protestors were sent to interrupt the services. Week after week, rough-looking young men and women muscled their way into the back of the hall to heckle, whistle, and disrupt.

"We should be glad," Pastor Solheim said. "Better a rowdy audience that cares than a silent one that only pretends to listen!"

Richard and Sabina decided to adopt a street-preaching strategy. If some people were too shy to come to church, then church would go to them. A small group would meet on a street corner to sing hymns, a foreign practice to the Romanians. A curious crowd always gathered, and with an audience, Sabina would deliver a gospel message. The sermons needed to be short and concise to avoid drawing the swift attention of the ever-present Communists.

Outside the Malaxa locomotive factory one afternoon, Sabina found herself amid a protest against the Communist take-over. She spoke to the gathered workers about the gospel, and for some, it ended up being their last opportunity for salvation.

The next day police opened fire on a factory crowd, and many workers were killed. In Communist Romania, time was precious and fleeting.

On one especially successful afternoon, Sabina spoke from the steps of the University of Bucharest. The growing crowd soon filled the entire square, causing a massive traffic jam along the adjacent boulevard. The people cheered and applauded Sabina's gospel message. As she was recounting the success to Richard, Anutza burst into their house.

"It's all over town that Ana Pauker made a speech outside the university!" No one could figure out why Comrade Pauker, a staunch officer of the Red Army, would tell the crowd to repent of their sins. Richard, Sabina, and Anutza roared with laughter.

In the years to come, Sabina held daily devotions for hundreds of Romania's religious leaders from all denominations. She preached on the streets to large gatherings. A powerful and charismatic speaker, the tiny woman became a towering giant in God's kingdom.

• • • •

Because of the piercing eye of the Communist government, it was becoming more dangerous to conduct the Wurmbrands' ministry out in the open. As had happened in Russia, Christians in Romania soon created a different version of church to evangelize, preach the gospel, and reach children for Christ. While the official church of Romania complied with the Communists' prohibition against Christian activity, the new band of Christians didn't … and their ministry flourished.

Together with other faithful Christians, Richard took his work "underground." Above ground, he held respectable official positions—pastor of the Norwegian Lutheran Mission and representative of Romania's branch of the World Council of Churches relief organization—and these positions provided cover for his real ministry work. No one would suspect the upstanding Richard Wurmbrand of subversive activity. In secrecy, through the underground church, Richard and Sabina began an effective, spirited ministry to the Russian soldiers and the enslaved people of Romania.

• • • •

On the day of his conversion, Richard had prayed for God to allow him to reach the Russians with the gospel of Christ. But instead of sending Richard on the long journey to Russia, God brought the Russians to him. And while Richard, with his command of the Russian language, could talk easily with the country's new residents, Communists didn't always understand his message.

In a shop one day, Richard met a male captain and female officer when he offered to translate for the Romanian salesman. After purchasing the needed goods, the pair agreed to join Richard at his home for lunch.

"You're in a Christian house, and we have a habit of praying," he explained before the meal. Impressed by Richard's Russian prayer, the Russian officers lost all interest in food and asked question after question about God, Jesus, and the Bible.

"How can He have a hundred sheep?" they asked when Richard told them the parable of the lost sheep. "Hasn't the Communist collective farm taken them away?"

When Richard presented Jesus as king, they said, "All the kings have been evil men who controlled their people, so Jesus must be a dictator also."

When he explained the parable of the wicked tenants, they responded, "Well, they were smart to rebel against the vineyard owner. The vineyard has to belong to the collective!"

To preach the gospel to the Russians, Richard realized that he had to adopt an entirely different approach. Years of brainwashing had ingrained their Communist ideology, so Richard changed tactics and used Marxist language as a point of contact with the officers. He wouldn't have been successful on his own, but with the Holy Spirit, the pair became Christians the following day and eventually became instrumental in Richard and Sabina's underground ministry to the Russians.

• • • •

The Wurmbrands and their church secretly printed and distributed thousands of Russian copies of the gospel of John and other Christian literature. Through converted soldiers, they smuggled

Bibles and sections of the Bible into Russia. Eventually the Wurmbrands would publish more than one hundred thousand Russian Gospels and more than one hundred thousand Christian books that were then distributed in parks, on trains, in cafés, at railway stations, and anywhere Russian soldiers were found.

They also took advantage of the tenderness in soldiers' hearts—a fondness for children and a longing to see their own children again. Mihai Wurmbrand and other young children would approach the soldiers in parks and on the street. The soldiers would engage them with loving questions and gentle pats on the head, offering them chocolate or candy. In exchange, the children would give them a Bible, which at that point the soldiers were eager to accept. What was too dangerous for adults to do, children could do openly and in complete safety. These young Christians became missionaries to the Russians.

The work wasn't without great risk, however. Many Christians in the underground church were caught and beaten mercilessly, but they never betrayed the ministry.

• • • •

In the early days of the Russian occupation, Christians throughout Romania took great risks to equip their brothers and sisters in neighboring countries, using the strategies Richard taught them.

On one bitterly cold winter night, a group of four Romanian Christians began the dangerous trek across the border into

Ukraine, by now part of the Soviet Union. Bundled in their arms were Bibles for Christians on the other side. Their journey through the snow was complicated by their curious decision to walk not forward but backward.

A Russian guard stationed along the border between Romania and the Soviet Union strolled through his routine patrol, one of the countless men tasked with preventing two paramount threats: Soviet citizens trying to escape and smugglers trying to bring in illegal items. As he walked slowly in the peaceful cold, he ran his flashlight back and forth over the freshly fallen snow.

Suddenly he drew a sharp breath as his light struck some indentations in the snow. Footprints! Headed into Romania! He raised his whistle and sounded a long, steady, shrill alarm. Within seconds, other guards with dogs surrounded him as the four Romanian Christians froze in the nearby darkness and listened intently.

"This way! This way!" The guard jumped and shouted, waving at the four sets of footprints. "They can't be far! Maybe we can catch them before they reach Romania!"

As the guards disappeared into the night air and the shouts and barking slowly faded, the four Christians smiled at one another. At the nod of their leader, they continued their journey, carefully walking backward into Ukraine with their precious cargo of Bibles for the underground church.

• • • •

Soon after the Soviets occupied Romania, Richard began to bring home Russian soldiers.

"Be careful, Sabina!" Anutza said. "What will you do if the German and Russian armies cross paths in your home?"

Richard and Sabina orchestrated a careful dance of hospitality. Richard started his outreach to the Russians by going to the Red Army barracks, posing as a black-market dealer in cheap watches. Romanians who wanted a watch had to purchase one from the army barracks, often buying back their own stolen timepieces. It was common for Romanians to do business in the barracks, so Richard had a solid cover. Once a group had gathered, he'd guide the discussion toward the Bible. Older soldiers would recognize Richard's maneuver.

"You haven't come to buy watches," one man said. "You've come to tell us about the faith. Sit and talk to us, but be careful. We know who to look out for." The man glanced at the soldiers sitting nearby. "The men around me are all good men, but when I put my hand on your knee, talk only about watches. When I remove my hand, you can begin your message again."

The Red Army was full of informers. They spied on their comrades and reported to their superiors. The young Russians knew nothing about God—they had never seen a Bible or been inside a church building. Sabina soon learned why Richard said it was "heaven on earth" to bring the gospel to the Russians.

One day two young soldiers knocked on the Wurmbrands' door. "Do you want to buy an umbrella?" one asked, offering three stolen samples.

"Ah, we're Christians," Richard replied. "We don't buy, but we have something to sell."

He invited them in, and Sabina brought them glasses of cold milk. The older of the two, a fair-haired man not more than twenty, gaped at Sabina.

"You're the one who gave me the Bible!"

At that moment Sabina recognized him. "You're the sergeant from the first tank into Bucharest!"

The soldier, Ivan, still had the Bible, tucked away in his barrack locker, and he had read it. Over dinner Ivan told Richard and Sabina about a Jew he'd fought with as his unit made its way across Eastern Europe. An older man in the unit used to torment the Jewish soldier: "You killed Christ!" he'd yell. The Jew thought he was crazy.

"He'd been killing people all the way from Stalingrad to Bucharest," Ivan explained. "How did he know who he'd killed?" The name of Christ was totally foreign to the Jewish soldier.

Ivan brought the man to the Wurmbrands' home, and Richard explained the entire Bible, from Genesis to Revelation. Over time Stalin ceased to be their God, and the soldiers visited Richard and Sabina often.

When his regiment moved out, Ivan left the Wurmbrands a farewell gift—a shiny, brand-new electric stove. Sabina glanced at Richard; the stove was obviously stolen.

"It's beautiful!" said Anutza. "Just what the Liebmanns need!"

The family had returned destitute from Auschwitz, and Richard gave them the stove. Ivan had stolen it out of gratitude for being shown the way of Jesus Christ.

A simple soul's love often shows itself in strange ways, Sabina thought. How good that the blood of Jesus covered even Ivan's theft of a stove.

15

In 1947 the arrests began. The Communists rigged elections with fraud and violence, taking total control of the country. Opposition leaders, police officers, and civil servants were liquidated in a swift wave of terror. Then the Communists focused their sights on the church. Catholic bishops and countless clergy, monks, and nuns were targeted next. Tens of thousands of ordinary people disappeared, sent to jails and labor camps. Others absconded to the mountains to join freedom fighters. No one's life remained the same.

In the earlier days of Russian occupation, the Jews had been able to leave Romania. Thousands had fled, leaving all their possessions and preferring the life of destitute refugees to the "freedom" the Soviets offered. Now they were trapped.

Anutza feared she was on the list of Jews to be arrested, and she planned to escape into the unknown life beyond the Communist walls. It was a wrenching farewell for Sabina and her dear friend.

"I'll work to get you both out of the country," Anutza promised. "We'll meet again in freedom." She worked tirelessly, but it would be nearly twenty years before the friends met again.

Terror spread through Romania. Secret police would charge into homes and search for hours, eventually taking the residents off to "make a statement." The promise of being gone for only a few hours never proved true. Vans marked Meat, Fish, and Bread cruised the streets of Bucharest, and foreign journalists reported that the Russians were providing food for the people of Romania. In actuality, the vans were transporting prisoners to captivity.

The Wurmbrands received their first warning when a plainclothes policeman found Richard at the mission headquarters.

"Inspector Riosanu," he said, introducing himself. "You're Wurmbrand?" The two men shared an acquaintance, and the inspector put the puzzle pieces together when he came across suspicious paperwork in his office. "I've come to give you a tip."

Richard furrowed his brow and waited for the man to continue.

"There's a big fat file on you at secret-police headquarters. I've seen it. Someone's informed on you lately. Been talking to a lot of Russian friends, haven't you?" Riosanu rubbed his calloused hands together. "But I thought we might come to an agreement …" His voice trailed off as he looked pointedly at Richard. For the right price, he would destroy the report.

Sabina joined the conversation, and the trio agreed on a sum.

Folding the bills and stuffing them into his pocket, Riosanu said, "You've got a deal. The informer's name is—"

"No!" Sabina interjected. "We don't want to know."

If Richard and Sabina didn't know the informer's name, they couldn't resent him. In those days, they couldn't have known the countless lives informers would destroy.

The inspector shrugged and placed his hat on his head. "As you wish." With that, he disappeared into the night air as quickly as he'd arrived.

Soon after, Richard was brought to police headquarters for questioning. But in the absence of an official charge of subverting the Red Army, the Wurmbrands' influential friends were able to secure his release after roughly three weeks. The release certainly didn't feel like the end of the road, though. Almost daily, more and more friends were arrested. And often with those arrests came torture.

• • • •

Though Jews throughout the country were now trapped in Romania, it wasn't too late for the Wurmbrands to leave. Thousands were still buying their way out. Sabina knew Richard didn't want to leave, but he warned her, "Under Antonescu's rule, we were never imprisoned for more than two or three weeks at a time. With the Communists, it could last for years. And they might take you too. And Mihai—who will look after him?"

Odd conversations with friends and acquaintances seemed to reinforce the wisdom of leaving, and the Wurmbrands wondered if these were messages from God.

"If we go to the West," Richard said, "won't we be able to do *more* for the church in Romania? If we stay, I'll follow the others into prison. It'll be the end of our life together. I'll be tortured, perhaps killed. And if you're imprisoned too, it's the end of the mission. The Solheims are foreigners—they won't be allowed to stay. Mihai will be raised on the streets as a Communist. What good will it do anyone?"

One night Richard and Sabina's answer became clear. Fifty believers had gathered for a secret prayer meeting in the home of a neighbor. At nearly midnight, a kneeling woman suddenly cried out, "And you, the one who thinks of leaving! Remember that the Good Shepherd did not desert His flock. He stayed until the end." She knew nothing about Richard's dilemma, and the Wurmbrands looked at each other in surprise.

When dawn came, Richard and Sabina walked home through the cold streets. It was January, and fine specks of snow were falling. "We can't leave now," Sabina said, and her husband agreed.

Many years later, when Richard regained his freedom after years of imprisonment and torture, the same woman met him at the train station to welcome him home, flowers in hand.

"I don't regret taking your advice," Richard told her. "I'm thankful for it."

• • • •

In the years to come—years bookended by persecution and unspeakable torture—Richard and Sabina left Christ's mark on the people of Romania. They disguised Christian literature, inserting books behind Communist propaganda, and distributed them in cafés and on the streets. Richard and Sabina sheltered orphaned children, former Nazis, ex-convicts, and Christians who were about to be exiled to Siberia. In a soup kitchen, they fed hundreds of war victims each day as the country suffered unrelenting drought and famine, and they held two summer camps for Christian leaders of all denominations in the Carpathian Mountains.

As their Bucharest church grew, topping one thousand Jewish converts and other Christians, the Wurmbrands' ministry drew the ire of the Communist regime.

16

February 29, 1948, began on a leisurely note. Richard bent down to kiss Sabina good-bye and stepped from his home into the brisk Bucharest air. The lanky thirty-nine-year-old pastor set out on his short stroll to church, winding from Olteni Street through the picturesque Vacaresti neighborhood.

It was a familiar walk peppered with parked cars. Signs of life at that early hour were few. The quiet Sunday venture freed Richard's mind to think about the main points of his morning sermon. Historic buildings loomed over his head, flanking the street and reminding him of his city's rich history. He zigzagged his way to his Lutheran church, where his wife would meet him in a half hour. Later that afternoon, he would officiate the wedding of their young friends, but for now his soul—like his soles—followed the topography of his Sunday-morning routine.

When a black Ford van approached and two men jumped out and grabbed him, Richard quickly realized his plans were futile. There would be no meeting his wife, no preaching his sermon, no officiating the afternoon wedding. Moments later, he was forced into the back seat of the van with a gun at his temple, the captive of a cadre of secret police. The Ford barreled down the street toward an unknown destination. Richard stole glimpses of his surroundings through the windows, but the brutality of his captors robbed him of the ability to focus clearly. The vehicle raced through the city center and then slowed as it approached a towering set of steel gates.

Richard couldn't tear his thoughts from the politician he knew who committed suicide in his prison cell only weeks after his kidnapping and arrest. *Will I suffer the same fate?* Richard wondered. Then he remembered the message "Do not fear" occurs exactly 366 times in the Bible, one time per day for an entire year, including leap year. For Richard, it was providential that he was abducted on February 29, a reminder that he wouldn't need to fear what men could do to him. Fear was one emotion he would not allow to enter his prison cell. With God's help, he could endure torture, ill treatment, disease, and even death so long as others could see Christ in his eyes.

The previous evening, Richard and Sabina had hosted a few friends at their home when one of them said about the politician, "He must have gone through hell."

"Richard, what do you think hell is?" another friend asked.

As the bars of the gate slammed shut behind the vehicle, Richard assumed it would be one of the last sounds he would ever hear.

"Hell is to sit alone in darkness remembering evil you have done," he had replied.

• • • •

Thirty minutes after Sabina kissed her husband good-bye, she departed for church as well, following the route Richard often took. When she arrived, she found Pastor Solheim, the head of the mission, pacing in his office, distracted and distraught.

"Richard hasn't shown up," he said. "But he has so much on his mind. He must have remembered some urgent appointment and forgotten he has to come here."

Sabina wasn't aware of another appointment. "But he promised he'd see me here in half an hour," she said.

"Maybe he met a friend who wanted help," he replied nervously. "He'll come."

While Pastor Solheim led the worship service without Richard, Sabina telephoned her friends, but they didn't know where her husband was.

"Now, don't worry," Solheim said after the service ended. "You never know with Richard. Remember the time we had that summer camp and he went off to buy a newspaper in the morning and then telephoned at lunchtime to say he wouldn't be back for breakfast?"

Sabina nodded, but fear escalated in her heart.

Her friends enjoyed the customary Sunday lunch Sabina prepared that afternoon in her apartment. It was the highlight of the week for many, but her appetite had long since vanished. As her guests ate and sang, she hoped Richard had remembered some pressing task and would return soon. She imagined him opening the door, laughing and apologizing for being late. She would forgive him, and all would be right again.

After Pastor Solheim officiated the wedding, Sabina telephoned all the hospitals in the city. Thinking Richard might have
been hit by a car, she searched frantically through numerous emer-
gency rooms, but to no avail. There was no sign of her husband,
only the memory of his promise to see Sabina thirty minutes after
he departed for church.

As the afternoon turned to evening and the evening nestled
into night, Richard still hadn't returned. Silently Sabina waited by
the door. The hours crept by until what she feared became the only
possible explanation for his absence.

• • • •

The Communist secret police manhandled Richard from the
van into their headquarters. They ripped off his tie, emptied his
pockets of identification and papers, and stripped off his clothes.
The laces of his shoes—which prisoners often used to hang themselves—were roughly removed.

"From now on," said one of the officials, "you are Vasile
Georgescu."

The name was generic enough to disguise any prisoner's
identity. Given Richard's popularity and knack for escaping pros-
ecution, even the guards wouldn't be able to identify him when
questioned. Richard would simply disappear without a trace.

This prison, beneath one of Bucharest's main streets, Calea
Rahovei, was new and relatively unknown. As its first prisoner,

Richard knew his supporters would never think to search for him there.

His concrete cell was narrow and primitive. A small box of sunlight entered the room from the window cut too high in the wall for prisoners to escape through. Richard sat on a plank bed next to a bucket in the corner and waited for the interrogators to enter. The waiting was always the hardest part of prison—the hellish part. He imagined the questions his interrogators would hurl at him and the torture techniques they would apply to weaken his resistance.

The threat of physical pain had extracted much information from other prisoners, but the fear Richard felt during his abduction had departed. In its place was a hardened resolve to suffer anything for the sake of the gospel. Richard believed God would empower him to stand up to the worst physical agony his abductors could impart.

Richard sat in the silence. Motionless as the stones surrounding him, he began to thank God for bringing him to this prison. Each passing second became an answer to his and Sabina's prayers to let them bear a cross. What strange and wonderful opportunities would blossom within these walls? What friendships with the guards could he build? Richard didn't know. But he hoped God would shine through him as he suffered in isolation in the foreboding Calea Rahovei prison.

• • • •

The Communists had taken not only Richard's identity, but like her husband, Sabina too ceased to exist. As the wife of a political prisoner, she received no ration cards, nor could she be employed. Acquiring food became a weekly challenge.

"How am I supposed to live?" she asked the officials. "And my son?"

They always replied, "That's your business."

For months Sabina searched for Richard, wandering from one office to the next in hopes of gathering information. Officials of every rank denied her requests and refused to acknowledge her husband's imprisonment. In the evenings at home, Sabina sat by the window, waiting and weeping. *Perhaps tonight he'll return,* she mused. After all, in the past the fascists usually released him after a week or two of confinement.

But the fascists were no longer in power, and the Communists were proving more aggressive than the Nazis. Resolved to take the matter to the highest authority, Sabina set out for the ministry of the interior. She knew that high-profile prisoners were often detained in the office basement, and she had seen the building swarm with families seeking information about their loved ones.

As Sabina made her way to the information office on the second floor, she ascended a staircase that was crammed with mothers and children waiting in line. A slogan on the wall above declared, "WE WILL BE RUTHLESS TO THE CLASS ENEMY."

Sabina overheard the conversations of the women ahead of her in line. The officials listened to their heartfelt pleas and even rifled through their files, pretending to search through pages of typed names. Filing cabinets were opened, notes were jotted down, but the answer was always the same. There was no trace of their husbands in the records.

Sabina's inquiry was met with the same staged performance, and she left the office feeling deflated and defeated. She decided to approach the Swedish diplomat, Mr. Reuterswärd, for help.

Pastor Solheim accompanied Sabina to meet him. He had rescued Richard in the past, and Sabina was confident Reuterswärd could free him again. Against the better judgment of his superiors, the diplomat risked his reputation to glean any leads about Richard. He spoke to the foreign minister, Ana Pauker, who told him, "Our information is that Pastor Wurmbrand has absconded from the country with a suitcase full of dollars entrusted to him for famine-relief work. They say he is in Denmark."

The diplomat, unimpressed with the obviously false information, spoke with Prime Minister Groza, who said jovially, "So Wurmbrand's supposed to be in our jails? If you can prove that, I'll release him!"

Proof would be difficult to come by, but Sabina couldn't abandon her search. Having exhausted all her resources and with no one else to intervene on Richard's behalf, she would have to resort to bribery.

17

The exchange of information for money led Sabina into the dangerous, crime-ridden neighborhoods of Bucharest. She was willing to pay anyone who promised to find out the whereabouts of her husband. Some said Richard had been kidnapped and transported to Moscow. Others spoke of his death, claiming that his funeral had already happened.

One day Sabina's childhood friend Klari Meir had an idea. "You know Teohari Georgescu, the cabinet minister?" she asked.

Sabina shook her head.

"His brother lives near us, and I've heard that he can open prison doors for the right amount of money. I'll talk to his wife for you."

Sabina met Mr. Georgescu in a squalid ghetto on the outskirts of the city. He was a short man wearing an expensive suit.

"I'm Georgescu," he said. "I arrange things. A word to my brother, and it's as good as done. Guarantee? You have my word."

Georgescu's price was high, but Sabina was able to raise the funds to pay him. No sum was too great compared with the life of her husband.

For weeks nothing happened. No word from Georgescu, no follow-up meeting. Sabina eventually concluded what her instincts had long since suspected. Once again a charlatan had swindled her.

For months thieves took advantage of Sabina's desperation. Criminals of all ranks and walks of life drained her funds, making it more difficult for her to raise support. She funneled the money she needed for food and necessities into the pockets of anyone claiming the ability to secure inside information. But each new contact turned out to be a fraud. Sabina soon came to expect the hollow promises all of them offered.

• • • •

One night a high-ranking politician came to Sabina's flat. "Who knows what's coming?" he said. "Perhaps the British and the Americans."

Sabina knew tensions between the United States and the Soviet Union were escalating, and for a brief moment, she found a glimmer of hope in the thought of liberation.

The politician helped Sabina as best he could, even offering a cash reward. But like the rest, his efforts proved futile. Sabina met another Communist official through a friend who had gone to school with him many years ago. The Communist official and Sabina's friend pretended to be lovers, meeting secretly without being suspected, but their negotiations rendered no results.

After endless meetings with criminals and fruitless months of investigations and bribery, Sabina received a knock on her door one evening.

The stranger was gruff and smelled of plum brandy—a scent Sabina knew well.

"I've met your husband," he said.

Sabina didn't believe him but continued to listen.

"I'm a warden," he said. "Don't ask what prison. But I take him his food, and he said you'd pay me well for a bit of news."

"It depends," Sabina replied. "How much?"

The stranger offered his price. "I'm risking my neck, you know."

The price was enormous, and Sabina doubted she could raise enough to pay him. Yet if this stranger could obtain tangible evidence that her husband was alive, she would try.

She told Pastor Solheim, who, though equally skeptical, met with the stranger. He handed the warden a chocolate bar and said, "Take this to Wurmbrand and bring back a message with his signature."

Two days passed without a word from the warden. Suddenly a knock interrupted Sabina's evening. When she opened the door, the warden removed his cap and handed Sabina the wrapper from the chocolate bar. She examined it carefully, unable to believe the words she read.

"My dearest wife, I thank you for your sweetness. I'm well. Richard."

The handwriting belonged to her husband! No mistaking it. She could have spotted his bold, clear letters a room away. Tears filled Sabina's eyes.

"He's all right," the warden said. "He sends you his love."

Sabina tried to imagine the horrible conditions Richard was experiencing and hoped the chocolate bar brought him some relief. She would have given anything to be with him, even if for a few minutes.

"Some can't take it in solitary," said the warden. "They don't like their own company."

Sabina knew Richard wasn't truly alone. As he often told her, in prison the presence of Christ was immediate. She had to continue encouraging him with messages, and she bribed the warden with everything she possessed.

"People have gotten twelve years for this," he told her. "You know, it's not just about the cash."

The warden risked his freedom to transmit verbal messages back and forth, and Sabina felt such gratitude toward him. He gave her hope that Richard was still alive.

"What do you do with this money we pay you?" Sabina once asked him.

"Get drunk!" he said, laughing.

If his inebriation could alleviate Richard's discomfort, the transaction would be worth the trouble. Richard was alive, and that was all that mattered. Sabina gave the warden enough cash to drown in brandy for months. Yet unexpectedly, he struck up a genuine friendship with Richard and smuggled extra pieces of bread to him when no one was looking.

When Sabina told Pastor Solheim and his wife, Cilgia, about the news of Richard's imprisonment, the couple dropped all other responsibilities and focused on trying to liberate him.

Solheim took Sabina to see the Swedish diplomat again, this time with a chocolate-bar wrapper as proof at last of Richard's plight. The diplomat immediately drafted a letter to the prime minister: "You promised to release Pastor Wurmbrand if we could prove that he is in a Romanian prison. I now have that proof in my hands."

Groza, astonished that his joke had backfired, relayed the information to Ana Pauker, the foreign minister, who requested a meeting with the diplomat. Furious and insulted, she berated Reuterswärd for insinuating that she was a liar, and once again she insisted that Richard had fled to Denmark. She wouldn't tolerate the diplomat's nosy meddling and refused to entertain his request for an investigation. Reuterswärd couldn't let an innocent man suffer and once again demanded her cooperation. But for the foreign minister, the case was closed.

The diplomat's superiors questioned the wisdom of his intervention, and he was declared persona non grata. With his reputation tainted and his leverage lost, he could no longer assist Sabina in her quest to find Richard, even though she had proof he was alive and imprisoned somewhere in Romania. Reuterswärd's career was over. He was recalled to Stockholm and retired under pressure from his diplomatic office.

Even more discouraging for Sabina was the tragic news that her closest friends, Pastor Solheim and his wife, could no longer remain in Romania. In her moment of deepest trial, Sabina had found courage and resilience through their encouragement. When she felt like giving up and believing the lies, they had bolstered her hope and confidence. How could she survive without them? But Solheim's missionary work had come to an end, and the little assistance they could now provide was from afar.

Before they left, though, God answered the months-long prayer of Sabina and her dear friends. Richard had finally been found!

• • • •

The rumor tore through the streets of Bucharest. Twice a week, in a particular government office on Calea Rahovei, relatives of missing persons could present themselves before the officials and learn about their loved ones' whereabouts. For this last-ditch effort, Sabina turned to her friend Bianca and asked her to appear on behalf of her "brother" Richard.[1]

Bianca wrote her petition and presented herself at what was later discovered to be the secret-police headquarters—the building above Richard's prison. Women waited in the outside courtyard to enter the office and learn if their relatives' names were on the official's list. As Bianca waited, the lady next to her pointed to one of the small windows of the building's basement.

"Look over there, at that window, but be careful not to be noticed," the woman whispered. "It seems like a man is there, and he's pointing at you, almost as if he wants to pass some message to you."

Bianca turned slowly and began to make out the face of a skeletal, unshaven man. She rubbed her eyes and tried to focus on the shadowy figure. It was Richard! He was alive!

Bianca hid her excitement, and Richard, apparently realizing she couldn't show that she recognized him, lifted up one hand and smiled at her.

Soon it was Bianca's turn to enter the office. "Wurmbrand, Wurmbrand … No, he's not on our list," the officer said. "That means he's not with us, and we don't know his whereabouts."

In a moment Bianca understood that this farce was yet another of the Communists' cruel and deceptive tricks to torture the prisoners' families even more. Every relative received the same denial.

But the official's information did nothing to dissuade Sabina. From the moment she learned of Richard's location, she arrived twice a week at the headquarters of the secret police, ostensibly to seek information on her missing husband. And each time as she waited in the courtyard, she "spoke" to Richard through glances and longing looks. As long as Richard remained at the Calea Rahovei prison, Sabina visited him.

But no one knew how long these visits would last.

18

To Sabina's surprise and joy, Israel officially became a state on May 14, 1948. In the wake of the Nazi massacre of Romanian Jews, the news prompted an exodus of families from the Communist-controlled country. Though Richard suffered in his cell, Sabina knew he would be excited about the fulfillment of God's ancient promise to the prophet Jeremiah: "Behold, I will gather [my people] from all the countries to which I drove them in my anger and my wrath and in great indignation. I will bring them back to this place, and I will make them dwell in safety" (Jer. 32:37). If, after nearly twenty-six hundred years, God could bring His people home, He could do the same for Richard.

However, as in the days of the Babylonian captivity, traveling to the Promised Land proved to be no easy pilgrimage. The iron grip of Communism held the population in place; few escaped its grasp. Russian soldiers frequently raided streets to arrest Jews and force them to labor deep in the Soviet mines. Romanians were rounded up as well. After the secret police abducted them, they were thrown into trucks and never heard from again.

In Sabina's hometown of Bukovina, a young man informed her, "My brother spent four months hidden in a hole behind a cupboard to avoid deportation to the Soviet Union. I got out with only the clothes on my back. I told a Soviet bureaucrat that he could have my flat with all its contents and every penny I had in return for a passport. I got it and left." The man sighed. "So much for Communism—it's simply the thieving of everything by everyone from everyone."

Exodus was on everyone's mind, but escaping was expensive. In desperate need of foreign currency, the Romanian People's Republic, spearheaded by foreign minister Ana Pauker, signed a pact with Israel that allowed Romania to sell their Jews to the new nation. Later, professors, doctors, and scientists were purchased for top dollar.

Crowds of Jews gathered outside Bucharest's visa office, eager for their country to sell them. The most vulnerable and undesirable—grandparents with babies in their arms—slept on the pavement outside the office, waiting for a chance, like everyone else, to flee Romania. A line of Jews hoping to secure Israeli visas stretched all the way from the police station to Parliament Square.

"What's this line for?" a stranger asked a Jew.

"Oranges," said the Jew.

"But in that shop across the street, they're selling oranges with no line."

"Ah," the Jew said, "but we want to eat them from the tree."

The topography of Israel, irrigated for the first time in centuries, promised enough produce to sustain a nation. Throughout Romania, cargo trains crammed full of Jews departed the country by the dozens. Even non-Jews sought freedom, paying exorbitant amounts of money for forged visas. Because the government sought to keep Operation Israel secret, the trains weren't allowed to leave from Bucharest's central station. Instead, they departed under the cloak of night from obscure suburban stations. Sabina went to these rail stations weekly with tears in her eyes, wishing her friends good-bye and Godspeed on their journeys to new lives.

Sabina considered leaving the country too, but not without Richard. No matter how many years it took to gain his release, she wouldn't abandon him to suffer his exile alone.

"Next year in Jerusalem!" was the cry of the Jewish heart from every ghetto and synagogue in the city. Sabina cried for this too. She yearned to travel by train with Richard and Mihai to Israel—to experience the holiest of homecomings in the land God had promised them.

Even soldiers and guards risked their lives to escape service in the military. A top-ranking police officer once told Sabina, "If you give me money and help in getting a visa as a Jew to leave the country, I can get your husband out of jail."

Sabina's friend, whom she trusted wholeheartedly, affirmed the policeman's sincerity and assured her he could fulfill his promise. Mihai leaped with excitement at the news. He would finally see his father again. Tall for his age and mature beyond his years, Mihai had developed a reputation among his peers as an outcast. He struggled to explain to other students at school why his father was so often imprisoned. The rejection Mihai experienced never escaped Sabina's notice.

"Mummy, I had a dream," Mihai said the morning after learning of the policeman's offer. "I saw our neighbor holding out his hat and begging two birds to land in it. They fluttered around, and then they flew away."

Sabina knew the meaning of the dream. The policeman would fail in his attempt to free Richard. Several days later, the dream came true, and the policeman was arrested.

Mihai had other insights regarding the future, but his dreams—like many childhood experiences—usually ended in nightmares.

Jews disappeared every day, nabbed from the back alleys of Bucharest. On one occasion, a large number of well-known prisoners was released from prison. Ambulances delivered each man to his house so he could show his family his bruises and tell them about his torture. The next day they were all rearrested.

Sabina worried about Richard's ability to endure torture. The Communists were far more skilled than the Nazis at extracting information from prisoners. Jesus once said, "Do not fear those who kill the body but cannot kill the soul" (Matt. 10:28), but Sabina knew of pastors who denied Christ under torture and even betrayed their families and closest friends. Guards often used threats of amputation, castration, and other horrific practices with alarming success. At first the human body can withstand even the most severe physical trauma. But when the body is injured repeatedly, the memory of the pain accumulates until it gradually breaks the will.

Sabina feared Richard's resolve would collapse, especially after years of torture. He once promised her that he would die before betraying his friends, but Sabina remembered that even the apostle Peter broke his promise not to deny Christ. As resilient as Richard was, even the best of men could break. Jesus reminded His disciples, "The spirit indeed is willing, but the flesh is weak" (Matt. 26:41). If the worst-case scenario unfolded and Richard was killed during torture, Sabina knew she would see him again in heaven. They had previously talked about their desire to meet again in heaven at one of the twelve gates—the Benjamin Gate.

19

In 1948, in his underground cell beneath Calea Rahovei, Richard could barely glimpse the edge of the courtyard through the high window of his cell. He often wondered if his faith was resilient enough to withstand the cruel treatment to come. He comforted himself with the many Scripture passages he had long since committed to memory.

The interrogators were patient in their questioning. Like a well-stocked library, Communist prisons contained archives of data—but instead of data stored in books, it was housed in human bodies. Sensitive and timely information was gradually extracted from the prisoners when it was needed, and never all at once. Richard himself was a vast treasure chest of information in the eyes of his interrogators. But they would take their time extracting the names in his network of relationships with Western churches and in the World Council of Churches. His numerous affiliations were treasonous to the Romanian Communists. He was their political prisoner and would most likely die at the hands of his interrogators.

But unknown to his captors, Richard possessed a secret and powerful weapon—he'd been training for imprisonment for years. Like a soldier in peacetime, Richard had prepared his mind and body for interrogation, torture, and malnourishment. On the day of his kidnapping, he was in perfect condition to endure beatings, verbal harassment, and the brutal conditions of his cell.

Richard had spent many years studying how other Christians endured intense suffering. He even had become something of a "martyrologist," constantly adapting and adjusting his lifestyle to anticipate similar hardships. While less-prepared prisoners caved under the pressure of imprisonment and often fed information to the interrogators, Richard had gained a reputation among the guards for his resilience.

A commonly used line during interrogation went this way: "As a Christian, you must promise to tell us the whole truth about everything"—but it never worked on Richard. In fact, no strategy worked on Richard. Since anything he said might lead to incrimination—or worse, apostasy—he devised a plan: he would confuse and mislead his interrogators until they couldn't continue their investigation.

But first Richard found a way to send messages to Sabina and his friends to let them know his whereabouts. Pastors and church leaders in Scandinavia and Britain also expressed concern about his disappearance.

Even the bravest of men cowered before Mrs. Pauker, whom Richard knew personally. Ana's father was a clergyman called Rabinovici, who once told Richard with sadness in his voice, "Ana has no feeling in her heart for anything Jewish." Originally she studied medicine to be a doctor before teaching briefly at the English Church Mission. Ana gained enough familiarity with religion in her early life to attempt its destruction when she ascended to power.

After marrying an engineer named Marcel Pauker, she embraced Communism and was arrested by political opponents for her participation in conspiracies. A devout Soviet at heart, Ana and her reluctant husband moved to Moscow; however, during one of Joseph Stalin's prewar population purges, Marcel was executed. Ana quickly ascended the ranks as a Russian official before returning as the foreign minister in Romania. Her ruthless reputation landed her on the cover of *Time* magazine, where she was described as "the most powerful woman alive."[1]

So enraptured was Ana Pauker with Russia that, on a fair and beautiful day, she was seen walking through Bucharest under the shade of her umbrella.

"Why are you carrying an umbrella?" someone asked.

"It's raining in Moscow," Ana replied. "I heard it on the radio."[2]

20

Richard couldn't believe his eyes when his cell door swung open. The man who entered was none other than minister of justice Lucretiu Patrascanu, the politician responsible for bringing Communism to Romania. What an honor to be interrogated by such a high-ranking officer.

But when the door slammed shut behind him, Richard caught a glimpse of Patrascanu's shoes—no laces. His shirt, devoid of a necktie, hung untidily around his neck. He was a prisoner too.

Patrascanu sat on the wooden bed across from Richard. His straight-laced demeanor revealed how highly respected he was accustomed to being. Prison would not alter the politician's usual poise. Richard knew the destructive role Patrascanu had played in the corruption of Romania and how much injustice he had caused. But as the two prisoners spoke, Richard saw his sincerity and believed he could talk to him man-to-man.

Patrascanu had been arrested several times before by previous leaders. His political enemies, jealous of his growing popularity, had conspired to rid Romania of his presence. A few days earlier, the minister of the interior, Teohari Georgescu, had succeeded in casting him as a bourgeois traitor. With the support of Vasile

Luca, the minister of finance, an accusation of helping imperialist powers was launched against Patrascanu.

Accounts of prisoners and counterrevolutionaries being tortured deeply disturbed him. When he inquired about these rumors, Patrascanu forfeited his good standing as a loyal Communist. The final nail in his coffin was hammered into place by his old friend Ana Pauker.

"As I left the hall," he told Richard, "I saw a new driver waiting at the car.' The driver said, 'Your chauffeur, Ionescu, has been taken ill, Comrade Patrascanu.'"

Richard leaned forward and listened.

"I stepped in, two secret policemen got in after me—and here I am!"

Instead of the sparse pieces of boiled barley Richard was usually served for dinner, the guard presented Patrascanu with a delicious spread of chicken, cheese, and fruit. A bottle of wine was uncorked for the minister, but the new prisoner had no appetite. He slid the tray over to Richard, who devoured the banquet ravenously.

Humorous stories poured from Patrascanu's lips as Richard ate. He reminisced about the Swiss senator who requested to become the navy minister. "But we have no navy!" said the prime minister.

"What does that matter?" the senator asked. "If Romania can have a minister of justice, why shouldn't Switzerland have a minister of the navy?"

Richard chuckled at the thought of landlocked Switzerland's fleet of ships. Patrascanu laughed too.

The next morning two guards escorted Patrascanu from the cell for interrogation. Richard wondered how a man of such standing could be brutally questioned. Yet that evening, Patrascanu returned to the cell to inform Richard he had not been interrogated at all. Instead, he had delivered a lecture about law at the university. His imprisonment had to be kept a secret. Even his wife was unaware of his confinement, believing he was traveling and staying in hotels. Because he believed Richard would be executed or kept behind bars indefinitely, the minister confided in him.

Patrascanu had become a Communist not because he was persuaded by its ideals but because of what had happened after the war. His father had supported the Germans in World War I, and after the Allied victory, his whole family was ostracized, and Patrascanu fled to Germany to receive university training. When he returned to Romania, the only political party that welcomed him was the Communist Party. He even married a Communist woman who had befriended Sabina while they were students together in school.

"You're like Marx and Lenin," Richard said.

The comment caught Patrascanu off guard.

"Marx felt genius within himself," Richard continued, "but as a Jew in Germany when anti-Semitism was rampant, he could find no outlet for it except as a revolutionary. After Lenin's brother was hanged for an attempt on the emperor's life, rage and frustration made Lenin want to overturn the world. It's been much the same with you."

Patrascanu didn't agree, but Richard could see his words had struck a nerve. The two continued to talk about justice, suffering, and the role of the church. Patrascanu spent no small amount of energy lambasting the corruption and abuses of the Borgia popes, the Spanish Inquisition, the evils of the Crusades, and the unjust persecution of Galileo.

"But it's the crimes and errors of the church that give us so much more to admire in it," Richard said, interrupting the tirade.

"What do you mean?"

"A hospital may stink of pus and blood," Richard explained. "In that lies its beauty, for it receives the sick with their disgusting sores and horrible diseases. The church is Christ's own hospital. Millions of patients are treated in it, with love. The church accepts sinners; they continue to sin, and for their transgressions, the church is blamed."

Richard continued, "To me, on the other hand, the church is like a mother who stands by her children even when they commit crimes. The politics and prejudices of its servants are distortions of what comes from God—that is, the Bible and its teachings, worship, and the sacraments. Whatever its faults, the church has much that's beautiful in it. The sea drowns thousands of people every year, but no one contests its beauty."

Patrascanu thought for a moment and said, "I could make much the same claim for Communism. Its practitioners aren't perfect—there are crooks among them—but that doesn't mean there's anything wrong with our theories."

"Then judge by results," Richard responded. "Sad deeds have stained the history of the church, but it has lavished love and care on people all over the world. It has produced a multitude of saints, and it has Christ, the holiest of all, at its head. Who are your idols? Men like Marx, who was described as a drunkard by his biographer Riazanov, director of the Marx-Engels Institute in Moscow. Or Lenin, whose wife tells us he was a reckless gambler and whose writings drip with venom. Communism has wiped out millions of innocent victims, bankrupted countries, filled the air with lies and fear. Where is its good side? Everyone knows that all your fellow travelers have been jailed, executed, or somehow destroyed in the past. How can you hope to go on using people and throwing them away?"

"Because they're stupid," Patrascanu retorted. "Ten years after World War I, the great Bolshevist thinker Bukharin opposed Trotsky's plans for making world revolution by force of arms. He argued that it was better to wait until the capitalist countries started fighting among themselves. Russia could then join the winning side and take the lion's share of conquered countries. If the West had known that half of Europe and two-thirds of Asia would become Communist as a result, the last war would never have taken place."

Richard couldn't be persuaded. "Don't you see, Mr. Patrascanu, that as you used people and then cast them aside, so your comrades have used you and thrown you away? Haven't you blinded yourself to the evil logic of Lenin's doctrine?"

Patrascanu couldn't conceal his bitterness. "When Danton was driven to the guillotine and saw Robespierre watching from a balcony, he called out, 'You will follow me!'"

Richard detected a spark of vengeance flaring in the man's eyes.

"And I assure you now," Patrascanu continued, "that they will follow me—Ana Pauker, Georgescu, and Luca too."

Within five years, Patrascanu's prophecy would come true.

21

On a night in 1948 in the Calea Rahovei prison, at 10:00 p.m., three guards burst into Richard's cell and demanded he get dressed. "Put your heavy coat on," Patrascanu whispered. "It might dull the blows." One of the guards named Appel strapped blacked-out goggles over Richard's face and led him through a long corridor to a room containing a table and a spotlighted chair.

As Appel removed the blindfold, Richard squinted into the light. The silhouette of a man across the table came into focus. Seconds later his face materialized, and Richard recognized him as Moravetz, a former police inspector who had recently been promoted to conducting interrogations.

"Vasile Georgescu," Moravetz said, "you'll find paper and pen on that desk. Take your chair over and write about your activities and your life."

Richard complied.

"As a priest," the inspector continued, "you've heard any number of confessions. We've brought you here to confess to us."

For the better part of an hour, Richard scribbled down his story, covering the major milestones of his spiritual biography.

Like his interrogators, Richard also had once been an atheist before his heart was changed.

"That's enough for tonight," Moravetz finally said, confiscating Richard's pencil.

After numerous similar interrogations, Richard soon learned his captors' methods and strategy. Instead of using police tactics that capitalized on the shock of arrest to glean confessions, the Communists preferred a much more patient approach—the prisoner must *ripen* first. The goal was to create enough guilt and anxiety to extract information gradually. Prisoners were rarely told why they were arrested, which threw them into a state of self-examination and uncertainty. Endless tricks created tension, doubt, and fear in their minds. Fake trials were scheduled and then postponed at the last minute. Firing squads were simulated in the courtyard outside the prisoners' cells. Tape-recorded screams and random shouts were played throughout the night.

After weeks of psychological games, resistance became more challenging. The mind began to break. Exhausted and guilt-ridden, the prisoner made false judgments, and one slip of the tongue became two. Names were given, friends betrayed. Before long, the interrogator had extracted the confidential information he sought.

Just before the mental breakdown, the interrogator switched his attitude and grew sympathetic to the prisoner's plight. Intimidation morphed into mercy. Promises were made to end the suffering, but only if the prisoner admitted guilt and confessed to his crimes.

Several days later, Richard was again retrieved from his cell and taken to a basement where two interrogators waited. Appel reached into his briefcase, removed a piece of toffee, and handed it to Richard.

"What were your connections with Mr. Teodorescu?" Appel asked casually.

"Teodorescu? That's a fairly common name. Which one do you mean?"

Appel didn't explain but quickly switched topics, asking questions about the Bible and the prophecies of Isaiah about the Messiah. He acted interested in Richard's perspective, nodding and raising his eyebrows. Then, at random and without warning, Appel inquired about the names of those who assisted Richard in distributing Christian literature to Soviet soldiers. Had they heard about the prophecies of Isaiah? Appel listened politely, more interested in Richard's reactions than his words.

The next interrogator, an insecure little man named Vasilu, was less cordial. "Write down the names of everyone you know," he demanded. "Tell where you met them and what your relations with them were."

Richard hesitated, careful and selective in the names he listed.

"Don't pick and choose," Vasilu snapped. "I said *everyone*."

Richard included names of Communist members of parliament and every random traveler he knew. If he accidentally surrendered the names of Christian ministers, their families would be arrested and savagely beaten.

"Question number two is to say what you have done against the state."

Richard looked into Vasilu's eyes. "What am I accused of?"

Vasilu slammed his fist on the table. "You know what you've done! Get it off your chest. Start by telling us about your contacts with your Orthodox colleague Father Grigoriu and what you think of him. Just write, and keep writing!"

Richard reeled off as many chapters from his spiritual biography as the interrogators liked. On other matters, he revealed as little as possible.

Richard was interrogated for weeks with little sleep. At night he calmed his conscience by repeating Scripture verses embedded in his memory.

God also sent small encouragements, like the barber who whispered that Sabina was doing well and was continuing the ministry work. Knowing his wife was okay provided double doses of strength. Richard could endure the interrogations, but the thought of Sabina being questioned and tortured was too much for any husband to bear. If Sabina were arrested, what would happen to Mihai? Countless children had already suffered that fate. He'd be orphaned and forced to live on the streets.

On one evening as he was trying to doze, the sound of a woman's sobbing voice emerged from a nearby cell. "No, no!" she pleaded. "Please don't beat me. Not again! I can't take it!" The corridor echoed with shrieks as the guards beat the woman senseless.

Richard listened intently until his eyes widened in horror. It was Sabina's voice! She had been captured and brought to Calea

Rahovei. Richard spent the night weeping and crying out to her in the darkness. Could she hear him? What were they doing to her?

Richard later learned that the woman's voice was not Sabina's but only a tape recording that was played for every prisoner, each thinking the sound belonged to his wife, girlfriend, or mother.

• • • •

The promise Richard had made to Sabina—that he would kill himself before betraying his friends—occupied his mind night after night. He remembered reading about a woman in the early church who had killed herself rather than lose her virginity to the barbarians who pillaged her monastery. If the church had canonized her, God could forgive Richard if his suicide rescued others from being slaughtered.

But the prison had confiscated his shoelaces. His cell was frequently checked for glass shards, cords, and razor blades. The doctors gave him one sleeping pill every evening, but the guards always checked Richard's mouth to make sure he had swallowed it. Perhaps if he could hide the pill under his tongue, though, he could amass a small collection. To hide the salvaged pills, Richard stored them in Patrascanu's straw mattress, tearing a few stitches to open it. Within a month, Richard had collected thirty pills—more than enough to make him sleep forever.

Suicide gave Richard power over his adversaries, but the sounds of the city begged him to reconsider: a young girl singing, a tram car squealing around the corner. Richard had dedicated his life to serving God. Was it wise to end it?

The interrogators shined lamps in prisoners' eyes to unsettle them, but God had His own lights too. One evening Richard peered into the midnight sky and saw a single star burning in the blackness. The light of the star had traveled across the whole universe to console him. Perhaps his life could also travel great distances to reach future prisoners suffering for the Savior. The star begged him to keep living, but Richard was still unsure. Maybe his death would do more good than his life.

The next morning the guards raided his cell and took Patrascanu's pallet to another prisoner. Richard's plans for suicide were suddenly thwarted. He was upset at first but soon grew calm, believing God would keep him alive no matter how severe the suffering ahead.

22

"You've been playing with us," Colonel Dulgheru shouted, delivering a blinding punch to Richard's cheek. "Can't you see that you're completely at my mercy and that your Savior, or whatever you call Him, isn't going to open any prison doors?"

"His name is Jesus Christ," Richard said, his face throbbing, "and if He wants to, He can release me."

"All right," Dulgheru said. "Tomorrow you will meet Comrade Brinzaru."

Richard, like all the other prisoners, dreaded that name. Major Brinzaru had a reputation for being a refined, intelligent sadist with arms as hairy as a gorilla's and a knack for extracting information. Before he became an interrogator, he had worked for a popular politician whose son was arrested for leading a patriotic movement.

"I used to hold you on my knee when you were a baby," Brinzaru had told the young lad. Then he killed him with his bare hands.

Richard knew the days of soft interrogations had come to an end. Brinzaru brought him to a room filled with a wide variety of torture instruments. "Is there anything here you particularly fancy?" Brinzaru asked, gesturing toward a table filled with curved knives and pliers. "We like to be democratic here."

Brinzaru forced Richard to stand on the tips of his toes with his arms touching the ceiling. When the blood abandoned his limbs, he collapsed, only to be beaten back into position. For several hours each day, Richard was forced to adopt obscene, crude, and ridiculous postures. If the goal was to steal his dignity, the guards succeeded as they laughed at each position.

The wall in front of Richard reminded him of a phrase in the Bible: "My beloved is like a gazelle or a young stag. Behold, there he stands behind our wall" (Song of Sol. 2:9). As the guards racked his body, creating countless welts, he imagined Jesus standing on the other side of the wall, comforting and suffering with him. If Christ could stretch out His arms on the cross, Richard could raise his own as well. Moses, the leader of the Israelites, also came to mind. As long as Moses's hands were raised, the Jews had triumphed in their war against the Amalekites (see Exod. 17:11).

Often blindfolded, Richard couldn't construct a mental map of the prison. But one room he knew well was the *manège*, the training ring, as the prisoners called it. Dreadfully small, the entire cell could be circumnavigated in twelve paces. After four steps, there was a wall. Then two more steps and another wall. Brinzaru forced Richard to walk in circles around its periphery for hours.

"Walk!" he demanded. "Keep going around!"

Richard obeyed, bruising himself as he bounced off the walls. He felt light-headed, and his eyes stung from sweat. After several hours, the room began to blur. Richard closed his eyes and slammed into the walls while trying to retain enough mental clarity to pray for the guards who were harassing him.

"Faster!" they told him.

One of the guards cracked a wooden club against Richard's elbow, sending radiating pain up his arm. "Get up! Get moving!"

The next day Richard was instructed to squat on the floor with his arms behind his back. The guard shoved a metal bar behind his elbows, lifted his body into the air, and lashed his feet, thighs, and spine with a nylon whip. The blacked-out goggles on his head prevented Richard from bracing for the impact of the lashes, causing the pain of each strike to double. After only a few beatings, Richard lost consciousness. But the guards brought him back to reality by hurling a bucket of ice-cold water in his face.

The following week Brinzaru came into Richard's cell and held a knife to his throat. The blade penetrated his skin several times and lacerated his chest. Richard awoke to discover his whole torso covered in blood.

When stabbings failed to inflict enough pain, Brinzaru inserted a funnel into Richard's mouth and poured water down his throat until his stomach almost ruptured. Then he ordered the guards to kick Richard until he vomited.

One day Richard was blindfolded, and two wolves rushed into his cell. He was told the beasts were trained to attack prisoners if they moved, and Richard sat motionless, feeling their hot breath only inches from his face.

As the months passed, the intensity of the torture increased. Guards pressed red-hot irons into Richard's ribs. His skin sizzled under the heat, and within a few seconds he fainted. Then the guards revived him with the searing pain of repeated burnings. Being branded with irons became an inferno as close to hell as Richard had ever experienced, and he pitied the guards who would spend eternity in similar torment.

To make sure Richard didn't die prematurely, a doctor always presided over the torture sessions. At times death seemed only seconds away. Richard was suffocated until unconscious, and his body was flogged until his lungs lacked the strength to inhale air.

Jesus was whipped also, Richard remembered. What a privilege to share in the very sufferings Christ endured. The cries and moans of nearby prisoners rang throughout the night, especially when their limbs were torn from their joints on a rack, a device that stretched the body until a prisoner's bones popped out of the sockets. The mere mention of the rack instilled fear and extracted many confessions.

"Where are the names of those you passed the secrets on to?" Brinzaru demanded.

Richard wrote down numerous names and addresses, but he never betrayed his friends. The names belonged instead to those who had already died or escaped to the West.

Before his arrest, Richard never dreaded mockery or humiliation. But all that changed when two guards spat and urinated in his mouth while others watched and laughed. Under torture, Richard was forced to confess to being a homosexual, an adulterer, a thief, a spy, and a traitor. At night he retired to his cell, weeping from the emotional trauma of the day and praying for strength to endure the next day's torment.

"Why don't you give in?" Brinzaru asked. "It's all so futile. You're only flesh, and you'll break in the end."

The Communists believed a man would do anything to avoid being put to death. A prisoner, they believed, would confess everything for his freedom. Richard sat alone in solitary confinement, dreading the torture the next day would bring, but he believed that life consisted of more than flesh, blood, and bone. His captors could brand, flog, mock, and humiliate him. But not even all the Communists in Europe combined—Brinzaru included—could rob him of his soul. His soul was held in hands too powerful to pry apart.

23

Richard sat in a lightless cell as currents of loneliness swept over him. The walls were as gray as the color of his uniform, and before long, solitary confinement had stolen memories of rivers, flowers, sun, and stars. Thirty feet below the Secretariat of State for Internal Affairs building in Bucharest, air entered his windowless cell through a small tube. With as little as one slice of bread per week, hunger became his constant companion. The food he was given contained only enough calories for him to breathe.

For the first three years of this eight-year imprisonment, Richard was alone. The silence was deafening. The only time he left his cell was to be beaten and interrogated. Even the guards muted their footsteps by gluing thin layers of felt to the soles of their shoes. In the absence of pen or paper, Richard even forgot how to write. The only words he possessed were those stored in his mind before his surprise arrest on the way to church in February of 1948, two years before his wife was imprisoned.

When Richard joined other inmates, life didn't improve. From 5:00 a.m. until 10:00 p.m., prisoners sat upright with their hands shackled behind their backs. Weak as skeletons, they lapped their food like dogs from dishes on the ground. For seventeen hours a day, they were unable to rest their heads or close their eyes. Blindfolded, beaten, and branded, Richard bore on his body the marks of his faith. Years later, when testifying before the US Senate, he would reveal deep stab wounds inflicted during his imprisonment.

"Around me were Jobs," he said, "some much more afflicted than Job had been. But I knew the end of Job's story, how he received twice as much as he had before. I had around me men like Lazarus the beggar, hungry and covered with boils. But I knew that angels would take these men to the bosom of Abraham. I saw them as they will be in the future. I saw in the shabby, dirty, weak martyr near me the splendidly crowned saint of tomorrow."

Brainwashing broke the silence. Hours of incessant interrogation were unfruitful as Richard refused to betray his brothers and sisters in the Romanian church.

The guards were not the only ones brainwashing Richard. At times he felt the presence of evil in his dark, cold cell. As a child Richard had seen Satan grinning at him, and now in the midst of isolation, the Devil returned to mock him. Richard could almost hear the taunts: *Where is Jesus? Your Savior can't save you. You've been tricked, and you've tricked others. He isn't the Messiah. You followed the wrong man.* Weaponless, Richard felt forsaken.

The guards drugged the inmates until their senses corroded. Richard struggled to focus his mind, and at times even the Lord's Prayer became too long to recite. Concentration escaped him. Once, he mustered what little strength he had left and mumbled, "Jesus, I love You."

You love Me? Jesus responded. *Now I will show you how I love you.*

Suddenly Richard's heart burned like the hearts of the two men on the Emmaus road. "I knew the love of the One who gave His life on the cross for us all. Such love cannot exclude the Communists, however grave their sins." The more Richard suffered, the more love he felt toward the guards. He believed in the all-embracing love of Christ, who desires the salvation of everyone.

At other times, especially during the black days of solitary confinement, Richard kept his mind alive by meditating on Scripture. Barefoot, he paced the three strides of his small cell all night, laboring to prepare sermons and deliver them in the presence of God and angels. In his small cell, biblical characters came to life. He saw Abraham and his camels, Jesus with His disciples, and Paul traveling on his missionary journeys throughout the Mediterranean. Food was scarce, but spiritual nourishment abounded.

Richard spent nights praying for other Christians around the world, and he also prayed for his captors. One day as Richard sat alone in his cell, his prayers were suddenly illuminated with brilliant beams of light. The gray walls of his chamber shone like diamonds. Music shattered the silence. The darkness vanished as God transformed his dungeon into a world of beauty, a world Christ Himself occupied. Richard later reflected, "The King of Kings, Jesus, was with us."

• • • •

Although he was utterly alone in his cell, Richard powerfully felt the presence of Christ. Persecution existed, but so did forgiveness. And there would be much to forgive.

In his darkest days, when evil seemed ever present, Richard composed a poem in his mind that thwarted the threats of the Devil:

> *Love is its own justification. Love is not for the wise. Through a thousand ordeals she will not cease to love. Though fire burns and the waves drown her, she will kiss the hand that hurts. If she finds no answer to her questions, she is confident and waits. One day the sun will shine in hidden places, and all will be made plain.*

The lightbulb above Richard's head burned throughout the night, but it didn't hum. Silence permeated his tiny cell. The world outside disappeared—the rain, the wind, the swaying of trees. All these sounds had vanished from Richard's memory. The cell even robbed him of Sabina's voice.

In the absence of noise, doubts passed freely through his mind. Had he truly experienced the power of God, or was his pastorate merely a performance? Did he really love others, or was he serving only himself? Shouldn't he have become a statesman, millionaire, or architect? Did God really exist, or were the Communists right? Where was God, anyway?

Richard wished he had a copy of his favorite book, *The Pateric*. He didn't eat or drink anything the first time he read its four hundred pages. The book described the history of fifth-century Christians who retreated into the Egyptian desert to preserve their faith and prevent pagan Roman society from corrupting it. One of the monks in the isolated desert asked his elder, "Father, what is silence?"

"My son," the abbot said, "silence is to sit alone in your cell in wisdom and fear of God, shielding the heart from the burning arrows of thought.... O, silence, in which one cares only for first things, and speaks only with Jesus Christ! He who keeps silent is the one who sings, 'My heart is ready to praise Thee, O Lord!'"

The silence burdened Richard at first. But soon it became a blessing. "In the silence," he later recalled, "I felt the kiss of Christ, and everyone is silent when he is kissed. Quiet and joy returned."

The memory of other Christians emboldened Richard. He was no longer alone. In his solitude, he sat in the company of thousands of pastors throughout the ages who enjoyed the presence of Christ. A cloud of witnesses enveloped Richard, and before long, he felt the encouragement of their testimonies and triumphs. Jesus Himself, after spending forty days and nights in the lonely wilderness, was attended by angels who comforted Him (see Matt. 4:11). Richard felt his own angels watching over him.

On the tree of silence hangs the fruit of peace. Richard came to believe this truth and dined on it daily. God *did* exist. He felt the presence of Christ every day. God *had* called him to be a pastor—to walk through the wilderness, to love and serve others, and perhaps even to sacrifice himself. Where was God in the midst of His children's suffering? Richard marveled at the thought. God knew what it was like to watch His own Son suffer. In fact, He sent Christ into the world to eradicate all suffering in the world to come. Richard was refreshed in his newfound belief that he *was* a believer. Every atom of his life belonged to God, every breath and beat of his heart.

But to keep his sanity, Richard needed to follow a routine. Every night at ten o'clock, a bell sounded throughout the prison, signaling that it was time to sleep. The bell also marked the beginning of Richard's regimen, a program he observed every night for more than two years in solitary confinement.

The routine began with a prayer that was rarely unaccompanied by tears. Like radio waves that travel more clearly through the night sky, the prayers Richard said seemed to zigzag quickly through the door of his cell, down the corridor, and into the sky to God's throne.

After his time of prayer, Richard preached a sermon the way he had done as a pastor standing before his congregation. But unlike the past, his sermons were now free from constraints—from the worry of what his congregation and bishop would think, from the fear of arrest, spies, or betrayal. Richard preached quietly so as not to alert the guards, but his sermons weren't soliloquies. He preached before God, angels, demons, and the faces scattered through his memory, especially Sabina's.

Richard aimed many thoughts at his wife, praying God would transmit them to Sabina's mind. He knew she was being pressured to divorce him. If she remained married and continued her work in the ministry, the Communists would arrest her, torture her, and worse.

After thinking about Sabina, Richard hugged his straw pallet good-night, pretending it was his son, Mihai. One night he couldn't bear the absence of his son any longer and bolted at the steel door, smashing his fists against it until the guards entered and sedated him with a tranquilizer. Richard awoke the next morning feeling hopeless. Was he losing his mind like so many other prisoners had?

He thought of Jesus's mother standing at the foot of the cross. Mary had been helpless too, Richard remembered. But she didn't complain. *Give me strength also*, he prayed, *to accept without complaining the fate of my son, Mihai.* God had sent His Son into the world, according to John, "that whoever believes in him should not perish but have eternal life" (John 3:16). Perhaps Richard could do the same.

John Wesley once claimed he was never sad even one quarter of an hour. Remembering Wesley, Richard obeyed God's command to be joyful and found strength to laugh, dance, invent jokes, and even play chess with himself. He crafted chess pieces from bread—darker pieces were matched against lighter ones. He didn't lose a single game of chess in two years!

Silence became essential for Richard's spiritual devotion. Solitary confinement became a sacred space where he could heal and pray in the presence of Christ. He could not verbalize the ecstasy of basking in the white-hot presence of God, but he felt like bursting with joy. Jesus had promised, "Blessed are you when people hate you and when they exclude you and revile you and spurn your name as evil, on account of the Son of Man! Rejoice in that day and leap for joy" (Luke 6:22–23). Richard leaped for joy and danced in his cell, filled with the Holy Spirit and privileged to suffer for his King.

Richard knew God's people, like caterpillars, must endure the dark cocoon before they can fly into the light. The cocoon of Communism had supplied Richard with a mission field. He resolved to love his interrogators, not as they should have been but as they were. If God could convert Saul of Tarsus, He could convert even the most brutal of captors. Many of Richard's guards would later profess faith in Jesus Christ and suffer the harsh penalties their salvation brought.

"It was in being tortured by them that we learned to love them," Richard later claimed. "The gates of heaven are not closed for the Communist. Neither is the light quenched for them."

24

The fear in her cousin's eyes alarmed Sabina. "He said he came from the Living Space Office," the young man told her, relaying information about the suspicious visitor who had stopped by earlier that evening. "He talked about putting more people in the flat, but I'm sure what he really wanted to know was how many exits you have apart from the front door."

Sabina exhaled slowly as beads of sweat dotted her brow. She knew what this meant, and it wasn't good. A police raid would soon be coming.

• • • •

Sabina's eyes flew open, and she blinked in confusion, trying to make sense of the hammering noise. Pounding knocks assaulted the front door, and she slowly identified the source of the sound. She sat up and felt the woman stir next to her, a dear female friend who had been staying with the small family. Sabina squinted as she struggled to see the clock. Five o'clock in the morning. The raid had begun.

She could hear her cousin's voice, mixed with angry shouts. Boots soon stomped on the stairs, heading up to Sabina's bedroom.

If Richard were here, he would know how to handle the policemen.
But Richard hadn't been here for two years now. Sabina and her
friend clutched the bedcovers and waited.

"Sabina Wurmbrand!" shouted a thick-necked man who was
obviously in charge. "We know you're hiding weapons here! Show
us where they are. Now!"

Before Sabina could protest, six men began emptying cabinets
and tossing drawer contents onto the ground. They pulled out
trunks and swept a shelf of books onto the floor. Sabina's friend
scrambled to collect them.

"Forget about the books!" the man shouted. "Get your clothes
on!" The two women dressed in front of the men as the officers
ransacked the room. "So you won't tell us where the weapons are
hidden? We'll tear this place apart!"

Emboldened by her anger but calm from the presence of the
Holy Spirit, Sabina said, "The only weapon we have in this house is
here." She picked up her Bible from a pile of debris under their feet.

The commander roared, "You're coming with us to make a full
statement about those weapons!"

Sabina placed the Bible on a table and said, "Please let us have
a few minutes to pray. Then I'll go with you."

The men gaped at her as they stood praying. Then Sabina
hugged her cousin and her friend. "Next year in Jerusalem!"

As the men led her to the door, she snatched a small package
from the sideboard table.

• • • •

The men shoved Sabina into the back of an Oldsmobile and jerked blacked-out motorcycle goggles over her eyes. The drive took only minutes. The men dragged her from the car and up a flight of stairs like a bound animal. Her shins cracked against a wall corner. Then one man ripped off the goggles, and the door slammed behind her.

Sabina looked around the long room crowded with women sitting on benches and the floor. She recognized a socialite from the newspaper, a film actress in a skimpy dress, and a lady-in-waiting from the palace. Sabina fit in with these "socially rotten" elements of Romanian society.

By evening several hundred women were crammed into the room. In honor of the anniversary of Freedom Day, as the Communists called it, they had rounded up countless subversives across the country. The women crouched under a single lightbulb dangling from the ceiling, each woman enveloped in her own fear. As the hours passed, no one brought them any food or drink.

How long would the interrogation last? they all wondered. What would happen to their children? Mihai had already lost his father, and now his mother had been taken as well. Their home and everything in it would be confiscated. Sabina prayed for Mihai, who would be cast on the kindness of friends. No one was safe.

Next to her, a woman leaped up and beat on the door. "My children! My children!" she screamed. No one answered.

"I'll be released," the actress said. "You'll see."

The door opened again, and the new captives shouted at the guards. "But I haven't done anything wrong!" each one insisted. As if their innocence would save them. The women seemed to forget that this was 1950 in a Communist nation.

Each had been told, "You're wanted by the police to make a statement." For some, that statement would last ten years.

· · · ·

Sabina passed the night in the crowded room. With the next morning came the clamor of brass bands playing for the paradoxical Freedom Day parade.

If the parade is passing below, Sabina thought, *we must be in the police lockup on Victory Street.*

The captive women could hear thousands of boots marching by and obligated celebrants rhythmically chanting ironic slogans:

"August 23 has brought us freedom!"

"Death to the thieves and traitors in prison!"

"Broken chains remain behind us!"

The women frowned at one another and murmured. Never in Romania's history had so many people been in chains.

Eventually the guards delivered black bread and watery soup to the detainees.

After their meager supper, the women settled down for the night. Sabina spent the long hours in prayer and fitful sleep.

25

The next day a sergeant entered the room and began calling out names. *Sabina Wurmbrand* was first on the list.

The guards again strapped black goggles over Sabina's eyes and led her to a waiting van. Later she learned that she'd been delivered to secret-police headquarters on Calea Rahovei.

"Any of you know this woman?" a female guard asked the occupants of a small cell. None did, and Sabina was allowed to join them. Communist policy required friends to be kept apart, preventing comfort or camaraderie. During the interrogation stage, the guards maneuvered an intricate shuffle of prisoners designed to avoid the formation of new friendships. Each new arrival in the cell could be an informer.

Aside from a young medical student, Sabina's new companions were peasant women. An unknown number of peasants had been executed at urgent drumhead trials conducted in the fields as Communists seized the farmers' land. Prison sentences awaited nearly one hundred thousand others.

Several days later, the guards moved Sabina to solitary confinement. Her tiny cell contained only an iron cot. As Sabina glanced around the cell, she had a terrible realization: there was no bucket to relieve herself. The food and stress of prison life caused constant intestinal distress, and Sabina soon learned the guards would allow her to use the latrine only every seven to ten hours at 5:00 a.m., 3:00 p.m., and 10:00 p.m. Between bathroom breaks, Sabina was at the mercy of her upset stomach.

It was August, but Sabina's cell was damp and cold. Iron bars obstructed a small windowpane high above her head. She shivered in her summer coat and the wool stockings she had grabbed on her way out of the house. She was grateful for even these light layers.

How long would it be before they called her? What would they ask? Sabina remembered Richard's earlier comment: "Hell is to sit alone in darkness remembering evil you have done." Sabina had many, and she wondered if they would be beaten out of her during the interrogations to come.

"It's thicker today," murmured an old warden as he delivered Sabina's daily boiled oats. He was kind to Sabina—the older ones often were. They seemed to think the Americans would soon put an end to Romania's troubles. Little did they know it would be decades before the Romanians saw freedom.

At night Sabina lay in bed trying to block her ears against the terrifying sounds around her—the crash of steel doors, the scrape of studded boots, and the incessant obscenities from the guards. In nearby cells, she heard the clang of metal as prisoners were taken for interrogation. Each time, Sabina believed she'd be next, but several claustrophobic days would pass before her time came.

• • • •

"Turn your back!" the guard shouted, opening Sabina's cell door and snapping dark goggles over her eyes. Darkened panic raged in her as two men pulled her through the invisible prison passages. Left, right, left, right. Would they shoot her? Would she die without warning in the dark?

Finally the journey ended. A guard ripped the goggles from her face, and she stood in a large room, blinded by sunlight. The warden guided her to a chair, and she steadied herself on the large oak desk in front of it. Sabina stared at the ink stains on its surface. Behind the desk sat two secret policemen—a heavy middle-aged major with a mustache and a younger blond lieutenant who had been present at the raid on Sabina's house. She looked at the lieutenant, and something about him seemed familiar. When he smiled, Sabina shivered. He looked just like the teenage boy she had loved so many years ago in Paris. The resemblance was extraordinary.

Sabina expected the charge against her to be read, but with weary patience the major said, "You know, Mrs. Wurmbrand, what your offense against the state has been. Now you will write for us a detailed statement about it."

"But what should I write?" Sabina asked. "I don't know why you've brought me here."

The major frowned. "You know very well," he insisted.

On a side table were a pen and some paper. To appease the officers, Sabina wrote a few lines saying she had no idea why she'd been arrested. The major glanced at her statement, nodded, and summoned the next prisoner.

All the way back to her cell, the guard shouted and pushed her, blindfolded, into the stone walls. Back in her cell, she saw his eye peeping through the small spy hole in the door.

"Now you'll sit and think until you write what the officer told you to write! If you don't, you'll get the treatment."

Sabina knew well what this "treatment" would entail. Torture. Bullying. Mockery. Humiliation. She would hear recorded voices screaming in nearby cells and the sound of a firing squad on loud-speakers in the corridors. Mental torture to soften the prisoner for interrogation.

But the torture would not stop at the mind. In these cells in the weeks and months that followed, Sabina would see the results of the physical torture the prisoners suffered.

The problem of what to tell the interrogators wasn't a new one. She had faced the same tactics during the Nazi occupation. Some Christians believed they could never lie—even to save others—and they acted on that belief. A person doesn't tell a thief where money is kept in the house, Sabina believed. And a doctor is right to deceive a madman who has a gun, so he may be disarmed. Communist hatred was an unreasoning madness, and Christians had a duty to mislead those whose sole aim was to destroy.

• • • •

The next morning the major and his lieutenant were waiting for Sabina. On a notepad the major had listed a string of questions, which he checked off one by one as he barked them at her in rapid succession. The aim was to extract information that could be used against Richard.

"Every man has his weak point," the major said. The Communists were looking hard for Richard's, and Sabina knew his interrogation would be ruthless.

The officers asked what Richard had said to his colleagues. Sabina replied that they had discussed religion not politics.

"Mrs. Wurmbrand," the major replied, smiling, "the Bible is full of politics. Prophets rebelled and complained against Egyptian rule. Jesus spoke out against the ruling class of His day." He looked pointedly at Sabina. "If your husband is a Christian, he must have clear views about the government."

"My husband doesn't interest himself in politics."

The major pressed Sabina, but she stood firm.

"Now, Mrs. Wurmbrand," he said, dripping with sincerity. "You're a very intelligent woman. I can't understand your attitude. You and your husband are Jews. We Communists saved you from the Nazis. You should be grateful. You should be on our side!" His eyes narrowed and his voice slowed. "Your husband is accused of counterrevolutionary activities. He could be shot. His colleagues have spoken, and they support the charge against him."

Sabina's mind whirled and her heart sank. He was lying, of course, and watching for her reaction. She tried to maintain a blank expression.

The major continued. "They may just be trying to save themselves. Perhaps *they* are the real counterrevolutionaries. We can't judge unless you tell us everything that people working with the mission used to say. Everything." He paused before continuing. "Speak out, denounce the real counterrevolutionaries, and your husband will be free tomorrow."

The major turned and smiled at his lieutenant, inviting him to join in the happy vision of the Wurmbrands' future. The younger man turned to Sabina and smiled encouragingly. "You could go home to your family."

Sabina warmed at the thought of returning to Mihai and her dear church family, but she pushed it away. "I know nothing," she insisted.

The major stood, staring at Sabina with steely eyes and a firm mouth. He walked toward her and raised his fist. She braced herself as the beatings began.

After returning to her cell, Sabina nursed her bruises. She lifted her legs onto her hard cot and felt her feet touch the footrails. *Poor Richard,* she thought. *He's so tall that his feet will be hanging over the end of his cot.*

What were they doing to him right now? It had been two years since she'd seen his face. Sabina wanted him to survive, but she also wanted him to resist, and the competing desires waged war in her heart all night.

• • • •

The major looked at Sabina through bleary eyes, but she also saw a flash of triumph. His line of questioning this time centered on the

Nazis. What Germans did she know? What were the Wurmbrands' connections with them? Didn't she know people were being shot for harboring Nazis? Why had Sabina hidden officers in her home?

Sabina could truthfully say she'd never hidden Nazis. To her, they weren't Nazis; they were simply men. They were people in need, and the Wurmbrands tried to help them in the same way they had helped so many others before them.

"You deny the charge, then," the major said, smirking. "Well, we have a surprise for you."

He pressed a buzzer on his desk, and the guards brought in a man Sabina immediately recognized. Stefanescu had lived with the Wurmbrand family in 1945, and he knew everything they had done for the Germans. Sabina's palms began to sweat as the man shuffled forward, nervous eyes flickering from the major to the lieutenant and then to Sabina. He swallowed and closed his eyes, blocking out the world.

"Now, Stefanescu," said the major, lighting a cigar and drawing a long puff. "Tell us how the Wurmbrands kept Nazis in their home." He nodded toward Sabina. "You know this woman, of course?"

"No."

"What!"

"I've never seen her."

"You're lying!"

"No, sir." Stefanescu closed his eyes again and braced for the berating to come. The major shouted and ranted, his face an inch from Stefanescu's. He screamed at the top of his lungs while his prisoner, dazed, repeated again and again that he didn't know Sabina.

The major finally relented, seemingly placated by the absurdity of a Jew hiding Nazi officers. He then turned to Sabina and questioned her about the Wurmbrands' work with the Red Army. Sabina managed to dodge the dangerous questions.

Lying awake in her cell later, she remembered the drove of gangly Red Army boys who had once filled their flat. With what wonderful simplicity they had heard the Word of God! She remembered one boy dancing around the kitchen with joy when Richard told him Christ had risen from the dead.

The day's events encouraged Sabina. Even alone in her cell, she felt the divine presence of God. He had given her the strength and wit to fend off questions about printing Russian Gospels and receiving relief funds. Maybe the worst was over.

With a piece of chalky plaster that had worked loose from the cell wall, she drew on her dark blanket a large white cross.

26

Sabina's next interrogator was a large sweating man with a bald head and hairy arms. As he perused documents in a brown file, Sabina stood in front of the ink-stained desk and waited. The blond lieutenant made notes from a thick textbook, occasionally looking up at her like a fox. He seemed to know something she didn't.

At last the interrogator began. He asked a series of personal questions about her family, friends, and travels abroad. He asked about her days as a student in Paris. His line of questioning was warm, friendly, and smooth.

"And now," he said, using the nondescript tone of a government grunt giving instructions on filling out a form, "we want you to write down your sexual history."

Sabina looked up, confusion wrinkling her brow.

He explained patiently. "Your sexual history. You have one, I suppose? Your first experience. The first boy you went with. How he fondled you. How you returned his kisses. What happened next? Did he take you on the spot, and which spot? Or was that left to the next one who came along? Tell us about *his* embraces.

Compare the two. Or three. Continue with your other lovers. We want a complete account … blow by blow, so to speak."

His calm, polite tone was like a slap in Sabina's face. The lieutenant looked at Sabina, his tongue passing over his lips until it found a small red sore at the corner of his mouth.

"Write it all down. We want every detail. I'm sure there are plenty."

Sabina tried to stay calm. "You don't have any right to ask me about this. You can accuse me of being a counterrevolutionary or whatever you'd like, but this isn't a morality trial."

The man's hairy fingers tapped the top of the desk. "This is whatever we choose to make it. The story has spread that you're some kind of saint. We think otherwise. We *know* otherwise. Now we plan to show your true colors—"

"—as a whore," the lieutenant finished.

"I won't do that," Sabina said.

"We'll see about that!" The bald interrogator fired a litany of obscene questions at Sabina, a stream of profanity pouring from his mouth. He punctuated his diatribe by slapping a meaty palm on the desk.

Sabina was drenched in sweat. Her head swam, and she refused to write. After an hour he stopped. After asking countless other women the same questions, he appeared bored.

"Time is on our side," he said. "Your husband has already confessed to being a traitor and a spy. You're on your way to the trash dump." He glowered at her as she trembled.

The guards replaced her dark goggles and dragged her back to her cell through the sour corridors. They ripped off the goggles a moment before pushing Sabina into her cell, and for the first time she saw the number above the door.

Seven.

She was in cell 7. The holy number. The number of days of creation. The number of branches on the menorah. Sabina fell onto her cot and sobbed. Eventually she grew calmer. Her body lay in darkness, but her soul rose above the walls of the prison. She was crucified with Christ, and a time might come for her to say, "It is finished." If so, she wanted to offer only words of love to parents and friends and the thief next to her. God was with her in her affliction.

• • • •

For months Sabina lived in solitary confinement, leaving her cell only to answer incessant questions from hardened interrogators. She ate the greasy midday soup and smiled at memories of her early days of marriage to Richard. How picky he'd been about food!

Each night in cell 7, Sabina recited passages from Exodus, reminding herself of how God delivered the children of Israel from slavery in Egypt. Somewhere she knew Richard was doing the same. God had delivered the Israelites, and He would deliver the Wurmbrands.

The bald interrogator continued his routine of obscene questions about Sabina's sex life, and she continued her routine of refusing to answer. Through exhaustion, she found the strength to say, "I will not tell you what you want to know." She knew that the worst "sexual history" would not prevent a person from becoming a great saint. The Old Testament, for instance, described Rahab as a harlot, but three New Testament passages referred to her as a revered and godly person of faith (see Josh. 2:1; Matt. 1:5; Heb. 11:31; James 2:25).

The interrogator finally gave up his line of questioning, and within days Sabina was transferred back to a communal cell. Winter was coming, and the room was like a freezer. Her scant summer coat and wool stockings were the envy of the cell, and she shared her riches with her cellmates. Her coat became a blanket, a dressing gown, and formal wear for interrogations. Sabina offered her threadbare stockings to a girl wearing only a thin cotton dress, and tears streamed down the girl's pale face.

• • • •

"You, Wurmbrand," a guard commanded, struggling to pronounce the *W* of her German name. "Put on the goggles."

The blind march along the smelly corridors ended in a room of men. Silence fell across the room, and Sabina could feel their eyes on her.

"Take off the goggles!" Bright lights blinded her, but she was eventually able to make out a long windowless room with ten uniformed officers.

"Do you know what's happened to your husband?" one asked. "Sit down. If you cooperate and answer all our questions, we may allow you to see him."

Sabina really believed they might. She and Richard had committed no crime. Maybe Richard had been tried and acquitted. How naive she'd been in the early days of her imprisonment.

With maddening repetition, the men peppered her with questions about Richard and their associates. Some she couldn't answer, and others she wouldn't. Her head whirled and her nerves stretched to the breaking point.

"You're not allowed to cry," one guard warned. But she couldn't stop. For two hours tears poured down her cheeks.

The officers made threats and then offered freedom. They made promises and offered money.

"Every woman has her price," the bald interrogator said. "You're an honest woman. You can raise your price. Judas was a fool to sell his boss for thirty pieces of silver. He could have held out for three hundred. Tell us what you want. Freedom for you and your husband? A good parish for him? We'd look after your family. You could be very valuable to us." If only she'd give him the names of traitors.

When he finished, silence enveloped the room.

At last Sabina spoke. "Thanks, but I've sold myself already. The Son of God was tortured and gave His life for me. Through Him I can reach heaven. Can you offer a higher price than that?"

• • • •

The Wurmbrands' wedding anniversary, October 23, came and went, and autumn soon turned to winter. Sabina thought about

Mihai. He always caught cold so easily. When he tossed the covers from his bed at night, who would put them back on? A hundred doubts and anxieties pierced Sabina's mind every day.

In November, the prison director came personally to the cell. He told a small group of women to be ready to leave in ten minutes. No questions were allowed. Sabina saw the trepidation on her cellmates' faces. They gathered their scant bits and pieces, expecting to be either freed or shot.

Years later Sabina would learn that, in fact, she'd been accused in a report of Gorge Boru, lieutenant of the Securitate: "As a servant of the Evangelical Lutheran Church at number 45 Olteni Street, she was carrying out activities hostile to the Communist government, she works against the Communist regime, and she fights off the Marxist ideas." The charges also addressed her faith, noting that she was asking those in her church to pray for those in jail. "She is fanatical in her faith. She is very persuasive and has a large influence."

Without a trial, she'd been sentenced to twenty-four months of hard labor in a prison labor camp. When that time ran out, a new sentence was added. She was one of thousands of prisoners classified as "administrative" residents of the prison camps whose work was essential to the Communist economy. In the newspapers, the government was congratulated for creating jobs; nothing was said about the arrests and imprisonments. The state did what it liked and published what it liked.

Camps had arisen all over the country, and "saboteurs" who failed to meet Communist norms—gypsies, criminals, priests, prostitutes, the wealthy—went there for "reeducation." Prisoners from the age of twelve to over seventy composed the permanent population of more than two hundred thousand men, women, and children. With this paradigm in place, "Socialist reconstruction" spread from the Soviet states across the world. Romania became an example of a country that had successfully solved its unemployment problems.

Before Sabina could partake in this successful solution, though, she was moved to a transit facility, Jilava—the most feared prison in the entire country.

27

A series of faint tapping sounds came from Richard's cell wall in Calea Rahovei. At first he thought it was only his imagination, but the tapping persisted. Soon he discovered a new prisoner occupied the cell beside him and was trying to communicate through code. One tap meant *A*, two taps *B*, and so forth.

"Who are you?" the stranger slowly spelled.

"A pastor," Richard tapped.

Cumbersome and frustratingly slow, a conversation unfolded over the next few hours.

"Are you a Christian?" Richard asked.

A minute passed, followed by, "I can't claim to be one."

Richard learned that his new friend was a fifty-two-year-old radio engineer awaiting trial for committing a capital offense. He had married an unbeliever, had backslidden in his Christian faith, and was deeply depressed. Every night Richard comforted him through a new system of communication. One tap indicated the first five letters of the alphabet, two taps for the second group of five, and so on. Thus the letter *B* was a single tap followed by a pause and then two more taps; the letter *F* was two taps followed after a space by one tap. Even this improved code didn't satisfy Richard's new neighbor. The radio engineer knew Morse code and passed on the letters one by one until Richard had learned them all.

One night the man tapped, "I would like to confess my sins." Through a staccato of taps, the man unburdened his heart, beginning with his memory of kicking a Jewish boy when he was seven years old. Myriad other sins unfolded. In response, Richard comforted him with Bible verses, which gladdened the man's heart. The two prisoners shared stories of freedom, made jokes, and even played chess together, tapping out the position and movement of the bread figures.

When the guards overheard the tapping between the two cells, they transferred Richard to a new cell. But Richard had acquired a new language and taught each new cellmate the code. The more the guards shuffled Richard around the prison, the more he spread the skills. Before long, most of the prisoners in solitary confinement learned to communicate with one another.

The confessions Richard heard through the concrete walls often began with the words "When I was a boy …" or "When I was at school …" Solitary confinement exposed the mind to long-forgotten sins of the past. Guilty memories of words said to fathers, mothers, brothers, and sisters animated the prisoners and produced shame. The faces of slandered friends, betrayed spouses, and beaten children manifested themselves, accusing each prisoner of his reckless behavior. Nothing remained buried for any length of time.

One morning Richard awoke to discover it was Good Friday. With a nail he found in the lavatory, he carved the name *JESUS* into the wall of his cell. Perhaps it would comfort the next prisoner who saw it.

"You're heading to the carcer," the guard said, catching Richard in the act.

28

Richard stumbled down the corridor as the guard threw him into a narrow cupboard carved into the wall. Only twenty inches around, the cupboard was studded with nails and prevented the prisoner from moving. When the guard slammed the door, a few small dots of light stippled the darkness—air holes. Richard leaned back, piercing himself. He jerked forward but was jabbed by a blanket of spikes. Panicked and impaled, he squirmed in pain as the nails penetrated his arms and chest. If he stood perfectly still, he could avoid being impaled.

Hours later the guard cracked open the cupboard. Lacerated and unable to stand, Richard collapsed. A brief rest, and then he was shoved back inside. At times he felt as if he was suffocating in the darkness. He tried to comfort himself with King David's words: "Even though I walk through the valley of the shadow of death, I will fear no evil, for you are with me; your rod and your staff, they comfort me" (Ps. 23:4).

But Richard was stuck. He couldn't even sway in the darkness, much less walk. He closed his eyes and imagined the Greek caves on Mount Athos. Cramped together in the carved-out mountain, the Christian monks who lived there wrote a prayer that was timed to match the beating of the heart: "Lord. Jesus. Christ. Son. Of. God. Have. Mercy. On. Me." Richard repeated these words for hours. Eventually his mind gave permission to his heart to repeat the prayer without thinking as his body endured the torment.

Richard spent two days in the carcer before a doctor demanded his removal. Due to the absence of sunlight and nourishing food, Richard's hair had stopped growing. His fingernails were soft and withered. He was thirty-nine and handsome when the guards abducted him on the street of Bucharest. But now, as he looked into a shard of mirror he found in the latrine, he didn't recognize the old man staring back. Richard was a stranger in his own body, a skeleton of his former self. Would his family even recognize him? The tin cup in the corner of his cell became his only reminder that he wasn't in hell. Water didn't exist in hell.

Hallucinations visited him nightly. Vast banquets were spread before him. Sabina brought him a plate filled with smoked sausages, his favorite meal. He could taste each salty bite, opening and closing his jaws in pleasure.

Suddenly the walls expanded to reveal a vast library. Millions of books towered above him. With delight he perused novels, books of poetry, biographies, and numerous scientific journals. Then the library disappeared. In its place, thousands of faces appeared, eagerly watching him and waiting for his speech, which they later applauded.

Richard saw darker visions too. He witnessed gruesome acts of violence and gore. He saw guards mutilate prisoners, and other unspeakable torments. He often lay awake, sweaty from the sexual fantasies and erotic dreams that tormented him. Like Saint Anthony of the desert, he saw women try to seduce him with their naked bodies. He couldn't even remember what it was like to make love to Sabina. His solitude, coupled with uncontrolled symptoms of tuberculosis, increased his sexual appetite. The more he sought to remove them, the more perverse the visions became. Richard almost began to feel that he deserved the torture inflicted on him. Frustrated and plagued with guilt, he cried out to God for relief.

God answered his prayer, and eventually Richard developed a strategy for shaking off the hallucinations. He had to think of them as hostile intruders—temptations not sins. Instead of blaming himself for his visions, he weaponized himself with cool reason. God had given Richard a brilliant intellect. Throughout his imprisonment, he produced a total of one hundred thousand words contained in three hundred poems. Throughout the course of beatings and being drugged and sleep deprived, he would forget them all. After his release, he began to remember them and wrote them down.

Richard soon developed the ability to block off parts of his mind during interrogations. That way he didn't have to worry about confessing the names and addresses of his friends. He honestly couldn't recall them. In the same way doctors use viruses to combat other viruses, Richard resolved to conquer his virtual opponents with their own ammunition. The Devil's arrows could be shot right back at the Enemy.

Day after day Richard enslaved his hallucinations by bringing them into intellectual submission. He refused to allow sinful
thoughts to dominate his cell and rested wholeheartedly in God's
promise: "No weapon that is fashioned against you shall succeed"
(Isa. 54:17).

29

In 1951, after three years of solitary confinement, Richard began to lose hope of seeing his wife and son again. Richard remembered a father he knew personally who, because of his imprisonment, left behind a sick wife and six children. On the verge of starvation and unable to gain employment, the two eldest daughters—ages seventeen and nineteen—became prostitutes to support the family. Seeing his older sisters sell their bodies, the younger brother lost his mind and had to be committed to an insane asylum. After the father's release from prison, he saw his family suffering and begged God, "Take me to prison again. I can't stand to see this."

Richard prayed for that family often, wondering why Christians in other countries didn't intervene to support their brothers and sisters suffering under the evils of Communism. Stories of other prisoners like Pastor Florescu expanded his prayers. Starving rats were pumped into Florescu's cell through a pipe, their bites preventing sleep and forcing him to constantly defend himself. The guards also made Florescu stand for two weeks, poking him with red-hot irons and cutting his body with knives.

Unable to acquire the names of his ministerial contacts, the interrogators kidnapped Florescu's fourteen-year-old son,

Alexander, and beat him in front of his father. Florescu couldn't stand the sight any longer.

"Alexander, I have to say what they want!" he said. "I can't bear your beating anymore!"

"Father," the boy replied, "don't do me the injustice of having a traitor as a parent. Be strong!"

The interrogators, furious with the teenager's stubborn resistance, bludgeoned Alexander to death, splattering his blood across his father's cell.

Richard heard about other atrocities too, like the young woman who was caught teaching children about Christ and smuggling Bibles to the underground church. The Communists targeted her but didn't arrest her until her wedding day.

Several weeks later, when the wedding ceremony began, the church door swung open, and the secret police stormed in. The guards approached the white-clad bride. Without hesitating, she extended her wrists to be cuffed. She exchanged one final glance with her groom, kissed the chains on her arms, and said, "I thank my heavenly Bridegroom for this jewel He's presented to me on my wedding day. I thank Him that I'm worthy to suffer for Him."

The police manhandled the bride down the aisle amid the cries and sobs of her friends and family. She was taken to a prison cell where, on her wedding night, the Communist guards raped her. Five years later, she was released back into the arms of her groom—a shattered woman who looked thirty years older. It was the least she could do for her Christ, she assured him.

The abuse women endured under Communism always exceeded what the men were forced to suffer. Richard thought of tiny Sabina, hoping and praying she would never be arrested and tortured.

In the winter, Richard was forced to wear handcuffs with nails poking into his wrists. Because of the bitter cold, his arms shook involuntarily, slicing the flesh and making it impossible to remain still. He saw Christians hung by ropes from the ceiling and beaten so badly their battered bodies swayed back and forth across the room as they writhed in pain. The guards burned so many cigarettes into the prisoners that their skin eventually rotted off.

In the summer, the guards stripped Richard half naked and forced him to sit in a frost-covered freezer. His fingers and toes went numb, then his limbs, until finally his torso lost the heat to keep him conscious. When the doctor assumed he was almost dead, the guards removed him from the freezer, wrapped him in blankets, and waited for him to warm back up. It took several minutes for him to stop shivering, but when he was stabilized, they threw him into the icebox again. Over and over this happened while the interrogator shouted at Richard to reveal his secrets.

"We're the Devil!" the torturers gloated.

One interrogator shared a secret with Richard: "You can't make omelets without breaking the shells of the eggs."

Richard knew he was becoming a broken man. During his time imprisoned in Calea Rahovei, the guards broke four of his vertebrae and many other bones. His skin was carved up, split apart, and scarred over from repeated knife attacks. Eighteen holes were burned into his muscle tissue. His malnourished frame and lack of sleep compromised his immunity. Pneumonia became a constant threat. Every day at dusk, Richard lay half dead in his cell, mustering up what little strength he could to prepare for the torture that came at dawn.

Yet even in his brokenness, he discovered a healing he had never before felt. With each interaction with the guards, he felt anger and hatred leave his body. Somehow suffering was producing sympathy. Unlike many of the other prisoners who spoke spitefully about the interrogators, Richard began to love them. He determined that God would judge him based not on how much torture he could take but instead on how well he could love his torturers.

The Communists weren't to blame for their crimes, Richard believed. The Devil was behind it all. Communism was Satan's weapon against the church. Richard rehearsed the words of Paul: "We do not wrestle against flesh and blood, but against the rulers, against the authorities, against the cosmic powers over this present darkness, against the spiritual forces of evil in the heavenly places" (Eph. 6:12).

Communism was not primarily a political movement. It was a spiritual movement—an evil uprising in Europe aimed at destroying God's work in the world. The interrogators were only actors in a larger drama. Richard regretted having been one of the actors as well, but because Christ had forgiven *his* sins—horrible as they were—he now possessed the freedom to forgive anyone's sins, even those of his enemies. If the Communists left no room for Jesus in their hearts, Richard would leave no room for Satan in his.

The stories of suffering from the nearby prison of Pitesti tested Richard's resolve. The Christians in that prison were tied to crosses on the floor while hundreds of prisoners defecated on their faces. Then, in jovial celebration, the guards erected the crosses for everyone to see, jeering, "Look at your Christ! How beautiful He is! What fragrance He brings from heaven!"

One priest was driven mad by the torture. Every Sunday guards forced him to consecrate human excrement and urine and serve them like the bread and wine of the Lord's Supper to other prisoners. After the others vomited up the sacrilegious substance, the Christians had to eat the contents off the floor.

In the midst of this darkness, heroes began to emerge. Milan Haimovici was one such hero, a pastor who valiantly endured beatings on behalf of other prisoners. Since the guards didn't know all the names of the inmates in the overcrowded prison, Haimovici volunteered whenever a name was called and was whipped up to twenty-five times each session. In doing so, the pastor won the respect of other inmates and demonstrated Christ's example in sacrificing himself to save others.

• • • •

The Communists learned that torturing the body produced confessions. But they also discovered the benefits of brainwashing the mind. Romania was the first Communist country in Europe to perfect the art of reeducation through brainwashing. Inmates who recanted their beliefs and betrayed their friends were rewarded with extra rations, and some of them were even promoted as lead interrogators. The ultimate goal was to convince prisoners to torture other inmates.

A reeducation project had been launched in December 1949 by the chief of the Romanian secret police, Alexandru Nikolski, and a prisoner arrested for helping organize the fascist Iron Guard ten years prior, Eugen Turcanu. After Turcanu's imprisonment, he spearheaded the Organization of Prisoners with Communist Beliefs project. Fifteen prisoners were selected for experimentation. If each could successfully complete four phases, he would be rewarded and promoted.[1]

The first phase was "exterior unmasking" in which the prisoner had to prove his loyalty to the Communists by confessing guilt and betraying friends outside the prison. The second phase, "interior unmasking," required him to betray his fellow prisoners who had helped him after his arrest. "Public moral unmasking" demanded each prisoner curse whatever he held sacred. He had to renounce his wife or girlfriend, family members, and close acquaintances. After completing these three phases, the fourth and final phase ultimately proved his loyalty. A prisoner would willfully attempt to reprogram his best friend by torturing him with his own hands.

Turcanu's reputation was on the line, and he used every means possible to motivate the recruits to successfully complete the four phases. Knowing that some of his prisoners were Christians, he desecrated their rituals. He baptized them in buckets of urine and excrement. He officiated masses during Holy Week and forced the prisoners to dress as choirboys and priests wrapped in robes of fecal matter. They performed pornographic acts during the liturgies and called the Virgin Mary "the Great Whore." For three years, Turcanu succeeded in his experimentation. His methods spread throughout Romania and became a pattern for other prisons experimenting with reeducation programs.

For seventeen hours every day—lasting months and even years—Richard was forced to sit alone in a room and listen to a tape recorder loudly playing Communist propaganda: "Communism is good! Communism is good! Christianity is stupid! Christianity is stupid! Give up! Give up!"

The effectiveness of this torture technique lay in its repetition. At first, after only one or two days, the mind resists the propaganda quite easily. But when days turn to weeks and months, the brain grows receptive to the statements. The words become like friends, sheltering the prisoner from crueler physical abuses.

Richard understood the power words could hold over the mind. He had spent years memorizing and repeating Scripture verses. After years of listening to repetitive Communist slogans, he discovered a weapon more formidable than even brainwashing—heartwashing. The head always obeys the heart, and if Jesus Christ has cleansed the heart, the brain is sure to follow. "For out of the abundance of the heart his mouth speaks" (Luke 6:45).

30

After his final year in solitary confinement, Richard became too unhealthy to torture. The blood he continued to spit up worried the doctor, who spied through the keyhole in the cell door. Richard would lose his usefulness to the Communists if he died. "We're not murderers like the Nazis," his interrogator bragged. "We want you to live—and suffer."

That night Richard was carried out of the bowels of the building into the open air. He had forgotten what the moon and stars looked like. The fresh air was foreign to his lungs, but he breathed it deeply as they put him in an ambulance. He even caught a glimpse of his house as the vehicle swerved through the city. *Am I being taken home to die?* he wondered.

When the vehicle came to a halt at the prison hospital, Richard was carried up a flight of stairs into a cell. A guard entered the room and eyed him suspiciously. He asked Richard what he had done to deserve imprisonment.

"I'm a pastor and a child of God," Richard said.

The guard leaned down and whispered, "Praise be to the Lord! I'm one of Jesus's soldiers!" He told Richard about joining the Army of the Lord, a branch of the Orthodox Church that had gathered hundreds of thousands of members. His name was Tachici. At the risk of being heard, the guard exchanged Bible verses with Richard. The consequences of being caught were brutal. Other guards like Tachici had been imprisoned and tortured for up to twelve years for so much as giving a prisoner an apple.

Bedridden and weak, Richard lay on the floor, fixated on the small window in the wall. For the first time since he could remember, he could see the blue sky. He had erased that color from his memory entirely. And green too. The grass beamed with light and life. A strange sound startled him—the chirping of birds. He told Tachici about Martin Luther, who, when strolling through the woods, said to the birds, "Good morning, theologians—you wake and sing, but I, old fool, know less than you and worry over everything, instead of simply trusting in the heavenly Father's care."

Exhausted beyond description, Richard fell into a deep sleep. But a voice soon woke him.

"I'm Leonte Filipescu. Who are you?"

Richard strained to hear his cellmate through the wall. It was one of Romania's first Socialists.

"Fight your illness," the man said. "Don't give in! We'll all be free in two weeks."

"How do you know?" Richard asked.

"The Americans are driving the Communists back in Korea. They'll be here in two weeks."

Richard hesitated. "But even if they meet no opposition, it will surely take them more than a fortnight to reach Romania, won't it?"

"No way!" Filipescu said. "Distance is nothing to them. They have supersonic jets!"

Richard let himself believe it for a minute but was snapped back to reality when the guards came into his cell. A trial had been arranged. A woman and four men sat as judges across a table from where Richard stood. "A lawyer has been appointed to defend you," the court president said. "He has waived your right to call witnesses. You may sit down."

The prosecutor launched into his attack, claiming Richard was an imperialist spy for the Scandinavian church missions and the World Council of Churches, he supported anti-Communist ideals, and he cloaked his subversion under the guise of religion. Delirious from fever, Richard felt the sting of an injection pierce his skin.

The defense lawyer proved useless against the waves of accusation. "Do you have anything to say?" the president asked.

Richard mustered the only defense that came to his mind. "I love God."

The ten-minute trial was over, and Richard was sentenced to twenty years of hard labor.

31

Two days after Richard's trial, Tachici leaned over his bed and whispered, "You're leaving. God be with you!"

The guards came into the cell, hammered fifty-pound chains around Richard's ankles, and escorted him to the main gate. A truck containing forty prisoners pulled up, and Richard was lifted into their company. One of the girls from his congregation wept beside him.

"You don't remember me?" she asked.

Richard remembered the girl well and listened between her sobs to her sad story. After her arrest, she had resorted to stealing food and supplies.

"I'm so ashamed," she cried.

"I'm a sinner too," Richard assured her, "saved by the grace of God. Believe in Christ, and your sins will be forgiven."

She bent down to kiss Richard's hand, promising upon her release to let Sabina know she had seen him.

The truck deposited the prisoners on a train bound for Tirgul-Ocna, a sanatorium for prisoners diagnosed with tuberculosis. The two-hundred-mile transit lasted a full day and night. Richard was taken to a large building at the edge of town where a Christian named Dr. Aldea examined him.

"I'm a prisoner myself," he said, "but they let me work as a doctor."

Only one physician, Richard wondered, *for a sanatorium crowded with tuberculosis patients?*

"I won't lie to you," the doctor said. "There's nothing we can do. You may have about two weeks to live. Try to eat what they give you, although it's not good."

Over the next few days, two prisoners died. Richard overheard another patient pleading with the doctor. "I swear I'm better, doctor," he stammered hoarsely. "The fever's going, I know. Listen, please! Today I coughed up blood only once. Don't let them put me in room 4!"

"Room 4?" Richard wondered aloud.

"That's where you go when they know there's no hope," explained the man who brought Richard his watery soup.

Richard tried to consume the liquid but kept throwing it up. When spoon-feeding failed, the doctor relayed the sad news. "I'm sorry, but they insist," he told Richard. "They're moving you to room 4."

• • • •

Guards led Richard to a sizable room with twelve beds crammed around a few tables. The windows were barred with iron but presented a view of a vegetable patch enclosed by walls and barbed wire. The fear of contagion prevented Richard and the other patients in room 4 from interacting directly with the guards. Because no one was expected to leave the room alive, criminals delivered food to the door—mainly cabbage, beans, and gruel made of barley.

While other prisoners were allowed to work in the garden outside, Richard spent the next thirty months in the Death Room, wavering between worlds. At times he descended into a coma before awakening to choke on his own blood. Bedsores spread across his back, oozing pus. Some prisoners in the room considered Richard as good as dead and crossed themselves when passing by his bed. Other prisoners helped ease the pastor's agony by turning over his body as many as forty times per night, repositioning his limbs in hopes of alleviating his discomfort.

Within two weeks, the four men who were quarantined with Richard died. Dozens more would succumb to the sickness, their beds quickly refilled with other prisoners.

Tuberculosis was again making considerable progress in Richard's body. His chest swollen and gurgling, Richard struggled to cope with the fluid filling his lungs. King David once said, "There is but a step between me and death" (1 Sam. 20:3), and Richard almost took that step many times. When he closed his eyes, he had no idea if he would open them in this world or the next.

"If only we had some modern drugs," said Dr. Aldea as he monitored Richard's symptoms. Rumor had it that the Americans had discovered a new tuberculosis medicine called streptomycin, but the Communists questioned the legitimacy of the rumor, chalking it up to Western propaganda.

Miraculously, Richard's health improved. To the astonishment of the doctor, his patient's mind became clear, the fever diminished, and his lungs began to heal. Richard began to eat again, and he shared his faith with unusual fervor. Every week death reached into room 4 to snatch another victim, but none of the prisoners died as atheists. Richard had become their provisional pastor, helping even the staunchest of unbelievers make peace with God before their final breath. Death gave Richard a new congregation—a flock of murderers, thieves, sinners, and fascists—and each grasped a hope Communism couldn't provide.

For a time, Richard's bed was between a man named Vasilescu, a common-law criminal who had been put in charge of a group of priests enslaved in a prison camp on the Danube Canal, and one of the abbots he had tortured. Now, in room 4, both men were dying.

Tuberculosis wreaked havoc on young Vasilescu's lungs, and one night he woke up gasping for breath. "Pastor, I'm going to die!" he cried. "Please pray for me!" He dozed fitfully throughout the night, waking again and crying, "I believe in God!"

At dawn Abbot Iscu called two prisoners to his bed. "Lift me out!"

"You're too ill to move," they protested.

"Let us do it for you," others said.

"Lift me out!"

So they picked him up.

"To Vasilescu's bed," Iscu directed.

The abbot sat beside the young man who had tortured him and put a hand gently on his arm. "Be calm," he said soothingly. "You're young. You hardly knew what you were doing." He wiped sweat from the boy's forehead with a rag. "I forgive you with all my heart, and so would other Christians. There's a place in heaven for you also." Abbot Iscu received Vasilescu's confession and gave him Holy Communion before being carried back to his bed.

That night both the abbot and Vasilescu died.

32

The Jilava prison was a nineteenth-century fort with a maze of cells deep underground. Surrounded by a moat, the damp prison, with an intended capacity of six hundred prisoners, now held three thousand. Jilava was familiar to Sabina. She'd visited the prison twice—once with a girl searching for a friend who was an inmate and once in search of Richard. Both times Sabina had been turned away without information. Now she was a prisoner herself.

The truck from the secret-police headquarters dipped suddenly down a ramp, causing Sabina and the other prisoners to squeal. The vehicle came to a stop, and the women waited.

Finally the command came: "Take off the goggles!"

Sabina looked around at the large underground basement. The walls reflected the dampness, and uniformed female guards milled around. A stocky, muscular woman with red hair barked at the group and directed them to her colleague, a clerk with a ledger.

"All superfluous articles of clothing," Sergeant Aspra bellowed, "are deposited here upon joining this establishment."

The guards took Sabina's summer coat and recorded the transaction in the ledger. Sabina remembered a conversation with two schoolgirls weeks earlier in her interrogation-center cell. "God help you if you ever get to know what it's like at Jilava in cell 4," whispered the older of the two.

As Sabina's group now approached a heavy, iron-barred door, she heard the dreaded words: "This lot for cell 4!"

Inside the cell, two long tiers of wooden bunks lined the walls. A narrow corridor ran down the middle of the room, and a dim lightbulb hung from the vaulted ceiling. The one window had been painted over and barred, and heat and stench smoldered in the airless cell. Dozens of eyes stared down at Sabina from their bunks.

"I'm Viorica, your room chief. Give her the bed at the end."

Sabina made her way to the darkest end of the room, where the lone lavatory bucket—a bucket shared by fifty women, most with bowel trouble—stood next to an open drain. Bodies hung from the beds, torture scars marking their limbs and torsos.

On her first morning in Jilava, Sabina heard someone singing a hymn. Nuns made up a portion of the prison population, and the guards despised their singing.

"Are you allowed to sing?" Sabina later asked one of the nuns.

"We're allowed to sing," Sister Veronica replied, "and they're allowed to beat us."

• • • •

At 11:00 a.m., Sabina joined her cellmates in line for soup. Each woman received a scoop of steaming liquid and a slice of black bread. The moment the soup keg left the cell, tempers raged over inequities in serving size, the cellblock raging with ferocious howls until the guards rushed in with their batons.

Sergeant Aspra roared, "We're too good to you! If this goes on, you'll starve tomorrow!"

Spilled soup lay in tiny puddles on the floor, and sobbing poured down from the bunks. The second the guards left, chaos returned.

"There'll be no more food today or tomorrow either!" Aspra bellowed.

The girl next to Sabina touched her arm. "You poor thing. You didn't eat."

"It's okay—it wasn't very appetizing."

"It's the rotten carrots," said the girl, Elena, wrinkling her nose. "The state vegetable trust dumped three hundred tons here. Nobody would buy them, not even for pigs. We've been eating them for weeks."

A large, imposing woman peered at Sabina. "And who are you? Why are you here?" she demanded. "You haven't said a word since you arrived." The women around her looked on with interest as the commanding woman glared down from her bunk.

Sabina told them her name and said she was a pastor's wife.

"Religious, eh? Know any Bible stories?" asked a gray-haired peasant woman.

"Yes, please tell us something!" rang other voices. "It's so boring here."

The masculine woman became more hostile. "You'll turn this place into a vicarage!" She stormed off, stiff with rage.

"Don't mind Elsa Gavriloiu," Elena said. "She's an old party member." Even in the dark cell, Sabina could see Elena's eyes sparkle. "She's ever so grateful for the chance she's been given to study her ideological errors in the Jilava reeducational institute!"

To cheer up the hungry women, Sabina told the story of Joseph and his brothers, reminding them that the wheel of life can turn when everything looks hopeless. A handful of women listened as the rest of the cell hummed and squawked like an aviary. Sabina caught a cautious glance from redheaded Viorica.

"Be careful," she whispered. "If Aspra hears you talking about God, there'll be trouble."

• • • •

The next morning Viorica appeared in the aisle between the bunks. "I finally figured out who you are!" She pointed a finger at Sabina, who froze and stared back. "I knew your name was familiar. I asked myself, *Where have I heard that name?*"

The other women stared as Sabina perched on her bunk, awaiting judgment.

"Yes!" said Viorica triumphantly. "She's a preacher—the wife of that Pastor Wurmbrand!"

The room chief proudly explained that her uncle had charge of an Orthodox church in Bucharest and had heard Richard's speech at the Congress of the Cults. "The only one in four thousand to stand up and speak like a man of God," Viorica said. "You know they fired the minister of cults afterward?" She turned to Sabina. "I've been to your church. I thought the service was lovely."

Sabina became the heroine of the hour, and Viorica found her a better bunk, ten feet farther from the lavatory bucket.

For breakfast Sabina received her first dish of *tertch*—corn boiled in water—and looked around for something to eat it with.

"She wants a spoon!" jeered Mrs. Gavriloiu. "Lap it up!"

Sabina tried to eat the thin, damp-smelling gruel from the shallow tin dish, but it dribbled down her chin. To lap seemed too animalistic, so she gave away her morning *tertch*. Later, though, she remembered Gideon, the biblical general whom God told to staff his army only with those who lapped the water "as a dog laps" (Judg. 7:5). And Jesus had humbled Himself to the utmost. If they could accept these humiliations, so could Sabina. When the next meal came, Sabina lapped her food. Even lapping, the women consumed hardly enough calories to survive.

Starvation was the official policy for the Communists. It made the prisoners listless and less troublesome. It also provided the Communists with eager volunteers for the labor camps and their promises of heartier sustenance.

• • • •

Sabina and other Christians often gathered around the nuns' bunks, singing quiet songs and caring for the other women in the cell. Most of the women were Orthodox, and the illiterate countrywomen feared dying without the priest's last rites. The nuns repeated the funeral service words to the dying, offering what bit of hope they could.

"Put your experience with the ladies' guild to work," said Mrs. Stupineau, Elena's closest ally, to Sabina. "Keep us from bickering."

Mrs. Stupineau was a tall, stately woman who'd been a wealthy widow until the Communists took everything. Impoverished, she had to sell candles and sweep the church where she'd once been a generous patron. Mrs. Stupineau had been betrayed by a French seminarian she'd welcomed to the church. Armed with the woman's stories of religious persecution, the secret-police informer reported her. At forty-six, after a year in Jilava, her hair was already white.

• • • •

Jilava was a place of injustice and terror. Sergeant Aspra's deputy, Corporal Georgescu, was a dull, daft girl with a flat face and flat voice who mustered the women for exercise. "When I say to get outside, no one is to be last. All out together!" Fifty women couldn't use the door simultaneously, but Georgescu rejected the logic. "When I give an order, you obey." It was always the old and infirm who received her beatings.

"Don't you know what pity is?" Sabina cried. "It's written in the Bible that those who show no pity will have none from God in the end!" (see James 2:13).

"No, I don't know," Georgescu droned. "And I don't want to know."

Sabina was used to people who loved and hated, but these wooden girls in uniform had been turned into puppets. If the order was to beat, they beat. They had passed through security-police schools, where blind obedience was drilled into them. Most were peasants who had never owned anything as nice as their new uniforms or as expensive as their revolvers. They ruled Romania, and Romania was their world.

Torturous flashbacks plagued cell 4 of Jilava, a lone woman's distress often setting off the memories of the entire cellblock. For hours the women writhed and screamed, echoing the horror they had experienced time and time again. Sabina fought off the madness with prayer.

"Lord," she said, "if You've given me some influence among these women, give me wisdom as well to win their souls for You."

Her chance came the next morning.

• • • •

Sabina came face-to-face with Elsa Gavriloiu, the old party member. "Start that preaching in here again, and I'll hammer on the door until the guard comes," she threatened.

"Elsa, do you still believe in the party?" Sabina asked.

"Certainly." She sneered. "I haven't changed my beliefs. My arrest was all a mistake."

"Nor has my arrest altered my faith," Sabina said. "In fact, it's stronger. I want to tell people about the friend they have in Jesus."

"You'll get the whole cell punished," Elsa warned. "I don't intend to suffer for you and your God. He hasn't helped you much anyway."

"This God you dislike," Sabina said. "Tell me about Him."

Elsa described a fanatic who squelched science and squeezed money from the proletariat, using the stolen funds to commission churches.

"What you call God is certainly very unlovable," Sabina said. "The God I love is totally different. He shared the poverty of the workers. He was brought up among the oppressed. He fed the hungry and healed the sick. He teaches love. He died for us—"

"Love!" Elsa's voice cracked. "What good is that? I'm all hate. If you knew how I hate those treacherous comrades who put me here—I hope they burn in hell! I gave my whole life to the party, and this is what they do to me." She lowered her head and a tear slid from her eye. "Praying? Forgive them, Father?" She spat the words. "I don't accept forgiveness—it's lies."

Elsa began to weep. "It's all the same. If the Americans come, I'll be hanged. If the Communists stay, I'm stuck in jail. Forgiveness!" The tears ran down her cheeks.

After a while she sat up and wiped her gray face with the edge of her skirt. "Sabina Wurmbrand," she said, her eyes widening, "you're sneaky. I tell you to stop preaching, and in five minutes you're preaching to me."

• • • •

Overcrowding in Jilava grew worse. Cell 4 had space for thirty people, but by Christmas there were eighty. Sabina continued to share the gospel with her cellmates and taught French and German lessons by writing in the DDT insecticide powder with a splinter. Her friends suffered greatly, and many died. Rumors of American emancipation swirled around the cell, but the hope was never realized. But perhaps in cell 4, cocooned in suffering, future saints were being made.

Corporal Georgescu arrived one morning with a sheet of paper. "Everyone on this list must be ready to move at once!" Names were read, but no reason was given for their departure. Few now believed they were going home, but nothing could be worse than Jilava.

Sabina waited, day after day, for her name to be called. On January 6, 1951, Mihai's twelfth birthday, her chance arrived. By 8:00 a.m., she was outside in the bitter cold awaiting the trucks that soon drove the prisoners to Ghencea, a transit camp near Bucharest. After so many months underground, Sabina relished the clear view of the night sky.

"Release?" cried a lanky girl with dark eyes, overhearing the hopeful murmurs from the new arrivals. "What an idea!" She stared at Sabina. "This is the departure point for the canal."

In a switchyard near Bucharest, the women boarded a train for the Danube Canal. Finally they would be able to work outdoors. And finally their food would be sufficient. Hours later the train stopped, and Sabina tumbled out, tired and aching. A sign on the platform read *CERNAVODA*, the name of a small town by the Danube. The camp was miles away, and they began the march through the wintry black night.

Little did Sabina know what horrors awaited her on the Danube Canal.

33

Sabina's eyes flew open, and her heart pounded as she bolted upright on the prison-hut floorboards where she'd slept.

"Beast!" shrieked the woman beside her. "It jumped on my bed!"

Sabina heard a scuttling and squeaking in the dark and recognized the acrid animal smell. Rats!

Her first night at Cernavoda was fitful. Arriving at the prison camp, she learned that on the canal, officials often granted prisoners permits for visits from relatives. With the hope of finally seeing Mihai swirling in her mind until the wee hours of the morning and the scurrying rats interrupting the few minutes she was able to sleep, Sabina now hoped for some rest and a chance to wash her filthy clothes.

But rest would not be granted by Docile Rina, the prisoner with a long criminal record who had been chosen to rule the entire female section of the camp. "All new arrivals will gather outside for a visit to the bathhouse!" she shouted.

Sabina lined up with the other women and was marched away over the frozen mud, armed guards flanking the column of prisoners. At the bathhouse, she disrobed.

The political prisoners of Cernavoda were educated women and young socialites, but the prison camp also held criminals, including a handful of prostitutes. Now, under the watchful gaze of the guards, the prostitutes squealed and shrieked, obscene gestures flailing from the naked mass of bodies. The guards laughed and stamped their boots. Cackling, Rina urged them on.

Exhausted, starved, and shamed, Sabina felt the world spin around her. Her face smashed into the wet concrete floor, and everything went black. Women carried her back to the prison hut and laid her on a bed. Someone threw her a jacket and sack-like skirt with dirty gray and white stripes. Sabina struggled to put on her new clothing, her head throbbing from hitting the hard bathhouse floor.

With her dark hair and Jewish beauty, Sabina's new look elicited curious stares from her fellow prisoners. The elite political prisoners knew Sabina did not look like one of them and surmised that she must be a gypsy. From that point on at Cernavoda, Sabina was an adopted gypsy.

• • • •

The next day, early in the morning, the prisoners prepared to march from the camp toward the Danube Canal. A bitter wind blew across the plain from the Black Sea, piercing the prisoners' thin garments. Guards in warm winter coats beat the women who dared to stir.

The line of women joined scores of men. "Taking out two thousand criminals and counterrevolutionaries!" the lead guard shouted as the group made its way to the iron watchtowers. The column of prisoners snaked its way into the distance like a single enormous beast, a being with a life of its own. Sabina thought of her forefathers in Egypt who had labored on the pharaoh's works.

The Danube, Europe's second longest river, flowed through countries caught in Communism's iron grip. Political prisoners and criminals in labor camps were forced to excavate the canal connecting the Danube with the Black Sea. For prisoners unable to meet the day's work quota, hunger and punishment waited. Many resorted to eating dogs, snakes, mice, and even grass to supplement their meager meals. Sabina's petite body was ill suited to shoveling frozen dirt and heaving heavy stones into the water. The jagged rocks would crush her tiny fingers, leaving them swollen and throbbing. Dreams of aspirin and relief would consume her nights. The project was called the Death Canal for a reason.

The Cernavoda prisoners were building an embankment along the canal. Women filled wheelbarrows with earth; then men pushed the loads two hundred yards before running with the weight up a steep incline to the parapet of the dam. After her first few loads, Sabina staggered as she tried to lift the heavy shovel of dirt over the side of the wheelbarrow.

A prisoner brigade chief oversaw each gang of workers, setting the norm for that day's work and checking on the progressing workload. If, after enormous effort, the crew managed to fulfill the norm, the chief raised it the next day. If they failed, they were punished.

"Come on! Wake up!" Rina's voice rang from twenty yards away. "Do you want a night in the carcer?"

Carcer was a word that froze the blood. Richard had endured two days in the spike-studded, coffin-like box at the Calea Rahovei prison. This was a common punishment in camps on the canal, and after an exhausting day's work, the prisoners found it torturous. The next day the prisoner went back to work again, this time even more fatigued and with an even higher chance of being ordered back to the carcer again that night for not working quickly enough.

At lunchtime the prisoners received a pound of bread and some soup and oats. It was an improvement on the meager sustenance of Jilava, but it fell far short of the necessary calories for backbreaking work on the canal.

After lunch, the workers toiled for another four hours. When the light failed, the great column formed again for the return to camp. Beleaguered prisoners collapsed, with slightly stronger men scooping up their companions before the guards noticed. The cold wind seemed to never stop blowing.

"Returning two thousand bandits!" the lead guard shouted as the column reached the gate. "Bracing breeze!" another called cheerfully, wrapped in the warmth of his thick overcoat.

Sabina was chilled to the marrow of her thin bones. Her blistered hands and feet throbbed as much as her aching muscles and head. The next day she would have a raging cold.

• • • •

The prison ranks of Cernavoda were full of broken, hardened criminals, and Sabina sought ways to slip words of challenge and encouragement into their steeled hearts using the stories of Scripture.

"One great man began life as a swindler," she told the women. "His name was Matthew. But when he met the Lord, he was so moved and so enchanted with His goodness that he left everything he had and became Matthew the disciple" (see Matt. 9:9). She looked from face-to-face, her own heart aching at the sadness in the women's eyes. "A thief became a saint, forgiven and loved throughout the world to this day. A martyr of the church, the author of the gospel read throughout the whole world."

Some women scoffed, but others clearly yearned to hear more.

The gulf between criminal and political prisoner wasn't often bridged. Straddling the two groups, Sabina was a gypsy Jewish Christian who spoke with love to the worst criminals and rebuked sin in the ladies of high society. Doing so naturally earned scowls from several sides.

Not all the people Sabina talked with were actually present with her. She often had imagined conversations with Richard, especially during his years of solitary confinement, and she sensed his responses to her. Separated for years, the Wurmbrands still moved as one.

Sabina asked everyone working on the canal if they had heard anything of her husband, dreading bad news but desperate to learn anything of Richard's fate. No one ever had. Then three women arrived from Vacaresti, a prison where many of the sick were taken.

"Every time you talk about God," one woman said to Sabina, "I remember Vacaresti. I was there only a short time, but we had a preacher there too."

Sabina's heart quickened as she listened.

"We were waiting on the landing to use the bathroom," the woman continued, "when we heard a man talking behind a locked door of a solitary cell. He was saying, 'Love Jesus and trust in God's kindness.' We were so surprised. Everyone in the prison asked who he was, but we never found out." Now that she'd met Sabina, she was certain the man had been Richard. He seemed deathly ill, and after several days, he stopped preaching. She heard he had died.

Back in her hut during a moment of solitude, Sabina sat weeping on her iron cot. Tears streamed down her face, and pain tore at her heart. But through her grief, hope grew. She continued to pray, asking the Lord to add years of life and health to the man who had served Him faithfully, even in the isolation cell.

• • • •

Sabina's tears soon dried as she looked forward to the day Mihai might come to visit her at Cernavodă. The guards provided postcards for the prisoners to write invitations to their families. Praying the cards weren't a ruse to trick prisoners into revealing their friends and relatives to the secret police, Sabina wrote to Mihai.

On the Sunday of his visit, Sabina woke long before daybreak. Ice crusted the windowpanes, and she longed for morning to come.

At last it did, and Sabina ran outside, hoping to see the visitors waiting in the faraway compound by the gates. Squinting her eyes and shielding her face from the rising sun, she spotted Mihai. There he was, tall and slim, wearing tattered clothes. Sabina recognized the man next to him as the pastor of their church. She waved ferociously, but they couldn't see her among all the other women lined up to see their loved ones.

Suddenly a fight broke out behind her. Rina was in the middle of it, screeching triumphantly. So many people had failed to fulfill their work norms over the past week that the visit was canceled.

Mihai and the pastor had traveled all night from Bucharest, spending their desperately needed savings for nothing. They couldn't speak to Sabina or even leave the food and clothing they had brought with them.

The small group of visitors, about thirty in all, waited all day at the gates in hopes the commandant would change her mind. She didn't, and by evening they were gone.

But the prisoners could write again. Several Sundays later, Mihai again made the trek to Cernavoda. This time there was no punishment, but the visits proceeded alphabetically. There was little hope the guards would make it to "Wurmbrand" in time. The prisoners around Sabina passed borrowed clothing among the group and tried to make themselves presentable. They rehearsed the words they would say to their families. They needed to make the fifteen-minute visit count, even though they would be separated by ten yards, with the guards hovering over every conversation.

Finally, near the end of the visit, Sabina's name was called. When she saw her son, she forgot she was a prisoner, forgot what she looked like, forgot where she was, and simply embraced him with her eyes. How thin he was, and how serious! She gazed at him, and he at her, and in a flash the fifteen minutes had passed. They barely spoke, but near the end of the visit and across the thirty feet separating mother from son, Sabina called, "Mihai, believe in Jesus with all your heart!" He'd been left like thousands of other boys and girls without a guide, and the Communists would profit from that.

Sabina wouldn't know it, but her words took root. They sprouted in Mihai as a tree from a small seed and emboldened him to cling to Christ.

The guard shoved Sabina's shoulder and led her back to her hut. For hours Sabina couldn't speak, the precious memory of her son a soothing balm for her weary, besieged soul.

34

When Sabina was a child, she hated the night. Now she longed for it as the one release from her unbearable work on the Danube Canal. Yet when darkness came, she couldn't sleep. She would sit up and pray for the women in her hut and in her camp, but also for the millions of prisoners in the Communist world and the Christians who slept peacefully in the West—for those she imagined were praying for Romanian prisoners.

Every Sunday at Cernavoda brought indoctrination lectures. In an assembly hall, weary workers gathered for verbal assaults on God. "Outside, everyone is now Communist," the room chief began. "Only you persist in this ridiculous religion, and we plan to educate you out of it. The party is in power now, and it knows best. You're not in *prison*—I don't even want to hear the word! You're in an institution for reeducation. You'll be building your own happiness! Working for future generations! And by surpassing the work norms each day, you may very well speed up your own liberty as a rehabilitated citizen."

After the indoctrination lectures came a propaganda concert, with cabaret singers and small-time actresses singing songs of praise for Communism. A German woman, once plump and pretty but now wearing the emaciated look of prison life, clasped her hands pathetically and sang, her voice cracking on the high notes. Officers in the front row howled with laughter. What could be funnier than a faded fräulein making fun of herself? Tears ran down her cheeks as she trembled and sang on.

Few resisted the charades. And those who did weren't completely unaffected by the hours of indoctrination. Some of the trash the guards threw at them was bound to stick.

Sabina refused to applaud at the lectures. "Go ahead and pretend—what does it matter?" her cellmates urged. "Is it worth a beating?" But when Sabina heard God slandered and saw beauty trampled in the dirt, she couldn't pretend. She buried herself among the people standing at the back of the hall. But she didn't escape.

• • • •

"I have information that you failed to clap during this afternoon's lecture and reeducation class, Wurmbrand," the commandant said, scowling at Sabina from under her peaked uniform cap. "All your behavior here has shown you to be a counterrevolutionary force, not amenable to proper reeducation." She licked her lips. "We've tried to be good to you. Now other methods will be used."

Instead of returning to her hut that night, Sabina was marched to the carcer. The iron door had a few holes to circulate air, and guards passed a small plate of food through a slit at the bottom.

On the Danube Canal, guards relished the chance to banish prisoners to the carcer.

After a few hours, Sabina's feet were burning. Each time she shifted, the stab of an iron spike pierced her side. *How many hours will they keep me here?* she wondered. She knew people had been driven insane in these torture boxes, allowing thoughts of horror to overcome them. But how could she escape?

Drops of water bounced off the top of the box, and Sabina decided to use the desolate sound to make time pass. She counted them—one for God, two for the tablets of the Law, three for the Trinity. She reached fifteen or sixteen before starting over. Eventually, as despair threatened to overwhelm her, she cried out, "One! Two! Three! Four! One! Two! Three! Four!" Soon the words became incoherent. Her mind moved from chaos to rest, and though her torment had faded into darkness, her spirit continued speaking to God. After an hour or two, her mind came back, rested. Sabina's sanity had been saved.

• • • •

Soon after Sabina's release from the carcer, Colonel Albon toured the canal camps, walking around Cernavoda and casting contemptuous glances at the ranks of gray and ghostly women. As he was about to leave, a gypsy girl accosted him. She'd been meeting clandestinely with a secret-police lieutenant and was now pregnant.

Albon's report prompted an inquiry from officials in Bucharest, and the decision was made to move the women from Cernavoda to a labor camp far from the men. Sabina would soon be introduced to Camp Kilometer 4.

. . . .

From morning to evening, the prisoners of Camp K4 loaded heavy rocks aboard a barge to be ferried into the river and dropped over the side. It was impossible to do this without making a huge splash, and within minutes of starting the work, everyone was soaked. The icy wind blew across the Baragan Plain and froze Sabina's clothes stiff. The rocks scraped her knuckles and bloodied her nails. She wondered if she'd ever be able to stand straight again.

In the evening the prisoners returned to the hut to sleep in their wet clothes. How Sabina longed for a little sunshine! She was skeletal, and the frosty gusts seemed to blow right through her.

. . . .

At 11:00 p.m., the door of the hut burst open, and half a dozen guards marched in. "Everybody up! Commandant's inspection!"

Dazed women jumped shivering from the gray blankets, fear reflecting in their tired eyes. They scrambled to gather their belongings. Maybe they were being moved!

"Women!" the commandant announced, her polished boots reflecting the overhead light. "I want all those who can speak a foreign language to take a step forward." Many women stepped forward, Sabina included, a cross section of the former bourgeois days. A guard recorded their names.

For hours the women guessed at the significance of the midnight interruption. "Translators—that's what it is!" one woman said. "The Americans are coming! And the French!"

The criminal prisoners were bursting with jealousy at the thought of the cushy jobs awaiting their privileged counterparts.

As she plodded to work across the plain the next morning, Sabina dreamed about her new prospects. *Could it be true?* she wondered. *Work as a translator in some warm office, out of this unyielding wind? Has some great international upheaval taken place?* The rock quarry buzzed with excited rumors.

Sabina worked that day next to a petite Jewish woman named Jessica. Eyeing the guards, the woman explained what had happened in her hut during the night.

"It happens in every hut and in every camp," Jessica said. "Sometimes they come in and ask who is a foreigner. And the Germans and Jews hurry to give their non-Romanian names, thinking they'll be allowed to emigrate." Jessica raised a large rock and heaved it onto the barge. "But there's no meaning in it at all. It's just to make you suffer."

Before long, Sabina knew the woman was right. It was simply another torment to exhaust the mind and sap the will.

• • • •

Between the tortured and the torturer, a love-hate relationship could arise. Guards beat and mocked the prisoners, and those same prisoners, who bore the bruises from the clubs, often called their tormentors by endearing nicknames. The younger guards had been taught that the prisoners were all "bandits" and repeated their harsh epithets mindlessly. Sabina learned to beware of blank-eyed girls in their early twenties. They could be more brutal than any man ... as long as their indoctrination lasted.

But then the young guards were dispatched to the canal, and for months and years they lived beside their prisoners. They marched the long miles to the quarries. They stood over the women as they labored. And sometimes they talked with them. After a while, they realized they were dealing not merely with "vermin" and "bandits" but often with simple peasant women like those in their own families. Throughout Romania, land and livestock were being torn from their owners to enforce collectivization, and the guards began to doubt as they learned that their own relatives were starving and being arrested. They lost pride in their jobs and then faith in their party. This rising revulsion against the consequences of Communism brought about a wonderful change in some of the guards.

Nina, a rosy-cheeked guard who had been kind to Sabina in the past, noticed the youth of some new prisoners at the slave-labor camp. "She's just a child!" she said about one. "They told me I'd be handling thieves and murderers, but she's so young!" Nina sneaked food to the inmates and smuggled messages to family members on the outside. Her confidence in Communism was starting to shake.

Sabina began to talk with Nina, chiseling through the parroted mockeries of religion. When she talked about Jesus, Nina scoffed. "But we Communists are the best friends of Christ! If there's a heaven and Christ is judge, we'll be the most favored of all. Your husband's a pastor?" she asked Sabina. "How many people do you think he's brought to Christ? A couple dozen? Maybe a few hundred?" She smirked. "We Communists make sure that every year Christ gets thousands of customers who die with His name on their lips. We're filling His heaven; He should be grateful."

Sabina absorbed Nina's scorn and told her about Saul of Tarsus, whose hatred of Christianity also laid the foundation for the future Paul, and how the Bible says that where sin abounds, grace abounds even more (see Acts 9; Rom. 5:20).

Nina eventually became a Christian, and it wasn't something easy to conceal. A traitor can work undiscovered for twenty years because evil is all around and he can hide in it. Under every stone is another cockroach. But goodness is a rare butterfly that strikes even insensitive eyes. No one can miss it, and some will want to kill it.

Sometime in 1951, Nina vanished from Camp K4.

"Don't take it so badly," Sabina said to her friend, who felt her actions compromised Nina's safety. "It was what she wanted to do in her heart. She'll have greater joy as a prisoner than she ever had as a guard."

Suffering would give Nina great authority to talk to others. But what if she died in prison? It would be for a good cause, Sabina reminded her friends. And God doesn't leave unrewarded even a cup of water given to someone in suffering. He would reward Nina too, for those who die for their faith leave behind the greatest legacy of influencing the world for good.

35

Male guards accompanied the column of prisoners to and from the camp, and these were the only men the female inmates ever saw. Sabina worked quietly along the banks of the Danube as women around her stained the silence with lewd jokes.

"Peter has hands like a gorilla! And all that black hair on his back. I'm sure he's covered in it from head to toe ... that is, if anyone could ever see it!"

"There's women here who have!" a prostitute shrieked, her gold teeth flashing in the sunlight.

"Though who knows what attracts them to us?" another woman wondered.

"I can't imagine! Can you picture a more unappetizing and sexless band of creatures than ourselves? I'm sure we all stink dreadfully!" Screams of laughter swirled around Sabina.

"Our little saint doesn't like nasty talk!" said the prostitute.

The guards, smoking and lounging as the women worked, grinned at Sabina. Little did she know what consequences the women's loose chatter would have later that day.

• • • •

"Fall in! Fall in!" bellowed the guards. The women marched to an assembly point where the trucks waited. The muddy path ran along the riverside.

Sabina was aware that Peter's eyes were fixed on her. An ugly grin narrowed his gaze. He nudged the man next to him and stuck out his boot so Sabina fell in the mud. The female guards roared with laughter. A hand reached out and dragged her up. Slippery with mud, Sabina struggled and cried out in Peter's grasp.

"What you need now, my lady," he growled, "is a wash."

Sabina screamed as Peter squeezed her narrow wrist. "Chuck her in the Danube!" someone yelled. A second guard grabbed Sabina's muddy ankles and jerked her into the air. Exhausted prisoners watched as the guards swung her helpless body toward the icy waters. On Sundays the guards delighted in tossing inmates into the frigid Danube, fishing them out only to mock their exposed frames.

Spring had replaced the harsh Romanian winter, but dark chunks of ice still floated down the Danube. After one swing, the men released their grip, and Sabina braced as the black water approached.

Shards of sun penetrated the waters as Sabina gasped for breath. She had landed on the rocks of the shallow riverbank and was at the mercy of the current. Icy liquid stole her breath as she scraped across the sharp rocks. The more she thrashed, the more she injured herself. Attempts at standing were futile, and every time she found her footing, the Danube overpowered her.

A guard stood over her, his menacing grin mocking her struggles to get out of the freezing water. "So where is your God now?"

The guards couldn't return to camp with fewer prisoners than they began with, so two hands reached into the river to grab her, but even the guard slipped on the stones. Dazed and dizzy, Sabina lay lifeless on the shore. Waves of sickness came and went, and she wondered if the sound of rushing water belonged to this world or the next.

The guard continued his mockery. "Why didn't He save you?"

Sabina looked up from the frozen ground. "He did save me. By your hands I'm still alive."

"She's all right. Get up!" another guard interrupted. "Get moving, or you'll freeze."

The young woman pulled Sabina to her feet, and Sabina wrung out her waterlogged skirt. As she limped back into line, fellow prisoners greeted her with sympathetic glances. Blinding pain radiated from her ribs. Years later doctors would confirm evidence of two untreated fractures. Sabina knew God had healed her.

"That's better," Peter said. "Nothing like a cold bath."

Sabina's clothes clung to her shivering body. The rocks had torn the skin from her legs and hands. The pain proved unbearable as she hugged herself to stay warm.

When the group arrived back at camp, Sabina twisted her soggy clothes with bloodied hands and examined her tender side. There would be little sleep that night as she shifted every few minutes, unable to find a comfortable resting position.

The next morning Sabina couldn't raise her arms above her waist. The large bruise on her ribs looked like a colorful map of Africa. She presented her battered body to "Doctor" Cretzeanu and awaited the dreaded pronouncement.

"Fit for work!"

36

With spring's arrival, Camp K4 began to thaw. The prisoners weren't allowed to eat the young blades of grass popping up along the quarry road, but they grazed on them like cattle when the guards weren't looking. Raw frog meat was another delicacy, and prisoners once fought off a wild cat for a chance at a fat green grass snake. Vitamin deficiencies plagued the camp, and diarrhea, scurvy, and infections ravaged the workers. Ulcers up to four inches in diameter formed on legs and feet, poisons spreading through their bodies and depleting what little energy remained.

But as the spring days began to lengthen, wonderful gold-and-crimson sunsets filled the sky beyond the Danube. It became a joy to march to work. Sprigs of nettle and pearly parsley sprang from the ditches, smelling moist and green. Trees dared to put out shiny young leaves. The balmy air affected the women, and as everything changed—light, leaves, grass, sun—they began to change as well. New friendships blossomed alongside the tiny flowers.

With so many different religious sects among the prisoners, they'd had their share of arguments. But now the virulence of former days was nearly gone. A new understanding had arisen among the women. Outside, they couldn't exist without quarreling. But here, in Camp K4, they shared a hut, a lavatory bucket, everything. They were sisters.

• • • •

Spring soon became summer, and the prisoners now worked, dizzy and wobbly, under the scorching sun. The hours passed slowly in the large field. Breath rasped in their throats, and their tongues turned to felt. They hoed the dirt for hours, moving like machines that could perform only one action.

One woman whimpered, "I'll faint if we don't get water soon."

Another responded, "Don't faint. They'll kick you."

The sun climbed higher, and Sabina remembered the small, thin-faced, tearful figure of her son. How many desperate prayers arose from mothers on the canal?

It was past noon now, and the prisoners hadn't had anything to eat or drink since dawn. Flies swarmed the makeshift latrines at the edge of the road.

A horse-drawn cart appeared, advanced, and then began to turn back. "It's the food truck!" a woman wailed.

"Water! We want water!" The mass of prisoners swarmed the truck, furiously throwing down their tools. The food truck arrived, but the frightened driver bounced carelessly over a rock. He pulled the wrong rein, and the horse veered, tipping the wagon onto its side. Guards yelled, trying to right the truck, and the horse reared.

Over went the canisters. Fifty pounds of boiled macaroni tumbled to the ground in a soggy heap. Frantic women charged the cart and fell on the precious food. They snatched sticky handfuls from the dirt and shoved them into their mouths. Others watched in horror at the spectacle.

No water came that day. As Sabina worked, a veil of darkness moved in front of her eyes. Her tongue seemed enormous as she remembered Jesus's words on the cross: "I thirst." Surely Jesus understood her torment.

• • • •

In Camp K4, Sabina cared for both the souls and the bodies of her sisters. She treated their wounds when they were beaten and carried their burdens when they couldn't take another step.

Word of her preaching made its way up the ranks, and Sabina was called before the deputy camp commandant, a red-faced woman with thick forearms and large teeth. "You've been preaching about God to the prisoners." She sneered. "It must stop!"

Sabina responded that nothing could stop it, and the woman raised a fist to strike her. Then she stopped. "What are you smiling at?" she demanded.

"If I'm smiling, it's because of what I see in your eyes," Sabina said.

"And what's that?"

"Myself. Anyone who comes close to another person can see herself in that person. I was impulsive too," Sabina explained. "I used to rage and strike out, until I learned what it really means to love—to sacrifice self for truth. Since then, my hands don't clench into fists."

The deputy commandant's hand dropped.

"If you look into my eyes," Sabina continued, "you'll see your-self as God could make you."

The woman sat like stone before Sabina. "Go away," she whispered.

Sabina continued to witness for Christ among the prisoners, and from that day on, the deputy commandant didn't interfere.

• • • •

Time stood still for the women at Camp K4. Slavery was their whole life, the canal their whole world. They had been worn down to a hopeless acceptance of their lot. Even the news from outside the prison camp never changed: hunger, shortages, oppression, and the endless hope the Americans would arrive and free the slaves.

Work levels fell as despondency rose, and the guards played cruel mind games with the women.

At a meeting they chose twenty women from the ranks. "You've been the hardest workers here," they told them. "For this, you'll be released."

The commandant made a farewell speech, and the twenty her-oines were loaded into the back of a truck, holding prized loaves of bread and waving red flags.

Ten miles down the road, at the next labor camp, the truck stopped, and the women were put back to work.

• • • •

Sabina was soon moved from Camp K4 across the country in an impossibly crowded and suffocating train. Prisoners near her discussed the American presidential election and how the outcome could affect Romania. They were certain Eisenhower would save them all.

Excitement gave way to claustrophobia, and the lurching black train car filled with sick women became unbearable. At one stop, a bag of rations was thrown in, but no more food came for the rest of the nearly weeklong journey. Soon conversations turned to Stalin.

"I know he can't last forever," speculated the woman next to Sabina, "but what makes a man into a fiend like that?"

"Often circumstances," Sabina replied. "They don't explain everything, but they explain a lot." She shifted in the airless metal box, seeking some semblance of relief. Then she explained what she meant.

Joseph Stalin was an illegitimate child. Some say his father was a police officer, and his mother had worked as a servant in the officer's house, eventually becoming pregnant. Stalin's legal father was a drunkard who knew the child wasn't his and beat him mercilessly. Stalin entered an Orthodox seminary where the students were more prisoners than scholars. Sabina could see how revolutionaries were made.

As day again turned to night, the train lurched to a stop.

"Out! Everyone out!" the guards shouted.

The train-car doors slid open, and the women blinked in confusion. Is this where they would finally be massacred? Crying and screaming, they tumbled onto the tracks.

"Line up! Stay near the sergeant!"

After an hour of chaos, the women were herded into the fields flanking the tracks. They marched through the darkness, spurred on by the guards' threats and blows. The journey seemed to last for hours.

Soon there rose in the distance the high walls of a new prison, long stretches of ashen drabness under the glare of electric lamps. The column of prisoners passed through the heavy steel-and-wood gates in straggly rows of five. Murmurs coursed through the courtyard: this was Tirgusor.

Why here? Why Tirgusor? It was a maximum-security facility where violent murderers were held. The prison was famous in Romania. What could this mean?

"It means they don't have any other prisons left," one woman declared.

• • • •

In Tirgusor, Sabina was assigned to the sewing shop. The prison held the country's most hardened criminals—murderers, sex offenders, swindlers, and sadists, some clearly insane. The woman on the sewing machine next to Sabina had stabbed a doctor to death with a pair of scissors, and Sabina watched nervously as the woman snipped her fabric.

Sabina learned that General Eisenhower had been elected president of the United States and heard that several Communist leaders had been overthrown and purged from the party. Was this the start of liberation?

Soon a rumor spread through Romania, snaking its way to Tirgusor through a witness who had been at Camp K4: the Danube Canal project was to be abandoned. Rumors hardened into fact, and the prisoners of Tirgusor learned that the canal engineers would be tried as criminals for stealing state funds. The same thought was in every woman's mind: *What use will they have now for tens of thousands of prisoners? Will we be set free?*

Weeks passed, and twice daily the prisoners were counted. Few guards could count, and fewer still could add the front ranks to those in the rear. The task took hours. Then came cell checks.

One day, though, the count passed with amazing speed, and immediately came the ominous call: "Gather your things!" The prisoners of Tirgusor were on the move again.

In open trucks they were driven to the collective farm of Ferma Rosie, where they turned their labors to the futile chore of covering the vineyard branches with dirt to protect them from the cold. It was too late in the year to preserve the vines, but no one seemed to care. The former granary of Europe faced famine.

One morning while slaving in the fields, Sabina collapsed and was taken to the prison hospital of Vacaresti. She knew the prison well. Richard had preached there in the old days, and Sabina had come at Christmas with decorations for a tree. Now she slept on the bare concrete of an isolated cell, her only company a dirty bucket in the corner.

The next morning she looked through the window of her cell to see male prisoners exercising. When they passed her window, she asked if they had heard anything about Richard

Wurmbrand. The first two men shook their heads, but the third replied, "Wurmbrand? The pastor?" Finally someone knew of her husband!

The man slowed to a stop outside Sabina's cell. "I met him," he whispered. "I don't regret my ten years in prison. They were worthwhile because the pastor brought me to Christ, and now I meet his wife!" The man knew Richard from Tirgul-Ocna, but he didn't know if Richard had survived. "He was in a cell for the dying," the man said. "He always talked about Christ."

Sabina didn't know if Richard was still alive, but she knew that while imprisoned, he had continued to be Richard, exalting Christ and winning souls.

• • • •

A kind doctor finally saw Sabina, treating her scurvy with improved nutrition and injections. Sores and scabs on her body began to heal, and her colitis and diarrhea ceased. Sabina's eyesight even sharpened. One evening the supervising political officer and his uniformed colleagues came into the hospital ward. "When such fine hospitals as this one were available," he asked, "who needed God?"

"Lieutenant," Sabina began, "as long as there are people on earth, we will need God, and we will need Jesus, who gives life and health."

Outraged, the man berated Sabina, but she didn't stop.

"Everyone who lives in a house knows it has been built by an architect, just like everyone who attends a banquet knows it was prepared by a cook. We're all invited to the banquet of this world, which is so full of wonderful things, and we know that the One who has prepared it is God."

The lieutenant snickered, scoffed, and walked out, banging the door behind him. The next day a guard told Sabina to pack. She was being returned to the Ferma Rosie pig farm.

37

"The night is darkest before the sunrise," Richard said, glancing with compassion at Sergeant Major Bucar.

The sergeant lay feverish and dying, stewing in the guilt of his past crimes. Not acting under orders, Bucar had slain scores of Jews, including women and young boys.

"I want to confess before you all," he said. "I have sinned so much. I can't die thinking about it."

"You're no longer that murderer," Richard assured him. "A man can be born again."

The next morning Bucar's condition grew worse. Minutes from his death, he said, "I didn't tell everything yesterday. I was afraid."

The sergeant confessed to shooting children in the arms of their mothers. When his ammunition ran out, he clubbed the babies to death with the wooden stock of his rifle. He unleashed other horrific stories, recounting his thirst for blood and his need for forgiveness. Then he grabbed the cross around his neck and fell asleep.

Richard watched the sergeant's breathing grow irregular and difficult. The hard lines around his mouth—carved from years of brutality—relaxed. He had accepted Jesus Christ as his Savior and slipped away in peace.

A scholarly professor named Popp took his eyes off Bucar's body and said, "I have been puzzled to see so many convinced atheists turn into believers at the end."

Richard nodded. "Once, I lived near a railway and never noticed the trains by day because the town was noisy. But at night I heard their whistles clearly." He adjusted himself on the bed and continued. "So the clamor of life can deafen us to the quiet voice of conscience. It is when death approaches in the silence of the prison where there are no distractions that men hear the voice when they never have before."

Popp became Richard's closest companion. At night they exchanged endless stories and jokes. The two men shared a love for literature, culture, ideas, and philosophy. Popp helped Richard wash and dress.

"Where is God?" Popp asked. "Why doesn't He help us?"

Richard recounted the story of a girl who asked a fellow pastor the same question after losing her father. "The girl said, 'Where's the protecting arm of God you preach about, Pastor?'"

"What did the pastor tell her?" Popp asked.

"He said, 'It's on your shoulder, in the shape of your mother's arm.'"

Richard explained how Christ had not abandoned them in the prison. The Christian doctors represented Him. At the risk of torture, they smuggled medicine into the cells for the prisoners. Christ was represented by the pastors who selflessly ministered a gospel of healing to the sick and dying. Even the storytellers reflected the hand of the divine in their efforts to keep hope and imagination alive.

• • • •

Easter dawned on room 4 with unusual force. Richard's ministry had turned atheists into Christians, murderers into ministers, and prisoners into preachers. That morning, a prisoner smuggled in a package and handed it to Valeriu Gafencu, an Iron Guard trooper.

"Open it!" someone shouted.

Gafencu unwrapped the paper, revealing two small lumps of sugar. The prisoners couldn't believe their eyes. Years had passed since they had seen the enticing white substance. Their bodies, having wasted away from malnourishment, craved even the slightest taste of the sugar's sweetness. Everyone watched Gafencu as he decided what to do with the Easter gift. He rewrapped the sugar in its paper shelter and placed it beside his bed.

"I won't eat it yet," he said. "Someone might be worse off than I during the day."

Several days later, Richard's head throbbed from fever. He grew so faint he couldn't even sit up. The inmates passed the sugar from bed to bed until it reached him.

"It's a gift," Gafencu said.

Richard thought for a moment about eating it. Everything in his body yearned for the irresistible cubes, but he declined. A few days later, he gave the sugar to Soteris, an aged Greek Communist on the verge of death. Soteris had fled to Romania at the end of the Greek Civil War, and even though he was arrested for cowardly combat, he always seized the chance to brag about his exploits. At Mount Athos, where monks had not seen a woman for two thousand years, Soteris had brought a band of young ladies.

"You should've seen those old boys run!" he crowed, giddy with pride.

As death approached, Soteris begged God to save him. Richard guided the former atheist brute into eternity with gentle whispers of God's love and forgiveness.

For two years the prisoners shuffled the sugar cubes from one man to another, each surrendering the package to someone in a more desperate condition. Not one man was selfish enough to devour the precious white grains.

• • • •

Room 4 provided Richard with a respite. But when the reeducation program came to Tirgul-Ocna, the torture resumed and even escalated. A brief visit from Formagiu of the notorious Pitesti prison sent waves of fear through the prisoners. Formagiu intended to inaugurate his methods at the quiet mountain sanatorium, and no one was safe.

A fresh batch of Communist instructors, handpicked for their harshness, moved into the prison. They had once been prisoners themselves before proving their loyalty to Communism by torturing other inmates. The director of the prison gave the new instructors permission to bully and beat the tuberculosis patients whenever they wished. Any hopes of escaping torture diminished. For every fifty prisoners, there were ten to twenty specialized instructors.

Doctors carefully monitored the more aggressive torture sessions, injecting prisoners with special serum to increase their pain tolerance and extend the brutality. Madness swept through the prison. Richard and his friends were stripped naked, lined up on the cold stone floors, and drenched with buckets of icy water. The shock to their bodies nearly stopped their hearts and exacerbated their sickness.

When food rations were cut, starvation became commonplace. The guards tied Richard's hands behind his back and forced him to eat the rotting garbage usually served to pigs.

One of the newest prisoners in room 4, a Catholic priest, shared about his time at the Pitesti prison when he was thrown into raw sewage and instructed to officiate Mass.

"Did you obey?" Richard asked.

The priest began to weep. "I've suffered more than Jesus Christ."

With the reeducation system in full swing, prisoners divulged secrets previously hidden from interrogators. Wives, friends, parents, and pastors were betrayed. Thousands were arrested because of the prisoners' confessions.

The rate of suicide among the inmates also increased. At the nearby Gherla prison, prisoners had to find creative ways to kill themselves. Some leaped from tall staircases to the floor beneath. Others lacerated their throats with barbed wire or glass. If a prisoner could muster up enough energy, he could crack his skull against the cement wall of his cell. Others died from drinking cleaning fluid. An Orthodox father who couldn't manage other methods killed himself by leaping from his elevated bunk bed. It took him several falls to succeed.

Richard listened to other atrocities from Badaras, the latest prisoner to join room 4. He was an elderly farmer, battered and bruised from a recent interrogation. Badaras cursed the Communists and swore vengeance against them. He told of his latest interrogator, an especially cruel thug. "If I ever get my hands on that man," he said, "I'll skin him alive." He told Richard his daily prayer had become "In the name of the Father, the Son, and the Holy Ghost, God destroy the Communists, make them suffer. Hurt them, the pigs!"

"Why do you say those kinds of things?" Richard asked. "That's not what's expected of a Christian."

Badaras believed in hell because he wanted the Communists to spend eternity frying in its fire. "I say them because God won't let anyone into paradise who doesn't curse the bastards!"

"We can't give way to hatred," Richard said. "These men like Boris have broken under terrible pressure."

Boris, one of the most despised men in the prison, was a fierce interrogator who had beaten Dr. Aldea for resisting his sadistic methods. The doctor's shoulders and back were covered with boils from Boris's lacerations.

As the reeducation program found increased traction, forgiveness became a more challenging task. Prisoners were being executed daily. Rumors of protest and uprising circulated, especially among well-known prisoners who had been accustomed to giving orders prior to their arrests. Could an organized rebellion bring freedom? A debate unfolded in room 4. Should the quarantined tuberculosis patients participate in the riot or instead turn the other cheek, as Jesus commanded (see Matt. 5:39)?

"Jesus is usually portrayed as meek and mild," Richard reflected. "But He was a fighter too. He drove the merchants from the temple with a whip."

After much discussion, Richard resolved to assist the rebels in their uprising, and he convinced others to join him.

An opportunity revealed itself on May 1. Around 5:00 p.m. on that Labor Day, the prisoners were transported to the soccer stadium in the center of Tirgul-Ocna to watch a match. For some it was their first time outside the prison walls.

Not long after the match began, the sound of a shattered window could be heard in the distance, signaling the uprising. The stadium suddenly erupted as prisoners turned on guards. Those who were strong enough to fight bolted toward their interrogators. Pandemonium ensued as the guards lashed back at the prisoners with their clubs, killing many with devastating blows.

The game came to a stop as citizens from the town fled the stadium and spilled into the streets. For some of the prisoners who remained in the sanatorium, an escape became possible. Taking full advantage of the guards' distraction, they sliced their wrists with sharp objects.

When the guards regained control of the prisoners, they unleashed brutality on the ringleaders. The doctors were instructed to withhold medical attention from anyone in the prison. The rebellion had failed, but news of the revolt quickly spread. Throughout Romania, the uprising instilled fear among guards and inspiration among prisoners.

38

A hollow needle entered Richard's chest, passing between his ribs and penetrating his collapsed lung. The relatively painless procedure to treat the pneumothorax[1] lasted only two minutes and promised to introduce oxygen into Richard's fluid-filled organ. He awoke the next morning, surprised at how easily he could breathe.

Winter brought heavy blizzards to Tirgul-Ocna—the coldest recorded winter in the town in hundreds of years. Six feet of snow blanketed the vegetable garden outside the frosted window of room 4. Without additional layers of clothing, Richard shivered in his bed. Memories of being thrown into freezers came rushing back into his mind. The unexpected cold front also reduced food rations allocated for the prisoners. Bread became a forgotten luxury. Richard struggled to consume the rotten carrots submerged in his soup.

The usual quarrels, swearing, and laughter gave way to nostalgic sadness as the prisoners tried to celebrate Christmas Eve. Richard began to deliver a brief sermon, but his chattering teeth made his words incoherent. His limbs, frozen and limp, became useless. He was surprised that his heart could keep pumping blood to the beleaguered members of his aching body.

A young man named Aristar picked up the Christmas sermon where Richard left off. As a fledgling farmer, he had never received any kind of university training, but he spoke as naturally about the nativity as if Christ had been born in his own barn.

Within weeks Aristar would be dead, but on Christmas Eve his words—strong and eloquent—caused tears to well up in the eyes of all who listened. Soon someone in the room began to sing a Christmas carol. The voice started softly and then grew in volume as it passed over the beds of the tuberculosis patients. The melody swelled wonderfully and reminded Richard of the blissful winters once spent with Sabina and Mihai around the fire. The sound echoed down the corridor, and everyone stopped their activities to listen. Even the guards, huddled in their quarters around a glowing stove, didn't interrupt.

• • • •

In February, Richard and his friends dug a shallow grave for Aristar in the deep snow. The ground in the prison yard was solid as steel. When they returned to room 4, they greeted Aristar's replacement, a musician named Avram Radonovici.

Before his arrest, Avram had worked as a music critic in Bucharest. He graced the Death Room with long passages of Bach, Beethoven, and Mozart, which he hummed. The symphony of sounds ricocheted off the walls to the delight of every prisoner. Avram's tuberculosis had affected his spine, and the gray body cast encasing his torso prevented him from singing at full volume.

One day the musician surprised everyone in the room when he extracted from his cast a small, tattered book.

"Where did you get that?" Richard asked. Outside his visions, he hadn't seen a book in years.

"It's the gospel according to John," Avram said. "I managed to hide it in my cast when the police came for me. Would you like to borrow it?"

Richard handled the gospel as if it were a bird with broken wings. The brittle pages were more precious to him than any medicine. He turned each page, amazed and refreshed by its contents. His eyes chanced on passages he hadn't seen since his imprisonment.

The punishment for being caught with a Bible was worth even a few seconds of reading. Richard didn't care if they executed him. He held a fountain of life in his hands, and after taking a soul-satisfying drink, he passed the book around the room.

The weeks that followed were spent discussing the gospel. Prisoners memorized its paragraphs, mesmerized by its simplicity. Numerous conversions unfolded, including the conversion of Professor Popp, who had a reservation.

"I've tried to pray," he said, "but between reciting the Orthodox formulas I learned as a boy and demanding favors of the Almighty to which I have no claim, there's nothing much to say. My words fly up, but my thoughts remain below."

Richard shared a secret with the professor. "I like to think that Jesus stands near me and that I can talk to Him just like I talk to you."

Popp wasn't accustomed to such casual conversation with God and listened curiously as Richard continued.

"People who met Jesus in Nazareth and Bethlehem didn't recite prayers to Him. They said what was in their hearts, and so should we."

In one fell swoop, Richard had demolished the final barrier keeping Popp from faith. He gave himself wholeheartedly to Christ and said, "When I first saw you, I had a premonition that you had something to give me." The professor now returned the favor. "I've been keeping something from you since my return to Tirgul-Ocna. Dr. Aldea thought it might be too much of a shock in your condition."

Richard sat on the edge of his bed, eyes locked on the professor.

"Your wife is now in prison, and she's been at the canal."

39

Richard's heart plunged into despair. He knew the labor camps along the Danube Canal were notorious for abusing women. A commander named Kormos had raped thirty female prisoners. He was later sentenced to prison himself, charged with "damaging the prestige of the regime."

"She's been very ill, but she'll live," Professor Popp said. "She knows that you're safe."

Richard listened to the professor's words, unable to control himself. A prisoner from the Vacaresti prison hospital, where Richard had spent a month after his solitary confinement, had spoken with Sabina in the hospital. "They told your wife that you must have died in 1950," Popp continued. "But she said no; she believed you were alive despite the evidence."

For days Richard refused to eat. Sabina had come under the authority of the much-feared chief Colonel Albon at Poarta Alba, one of the labor camps along the Danube. Richard tried to imagine how scared Sabina must be, and his thoughts soon turned to shame. It was *his* fault for marrying her, for introducing her to Christ, for becoming a pastor, and for working in the underground church. If he had chosen a different career, his precious bride would be safe. *And what about my son?* Richard descended to a level of despair he hadn't felt in years.

Father Suroianu noticed Richard's misery and said, "It takes seventeen muscles of the face to smile but forty-three to frown!"

Richard had been fascinated with Father Suroianu ever since he first saw him in the prison yard with his long white beard waving in the wind. An aura of holiness and authority filled every room he entered. He never greeted a prisoner with "Hello" or "Good morning" but instead with the biblical command "Rejoice."

Suroianu had more reason to mourn than Richard or any of the prisoners. The husband of his crippled daughter was imprisoned. Another daughter was sentenced to twenty years of torture. His Christian son had died in prison, and his other son—who hated Christ—spent his life rebelling against religion. All his grandchildren had been orphaned.

"You've had so much adversity," Richard said. "How can you keep rejoicing?"

"Well, it's a grave sin not to," Suroianu replied. "There's always a good reason to rejoice. There's a God in heaven and in the heart." He looked tenderly at Richard. "Every day you don't rejoice is a day lost, my son! You will never have that day again."

Richard knew the wise man's words were true. In fact, he had often comforted other prisoners with the same advice. But with the news of Sabina's arrest, Richard had forgotten to rejoice. How could he pastor others while he himself strayed so far from the Shepherd's embrace?

With Father Suroianu's encouragements lodged in his mind, Richard prayed for the first time in days. He thanked God for saving Sabina's life and knew he would see her again, either in this life or in the next. He rejoiced that God had provided opportunities for him to share his faith with others.

Before Richard's arrest, church bells had to ring to collect his congregation. But now, in the tight quarters of quarantine, he had instant audiences. Instead of preaching once or twice a week, he could now minister the gospel every minute of every day—and not only with words. Richard's whole life, like Father Suroianu's, would become a sermon he would preach with a newfound fire and frequency.

• • • •

As the sun set on the Tirgul-Ocna prison in 1953, Richard suffered from a toothache that jolted waves of pain through his jaw. Pacing around the room promised relief, but fifty pounds of iron shackled his ankles. Beatings and poor nutrition took their toll, as did Richard's fever, weight loss, chills, and bloody coughing. Medicine was in short supply, and doctors, like dentists, were hard to come by after the riot.

Eventually guards allowed the prisoners of Tirgul-Ocna to receive monthly packages from home. Richard wrote requests to Dr. Filon, his former doctor who lived in Bucharest. On supplied postcards, he requested food and cigarettes. Although he disliked smoking, Richard knew it would be a comfort to other inmates.

On one occasion, Richard inscribed a curious request on a postcard. He prayed his doctor could decipher the clue: "Dr. Filon's old clothes."

The family doctor was not as tall as Richard, and his clothes would be of no use in prison. But Dr. Filon's access to streptomycin, the promising new drug from America, held the power to treat Richard's tuberculosis.

For two and a half years, Richard had battled tuberculosis. He was the only prisoner in room 4 who had not died. Dozens of men he knew succumbed to the symptoms of the dreaded disease.

Almost one month after Richard sent the encrypted postcard, he received a parcel containing one hundred grams of streptomycin, enough to treat one man's tuberculosis. Like with the sugar cubes, though, instead of taking the medicine himself, he asked General Stavrat, a fellow Christian prisoner and former member of the Romanian military, to administer the elixir to the direst case in the Death Room.

An Iron Guard fascist named Sultaniuc was nearest death. Stavrat shot Richard a disgusted glance. "Much better to take the stuff yourself," he said. But Richard couldn't be convinced.

Knowing an anti-Communist Christian had offered the medicine, Sultaniuc refused to take it. Convincing him would require clever tactics—and possibly a new friendship.

40

Sabina's time at the Ferma Rosie pig farm was the most difficult of her imprisonment. Food was at a starvation level, and at five o'clock each morning, the women dragged themselves from their beds, still wearing the filthy rags they had gone to bed in the night before. The pigsties were ankle deep with liquid filth, and a vile, nauseating stench hung over the place. Sabina and the other women filled their bellies with the husks the swine ate.

From Ferma Rosie, Sabina was transferred to Ghencea, the transit camp from which she had departed for the canal more than two years earlier.

"What crowds of women!" the prisoners whispered to one another. "This place is busier than ever. What's going on?"

Hundreds of women from camps all over Romania packed the huts of Ghencea. Either the officials planned some big new slave-labor system, or ... No one dared voice the hope. They had been through too much and fooled themselves too often.

On the second day, though, a rumor spread: in the offices at Ghencea, ten men from security headquarters were working on dossiers. Dossiers! Could this really mean freedom?

Guards began taking the women for questioning in the camp offices. The interrogations were similar to ones the prisoners had experienced in the past, but this time they were polite. Before the month's end, small groups of women began to leave Ghencea.

Eventually Sabina's turn came for questioning. The major behind the desk was stout and pink as a baby. He had hands like fat little bunches of sausages, and with them he kept clearing the objects on his desk while he talked.

There were a few special questions reserved for religious prisoners. "In this place, Mrs. Wurmbrand, you must know that I am more powerful than God. At least, He has not so far made any interventions in this office." His two assistants smiled appreciatively. "But have you really accepted this? Have you really seen through the sham of religion? Have you realized that in a Communist society, God is superfluous? That you don't need Him anymore? If you are ever released from here, you'll be astonished at the achievements of recent years. And we're only beginning!"

The glittering gold braids on his epaulets shook as he shuffled a file stuffed with papers.

Sabina drew a breath and replied, "I see that you're powerful. And probably you have papers and documents there about me that I've never seen, ones that can decide my fate. But God keeps records too, and neither you nor I would have life without Him. So whether He keeps me here or sets me free, I'll accept that as best for me."

The major banged both fists on the desk. "Ungrateful, Mrs. Wurmbrand, ungrateful! I'm sorry to see that you've failed to learn your lesson, and I shall make a report to that effect." He shouted in feigned rage for several more minutes.

But three days later, Sabina's name was read out. Higher authorities than the major were indeed deciding her future.

She soon stood waiting in the snow-covered yard with her poor bundle of possessions. Others waited as well. Even now, the women weren't at all sure they would be freed. It was only when they had been marched through the gates of reverberating barbed wire and were standing shivering in the road that the guard began the long process of handing out slips of paper.

In the brisk night air, Sabina heard her name. "Wurmbrand, Sabina, born Cernauti, 1913, resident at …"

She took the document ordering her release. "Certificate of Liberation" was the heading, but it was too dark outside to read. Sabina and the others piled into a truck and were driven the few miles from Ghencea to the outskirts of Bucharest.

Sabina climbed out of the truck and walked with her greasy, smelly bundle through the suburbs. For the first time in nearly three years, she saw people hurrying home after work and shopping for their families.

If home even existed—if anything existed anymore—she would be there soon. Mihai would be fourteen by now. What had the years done to him?

Shining lights and wafting smells flooded Sabina's senses as she looked for the number 7 tram stop. "Would someone be so kind as to pay my fare?" she asked the crowded group. A dozen people immediately offered money. Everyone, it seemed, had a friend or relative in prison.

As the tram passed near Victory Street, sad memories rose in Sabina's mind of the police station where she had first been held. Nothing had changed. The gigantic portraits of humankind's four geniuses—Marx, Engels, Lenin, and Stalin—still stared down on the crowds that tramped through the slush.

She exited the tram near a block of familiar flats and climbed the stairs of one. A friend opened the door. "Sabina!" She put her hands to her mouth and stepped back in shock. "Is it possible?" The two women embraced, and Sabina's eyes filled with tears.

Someone ran to fetch Mihai. Sabina's heart seemed to stop as she saw him come through the door. He was tall, pale, and extremely thin. A young man now.

As mother and son embraced, the tears began to flow down Sabina's cheeks. Mihai wiped them away with his hands.

"Don't cry too much, Mother," he said.

At that moment it seemed that all of Sabina's troubles were over. She would never need to cry again.

41

In Bucharest, immediately after her release in 1953, Sabina took Mihai to Cismigiu, the largest park in Bucharest. It was a spring day—heavenly, even—and the hyacinths were waking up from their winter slumber. At long last, after years of prayer and imprisonment, Sabina and her son were reunited.

But she didn't know Mihai anymore. He was fourteen years old and quite the man. She led him through the soft-bladed grass on the path they had walked when he was a child. *Does he still believe in God?* she wondered.

Sabina remembered when her precocious boy was only five years old—a keen evangelist even then. At seven he became a Christian when a professor in her congregation spoke with him about his need of a Savior. Since then, Mihai's life had been filled with trauma. Did the Communists who had robbed Richard and Sabina of their son also succeed in turning Mihai from the faith? Anti-Christian propaganda flooded the schools and often succeeded in converting religious pupils.

Sabina recounted her years of imprisonment. She told Mihai how the guards forced her to work on the banks of the Danube

Canal and how much she had missed him. Her son had not escaped her thoughts and prayers even for a day.

Then Mihai startled Sabina with the words, "We don't criticize nature for the fact that it contains both day and night, light and darkness. So I accept the badness of men. Let's try not to call them brutes."

Sabina rejoiced at the comment. Mihai hadn't wavered in his faith. Actually, he had come to resent the Communists and their false indoctrination.

And Mihai had a point. God had created both the sun and the moon—one to govern the day and the other to oversee the night. God even called the night good. But how could an adolescent respond to hatred with such maturity? Many adults couldn't offer forgiveness or mercy to their enemies. Sabina was amazed to see Mihai succeed where others had failed. His resilience astonished her, and in his voice she detected traces of his father's love and kindness.

Walking beneath fruit trees that had burst into bloom, Mihai said, "You, Mother, and Father too have chosen the way of the cross as the best way to serve God. I don't know if I would choose it too. I feel closest to God in a place like this. Somewhere there is beauty. Not suffering and shame."

Little children are often comforted by little joys, and Mihai was no exception. God had satisfied Mihai's young life with little pleasures. God's lilies, her son reminded her, cost nothing to look at.

Mihai asked, "Why not just stay in a garden, smell the flowers, and love God that way?"

"You know that when Jesus was crucified," Sabina said, "there was a garden nearby. What would you do if, being in a garden, you heard the shrieks of an innocent man being crucified? The jails of Vacaresti and Jilava aren't far from here. People are being tortured in them as we look at the flowers, and in the ministry of the interior down the street."

"Was it hard for you, Mother?" Mihai asked.

Sabina offered him an answer that in her younger years she wouldn't have believed. "Mihai, we are Hebrew, and we are children of God. What oppressed us most wasn't the physical aspect. It was that we were put to labor for the illusory world and were taken away from the spiritual. The story of the canal shows how illusive this physical labor can be if God isn't behind it."

Mihai nodded in agreement as Sabina continued. "The canal came to nothing in the end. So did the Roman Empire, the Greek republics, the first Jewish state, the ancient Egyptian and Chinese civilizations. Now the British Empire is going too. All belonged to the world of illusions."

Words didn't seem to matter after that. Mother and son enjoyed the rest of the stroll in companionable silence, reunited after giving up hope of ever seeing each other again.

• • • •

Later that evening, Mihai came into Sabina's room with a book in his hand—Plutarch's account of Cato's life. He read to his mother about the evil tyrant Sulla, who had a grand palace that served as nothing more than a place of execution. Many were tortured and murdered within its walls. Cato was fourteen too, Mihai explained.

When Cato saw the heads of illustrious leaders carried out of the palace, he asked why someone didn't assassinate Sulla. His teacher replied that people feared the tyrant more than they hated him.

Then Cato said, "Give me a sword that I may kill the man and deliver my country."

Mihai closed the book and told Sabina, "It's true. I feel a bit like Cato. I'd like to just enjoy life, but sometimes I wonder why so many young people don't *do* something. Just one boy like me could rid the country of a tyrant. That's what all the Old Testament is about. Is it not from God?"

Sabina thought for a moment. "It wouldn't help in modern circumstances," she observed. "And it wasn't the best way. We should try to kill the *tyranny* not the tyrant. We should hate the sin but love the sinner."

"Mother," Mihai said, "that will be the hardest thing."

Sabina nodded and kissed her son good-night. *That will be the hardest thing.*

42

Nearly a week after her release, Sabina awoke to the sound of bells ringing in Bucharest. At first the sound came from the cathedral tower of Saint Spyridon and then from the surrounding churches. Eventually all the medieval monasteries in the city chimed together in one lovely orchestra of lament.

Joseph Stalin had died. It was March 5, 1953, and Sabina stepped outside into the warm sunlight. Even though the winter had been the worst in thirty years, the air sparkled with newfound hope. The tram cars, usually squealing on their tracks, whizzed around the corners as if belonging in an amusement park. Despite the police ban on public gatherings, everyone stopped what they were doing and flooded the market squares to discover who had died.

Sabina walked along Victory Street, curious about the people who walked beside her. Every shop, school, and factory had closed its doors for the important announcement that suddenly crackled from the dormant loudspeakers.

"Dear comrades and friends! Workers of the Romanian People's Republic! The presidium of the Supreme Soviet of the USSR informs the party and all Romanian workers with deep sorrow that the chairman of the Council of Ministers of the USSR and secretary of the Central Committee of the Communist Party, Joseph Vissarionovich Stalin, died after a grave illness."

An audible gasp left the audience.

"The life of the wise leader and teacher of the people, Lenin's comrade and faithful disciple, is over."

Funeral music blared through the speakers, but for Sabina, it was the sound of new life. For the first time in a long time, she felt a wave of relief. The broadcast continued, informing the population that religious services would mark the end of the man who had spent so much time and energy destroying the Christian religion.

Years later his daughter, Svetlana, would recount the details of her father's final day on earth.[1] Stalin, she said, died a horrible death. He slowly suffocated as a brain bleed spread and suppressed the parts that controlled breathing. For the last twelve hours of his life, his breathing became more labored, his lips turned black, and he gradually choked to death. In the moments before he died, his eyes flashed open and cast a terrible, angry, fearful glance over the government officials, family members, friends, and medical professionals crowded into the room. Then suddenly he raised his left hand in a menacing gesture, and he seemed to point at something above him, as if he were calling down a curse on everyone in the room. In the next moment, he died.

If Stalin had devoted his entire lifetime to writing the names of the Christians he had killed, the atheist couldn't have completed the list.

When Mihai arrived home from school, he found Sabina in the attic listening to foreign radio broadcasts of Stalin's death. Mihai showed her a copy of the newspaper he picked up on the way home from school. The *Scintea*, the only newspaper in Bucharest, had published page-long eulogies and glowing reports of Stalin's legacy. Banners had flanked Mihai's walk through the city, hanging from every café and cinema along his route.

One of the stations aired a reading from Isaiah 14, which describes the demise of the Babylonian Empire that had once enslaved the Jews: "How the oppressor has ceased, the insolent fury ceased!" (v. 4).

"What do you think of that?" Mihai asked.

"I don't feel that way," Sabina said. "In a man's last moments, as he sees death before him, great changes can happen." Unfortunately for Stalin, those deathbed changes did not appear to have taken place.

Sabina wasn't sad Stalin had died. A new era would dawn in Romania. The slave-labor camps, the tortures, and many other evils the intolerant regime had imposed would finally cease. Not long after Stalin's death, the state decided to shift its priorities away from constructing social works like the canal to producing consumer goods, which promised to raise Romania's standard of living. Sabina empathized with the Jews who returned from slavery to Jerusalem. As she read the final eulogies of the *Scintea*, Mihai heard his mother whisper the Passover prayer: "We were slaves of Pharaoh in Egypt, and the Lord with a mighty hand freed us."

. . . .

On July 18, 1953, after four excruciating years of construction and with only one-seventh of the job complete, the Danube Canal project came to an abrupt halt. The rumors she had heard at Tirgusor were indeed true. The undertaking had promised to showcase Communist strength, but the human cost had been staggering. The barracks Sabina had known were closed permanently. Weeds claimed the dilapidated huts, and snakes—which the prisoners once hunted for food—now slithered across cracked concrete. For the tens of thousands of men and women enslaved on the banks of the canal, the work had been in vain. Countless thousands of lives had been lost, and thousands of families had suffered intolerable cruelties for nothing.

Romanian engineers believed the project would have failed anyway. There would never have been enough irrigation water to justify the construction. The chief engineers and architects of the project were arrested. Two of the designers were shot on the spot. Another thirty were imprisoned for twenty-five years each. Twenty-three years later, construction on the canal would resume, not with manpower but with state-of-the-art machines.

Babylon, too, once prided itself for creating irrigation systems that supported the famous hanging gardens—a wonder of the world the Jews would have seen. But like Babylon's destruction by the Persians, the Black Sea reclaimed the canal and erased any trace of its construction.

43

Sabina felt like a woman back from the dead.

"If I could only get out of here," Sabina had dreamed from prison, "I'd happily live on bread and water for the rest of my life."

After nearly three years of humiliation, starvation, and back-breaking labor, her dream became reality. Sabina reveled in her freedom. Her fractured ribs and bloodied fingers could finally heal. Guards like Peter no longer threw her into the icy river. The future looked bright again, but she couldn't see the shadows hovering on the horizon.

"Where's your work card?" the employee at the government office barked.

Sabina had waited four hours in line. "But I'm an ex-prisoner," she said.

"I can't help that," the man replied. "No work card and number, no ration book."

Sabina left the office, not knowing where her next meal would come from.

Her suffering did not cease once she escaped the banks of the Death Canal. Communists had confiscated her house on Olteni

Street in the historic Bucharest neighborhood of Vacaresti. After standing in lengthy lines and completing countless forms, she and Mihai were allowed to move into the poorly insulated attic of their former home. Sweltering summers and bitter-cold winters tested the attic's insulation. Blotches of fungus stippled the ceiling, and wobbly beds with severed springs made sleep difficult. Outside the lone window, a brick wall obstructed their view. There was no running water or toilet.

Ex-prisoners like Sabina were forced to live in tattered, congested tenements with frayed blankets to keep them warm. Food and electricity were scarce, and heirlooms were sold in exchange for basic necessities. One of Sabina's friends sold all her possessions—cutlery, sheets, rugs, and books—to purchase medicine for her ailing father.

A flood of friends visited Sabina, hounding her for information about their imprisoned relatives.

"Sabina, do be careful what you tell people," one friend pleaded. "There are informers *everywhere!*"

Janetta, a fellow worker in the underground church, soon shared a sofa with Sabina. Marietta, a young epileptic woman, also joined them in the crowded attic.

When Marietta first arrived, the shadows encircling her eyes were as dark as her matted coat. She presented Sabina and Mihai with a small box containing two pastries, a delicacy she had waited in line two hours to buy.

"How cozy you are in here!" Marietta said, smelling potatoes frying on the stove. Together they shared the meager meal.

"Well, Marietta, clearly this isn't a flat. It's just the old storage room we used to keep junk in when we lived downstairs," Sabina began. "But if you like, we could squeeze another bed in here. I'm sure we can find a mattress somewhere."

Thirty years later, Olteni Street would be leveled. Centuries of cultural and religious landmarks would be razed to make room for apartments and government buildings. But for now, Sabina and her son lived with their friends in the tiny attic behind the Iron Curtain.

44

When Richard learned of Sabina's release, his spirits were raised, and his primary mission became winning over Sultaniuc. Determined to sacrifice his own health by giving his streptomycin to the man, Richard struck up a conversation with his cellmate, Josif, a usually good-natured eighteen-year-old who had been arrested by the secret police while trying to reach his sister in Germany. Accused of being a political pawn, Josif was tortured severely and sentenced to manual labor on the Danube Canal, not far from Sabina, where he contracted tuberculosis. An ulcer now deformed his youthful face.

"I hate God!" Josif spat. "If you keep going, I'll call the guards. Leave me alone!"

Richard wondered if Josif was actually a secret informant sent to betray him. When interrogations failed to extract enough information from the prisoners, spies were sent into the cells. Josif might be a spy. But Sultaniuc was in danger of dying. The risk would be worth the reward.

Richard begged Josif to tell Sultaniuc that a fascist sympathizer had provided the streptomycin for him. Then Richard swore an oath to Sultaniuc, claiming the medicine didn't belong to him.

On the brink of death, the fascist finally accepted the powdered medicine, and within days his health was fully restored.

"The streptomycin is really not mine but God's," Richard later explained to Josif. "I gave it to God the moment it arrived."

An imprisoned Catholic bishop overheard the conversation and questioned Richard's ethics. "When the Communists interrogate you, Mr. Wurmbrand, do you not feel that you must tell the truth?"

"Of course not," Richard said. "I have no qualms about saying the first thing that comes into my head, as long as it misleads those who are trying to trap my friends. Should I give these people information that they can use to attack the church? I'm a minister of God! Here the ugly word *lie* is used for something that instinct tells us is right. I respect truth, but I'd 'lie' to save a friend."

"What do you call a lie then?" Josif asked.

"Why should you expect a definition from me? Your own conscience, if guided by the Holy Spirit, will tell you in every circumstance of life what to say and what to leave unsaid. You don't think the oath you carried to Sultaniuc about the streptomycin was a lie, do you?"

"Oh no," Josif said. A smile spread across his face. "That was an act of love."

Richard saw a softening in Josif's bitterness and asked, "Why do you say that you hate God?"

"Why?" Josif said. "You tell me first why God created the tuberculosis microbe."

"I can explain," Richard said, "if you'll listen quietly."

Josif leaned his head against his hand. "I'll listen all night if you can do that."

"One bacillus lives and makes dough ferment," Richard said. "Another lives and damages a child's lung. Neither germ knows what it does, but I approve one and condemn the other. So things aren't good or bad in themselves; we label them according to whether they're convenient to us. We want the whole universe to conform to us, but we're only an infinitesimally small part of it. What we call bad is often simply unfinished good."

"That'll take some proving in my case," Josif said.

"A man named Joseph lived four thousand years ago. His brothers sold him into slavery, and he suffered many other injustices in Egypt. Then he rose to be prime minister, and he was able to save the land and his own ungrateful brothers from starving in a famine. So until, like Joseph, you reach the end of the story, you can never know if what has happened so far will prove good or bad."

"And those who don't live to see freedom again?" Josif asked.

"Lazarus died in poverty and sickness, but Jesus tells us in a parable that the angels took him into eternal blessedness [see Luke 16:20–22]. After death, there comes to all of us a compensation. Only when we see the end of everything can we hope to understand."

A few weeks later, Josif received word that he would be released from prison. His plans for a future in America depended on mastering the English language, and Richard promised to teach him. But Josif wondered if his face—disfigured by tuberculosis—would hinder his employment opportunities.

Richard encouraged his young friend. "The Russian writer Nikolai Ostrovsky was blind, paralyzed, and so poor that he had to write his novel on wrapping paper. Schiller, Chopin, and Keats were tubercular like us. Great men have often been sick men."

"Pastor," Josif said after much thought, "if Jesus is like you, then I love Him too."

• • • •

The guard who entered Richard's cell demanded he get dressed before leading him in shackles down the corridor and into a large hall. A visitor waited.

Through the iron bars of a window, Richard caught a glimpse of a familiar but emaciated profile.

My son! Could it really be him?

Richard had spent years imagining what he would say to Mihai if he ever saw him again. He remembered when Sabina broke the news of her pregnancy and how the young couple danced with joy to welcome their firstborn son into the world. What would Mihai think of his father? Would he even recognize him?

The guards stood at each corner of the room, monitoring the conversation closely. But to Richard, everything disappeared—the walls, the windows, the interrogators who listened for information. As far as Richard was concerned, only two people sat in the room: a thin-haired father and his beloved son.

Richard looked with amazement into Mihai's eyes. The boy had been nine years old when Richard was arrested. Now, six years later, his son was a man and even had a fledgling mustache to prove it.

"Mom says even if you die in prison, you can't be sad, because we'll all meet in paradise."

"How is she?" Richard asked. "Do you have enough food at home?"

"She's almost well again," he said. "And we have food. Our *Father* is very rich."

Mihai peppered the conversation with Bible verses, revealing little information about Sabina to prevent the guards from informing on her. Richard's spirit soared to hear how God had protected his family. Unlike the wives of hundreds of other prisoners, Sabina had not filed for divorce. The good news was more potent a medicine than streptomycin. No matter how many years of darkness awaited him, Richard could endure the iron grip of Communism knowing his wife and son were finally safe.

45

By small degrees, Sabina regained her health. With every deep breath, however, she could still feel pain shooting from her broken ribs. The doctors, astonished that Sabina had survived the torture at all, assured her that the pain was only temporary and would subside over the coming months.

As Sabina walked one morning along Olteni Street, a short, shabby man with thinning hair passed by. He stared intently at her before brushing against her. Sabina didn't think much of the interaction until she reached into her pocket a few minutes later to pull out a folded leaflet.

He must have slipped it into my pocket! she thought. Sabina held the paper up to the light and read these words: "It shall come to pass in the day the LORD gives you rest from your sorrow, and from your fear and the hard bondage in which you were made to serve" (Isa. 14:3 NKJV).

Was the man an angel?

Sabina didn't know, but she felt love emanating from the letter. Everywhere she looked, she felt God's hand of mercy. Bucharest had become a blessing she had never known. The faces of people she passed on its streets sent waves of happiness through her body.

The war was not over, but neither was the encouragement God kept sending her from members of the underground church.

Only years later would Sabina realize the name of the Christian resistance she had joined. Under the iron grip of Communism, the underground church had no organized name or label. It boasted no towering cathedrals or cavernous church buildings. Its pastors wore no elaborate robes or garments. In fact, they couldn't even be identified by the degrees and theological training they once heralded. The members of the underground church did not comply with Communist laws, and that was their sole identification. They were Christ followers, performing their duties in the fear of God and obedience to the Holy Scriptures. Nothing more, nothing less.

Underground churches had always existed. Throughout the history of the church, God had raised up from the soil many Christians who could not worship freely or without fear of punishment. In numerous eras, congregations risked their lives to meet in clandestine cavities in the earth to worship the only true and living Christ.

Sabina knew as long as evil governments existed, underground churches would also exist. After her release, she spent her time testifying to God's gracious activity in her life. To those who were frightened, she explained how Christians are truly free—citizens of a city whose builder and architect is God. Teaching people this truth became Sabina's primary ministry, and her years of imprisonment only added to the credibility of her message.

Some of Sabina's friends avoided her. Afraid of losing their jobs, they didn't dare come near her apartment. Others disowned her entirely. When the authorities asked them about Sabina, they claimed never to have known her.

Once, Sabina passed by the university she had attended in her youth and saw a professor she knew. Sabina greeted him as one of the professor's colleagues walked by. The professor interrupted her and said, "You're making a mistake, madam. I don't know you." He turned his face away in shame, unable to make eye contact.

Two young Lutheran pastors now led the Wurmbrands' church. They tried to pastor the congregation to the best of their abilities, but their teaching was forged in books not in prison. They could recall vast amounts of knowledge from previous ages, but when it came time to apply that knowledge to Communist Romania, they struggled.

In stark contrast to these two pastors, Sabina inspired reverence from those in the congregation. At times the sheer number of people visiting *her* for spiritual guidance embarrassed her. Sabina continually opened her door to encourage hundreds of troubled souls who needed advice, comfort, and prayer.

Throughout Romania, Christians looked up to those like Sabina who had suffered greatly for their faith. As in the days of the early church, persecuted fathers and mothers were placed on lofty pedestals. Some worshipped them as heroes and saints. Every word that came from Sabina's lips was interpreted as gospel truth. But she resisted fame and idolization and stopped those who elevated her, reminding them that she was merely a servant of Christ.

Martyrs don't make truth, Sabina knew. Truth makes martyrs.

• • • •

"Mother, I'm finished with school," Mihai said. He had come home early one day, his eyes shining with confidence and determination.

"What do you mean 'finished'?" Sabina asked.

"I'm not going back."

Sabina didn't understand. "But you have to continue your studies."

"Not there!" Mihai replied.

He explained to Sabina that the Communist Youth Movement had nominated him to be a candidate of honor—an honor reserved only for the best pupils. But to accept the nomination, Mihai was instructed to wear a red tie. He had refused.

"I won't wear the red tie," he had informed his teacher. "It's the sign of the party that keeps my father in prison."

The teacher, although Jewish, feared she would lose her job and scolded Mihai before sending him home for the day. Sabina knew Mihai needed an education and encouraged him to go back to school the next day.

Most of the teachers—especially the Jewish teachers—hated their jobs because they couldn't teach their subject matter freely. The Communists forced every teacher in the country to insert Communist ideas into their lesson plans. But Sabina knew Romania was not truly a Communist country. It was a country oppressed by Communism.

The next day Mihai's teacher welcomed him back to the class. She was prepared to absorb the fallout. She gave Mihai a huge hug, and from that moment on, he became the most protected pupil in his school. Other teachers knew Mihai was the son of a political prisoner, and they respected his courage. From time to time, he even stood up in class to argue against the atheistic propaganda. Being only a teenager, he couldn't always win the arguments, but he defended his faith anyway.

• • • •

"Aunt Alice" had unofficially adopted Mihai when Sabina was imprisoned. "You'll be my mummy now," Mihai had told Alice.

She had cared for Sabina's son since he was eleven. She used to work as the head of an important teaching department before being relieved of her position when she refused to join the Communist Party. Now Alice managed to eke out a living teaching French and helping students like Mihai prepare for their examinations.

When an elderly couple became aware of Alice's plight, they traveled for two days undetected to give her a large sum of money. Every bit helped. A woman named Mrs. Mihailovici even risked her life to travel hundreds of miles from her village to Bucharest to give everything she had—a solitary bag of potatoes—to help Alice raise Mihai. When the militia found out, they beat the elderly woman so badly she never recovered from her injuries.

Alice's poverty didn't prevent her from including Mihai as an additional member of her family, even as she also cared for her aging father. The three of them lived in a single room, and Alice spent every penny she could earn providing for their necessities.

She also cared for other disenfranchised children whose parents had been killed or imprisoned. Her daring and boldness saved numerous children who would have lived on the streets, gone hungry, and likely died from exposure to the elements.

Because of Alice, Mihai was able to greet his mother after her release from prison with words Sabina would never forget: "Mother, I'm on your side, and I love the Lord."

But school proved difficult for Mihai. Teachers injected atheist propaganda into every subject—from science to literature and even mathematics. Children were brainwashed daily by Communist films. Lectures ridiculed Christianity. Every school bookstore had a "godless corner" that contained books, complete with full-color pictures, depicting priests and pastors caught in immorality and behaving badly.

Sabina helped Mihai fight the propaganda he was subjected to at school. Once an atheist herself, she knew how to combat Mihai's brainwashing. Richard had helped Sabina overcome her own doubts.

On one occasion, Richard had said that nobody ever asks for proof that nature exists—it's all around us. In the same way, spiritual beings are aware of hidden realities that are just as real and true and evidential as anything experienced in the natural world.

The Holy Spirit, for instance, cannot be seen with human eyes. But no Christian who is filled with the Spirit doubts His existence. Jesus compared the Spirit to the wind, saying, "The wind blows where it wishes, and you hear its sound, but you do not know where it comes from or where it goes" (John 3:8).

Sabina couldn't see the wind, but neither could she deny its effect. In the same way, she hoped to instill confidence in Mihai to see the invisible. To feel the power of his faith—a faith that, like a strong gale of wind, could hold him up when he leaned against it.

"The church has a human side as well as a divine side," Sabina said to Mihai after a particularly hard day at school. "God's power is manifest in a Christian's sinfulness through repentance and forgiveness."

The Wurmbrands came to know many pastors who had fallen into great sin, but Sabina told Mihai that the Communist literature at his school never reported the guilt and remorse the pastors felt after falling. "They show you just the sinful side," she said. "Anyone can go wrong. It's when we repent that God's grace truly shines."

One day Mihai's teachers told the class that King David was a murderer and an adulterer. Mihai came home from school and asked, "Why did King David want to marry Uriah's wife?"

"The Bible doesn't hide the truth," Sabina replied. "It tells of men who can sin and make mistakes. But when you read these stories for yourself, you see it's the Communists who are lying and distorting the truth."

Every Christian mother fought the battle Sabina was waging. Communism took territory in children's minds in the mornings, and the mothers reclaimed it in the evenings. The Marxists had all the weapons: teachers, literature, films, and radio. But Mihai had a weapon far more powerful than even those—a Christianity modeled every day by his mother. Theories and philosophies could be disputed, but no one could argue with the power of a praying woman.

Sabina and other Christian women learned to become just as ferocious as any warrior on the European battlefield. If they couldn't enlist to fight the enemy on the front lines, they would be sure to defeat its advances at home.

• • • •

Though persecuted, the underground church never forgot its duty to protect children who were orphaned.

Some church members left Bucharest, fearing they would become informants for the secret police. Others, however, caved to the pressure. The temptation to betray other Christians became so intense in Bucharest that on many occasions Sabina opened her door to a Christian confessing his or her crimes and seeking forgiveness.

"We're in a trap," one woman told Sabina. "We love the Lord—we love you and Mihai—but we can't resist all these threats and harassments."

Sabina listened to the woman, who confessed, "My husband will lose his job or be sent to prison. We have to report on everyone who attends church and what they say. We try to tell them only what won't harm you, but you have to beware!"

The Communists divided homes by pitting family members against one another. If the state couldn't succeed with children reporting on their parents, it could always find a nosy neighbor, colleague, or friend who would betray them. The secret police collected large amounts of information on every detail of Sabina's life—the food she bought, what she cooked, where she went, what streets she walked on, and people she talked to throughout the week. Police interrogated girls about the boys they dated. Every piece of data was cataloged and cross-referenced at secret-police headquarters in hopes of catching and imprisoning Christians.

Secrecy became the church's greatest defense. Every activity, from washing clothes to casual conversations, had to be intentionally regulated. Informants were everywhere. They were Christians who wore the red tie of Communism. Some even held reputable positions in the highest levels of the state, often traveling far away from their jobs to remote villages to be married by a pastor or have their son or daughter baptized by a member of the underground church.

Sabina spoke with hundreds of informants in her attic. She always told them, "Prove the sincerity of your repentance by telling us now about how we're spied on. Let's have the names of the officers you took orders from. Tell us when and where you meet."

The news Sabina gleaned from repentant informants saved many lives and prevented hundreds of arrests. She even launched a covert organization aimed at preventing the secret police from tracking down Christians. With the help of others in the underground church, Sabina spied on secret policemen, monitored their activities, and warned Christian families before it was too late. She spearheaded the charge to follow police through the streets and take snapshots of them with cameras while carefully studying their contacts.

Pinning down chief informants like Colonel Shircanu was risky, but Sabina pursued him as much as he pursued her. Every day Sabina left her house when he did, spied on him tirelessly, and calculated his patterns of behavior. Eventually, after uncovering a vast network of his friendships, Sabina's unconventional methods paid off, and scores of pastors and families who otherwise would have been interrogated were spared. The underground church must be defended at all costs, Sabina believed, even if it meant going on the offensive to hunt down informants one by one.

Mihai became an ideal spy. Young and unlikely to be detected, he kept his eyes and ears open, watching for the whereabouts of informants and reporting them to his mother. In addition to surviving the normal developmental struggles of a teenager, Mihai helped strengthen the underground church and brought encouragement to many.

But Mihai and Sabina knew that any misstep, no matter how great or small, could lead to their imprisonment—or worse.

46

Mihai came home from school with a smile on his face. Sabina noticed it, and Mihai told his mother the joke.

"Hitler, Napoleon, and Alexander the Great took a day off in hell to watch a parade in Moscow's Red Square. Hitler, noticing the line of tanks rolling by, said, 'If I'd known the Red Army was so powerful, I'd never have attacked Russia.' Alexander the Great said, 'If I'd had an army like this, I could have conquered the world.' Then Napoleon, carefully studying a Russian newspaper, said, 'If only I'd had a newspaper as obedient as *Pravda*, the world would not have known about Waterloo.'"

Sabina knew he didn't learn that joke from his teachers, but the humor did make her grin. Her fifteen-year-old had reached the end of his elementary-school education and couldn't go any further. Children of political prisoners weren't legally allowed to pursue advanced academic training, and Mihai suddenly had time on his hands.

One of his father's old friends heard Mihai playing the piano and offered him a job tuning them.

"I look after the instruments at the State Opera House," the man said. "I need an apprentice with fine fingers and a good ear."

Mihai had both. But to land the job, he had to complete a sixteen-page questionnaire. He had to provide the addresses of two neighbors from every street he had ever lived on. "You'd better be sure they know what to say when the secret police come around," the tuner warned.

One of the questions was "Has your father ever been arrested?" Mihai thought for a moment and wrote down his answer: "No." Then he whispered to himself, "Actually, my father was *kidnapped* in the street, which is not an arrest at all."

Mihai worked for the piano tuner for a salary of eight pounds per month, a massive sum for his impoverished family. He even received food ration cards so he could buy bread and other supplies at the local market. After several months of learning the trade, Mihai developed an excellent ear and could identify pitch quickly and without effort. His skills so impressed his father's friend that the man told Sabina, "Mihai's better at it than I am, and I've been doing this job for forty years."

Eighteen months later, Mihai lost his job. Someone had informed the authorities he was the son of a political prisoner, and the piano tuner had no choice but to fire him. Yet Mihai had become so gifted at repairing musical instruments he had marshaled his own clientele among the musicians in Bucharest and continued to earn money for his family.

Sabina also worked odd jobs to support her family. First came her venture at the silkworm rearing cooperative, which Marietta had read about in a magazine. The advertisement stated, "Rear silkworms at home. Supplement your income and help build Socialism."

Mihai couldn't help but smirk. "Marietta sees herself in a swishy evening gown all made from homegrown silk."

"No, seriously," Marietta said, overhearing the conversation. "Silk is worth a lot of money!"

Mihai grabbed the magazine and said, "Ah, but you have to take anything you produce to the state cooperative. What do you suppose *they'll* give you for it? Anyway, where could we put the worms? If you think I'm going to eat my meals with a box of dirty old silkworms in the middle of the table, you're wrong."

Everyone laughed.

"You could keep them under your bed," Sabina suggested.

"Under *your* bed!" Mihai shot back.

Nevertheless, the Wurmbrands began harvesting silkworms at their kitchen table. Mihai read the instructions aloud. "'When the silkworm is ready to change into a moth, it spins around itself a cocoon made of matter from its own body.'" He paused for a moment and looked at Sabina. "You'd better be careful, Mother. One day you'll take the lid off, and they'll fly away." Mihai read the rest of the leaflet. "'When the cocoon is unwound, it gives a silk thread many hundreds of yards long.' That's going to be a bit awkward in here, isn't it?"

Sabina kept the silkworm larvae in a cardboard box with air-holes punched into the top. Each ashy-gray worm was three inches long and was fed the mulberry leaves Mihai gathered from the nearby cemetery. After gorging themselves at an astonishing rate, the caterpillars rolled into cocoons made of their own silk thread.

Sabina eventually unwound the silk to sell. One hundred cocoons later, she took her fabric to the cooperative.

For all her work, Sabina received enough wages for only two days of food.

47

After Sabina's silkworming job, she decided to turn to other cottage industries like sewing and knitting. The money Mihai earned tuning pianos supplemented the family's wages, and the Wurmbrands were able to ward off the confiscation of their apartment.

The International Youth Festival was fast approaching, and Communist teenagers from all parts of the world were about to gather in Bucharest. For the three months leading up to the event, however, food became scarce. Shops were depleted of inventory, and long lines of hungry people stretched through the streets. After endless waiting, Sabina was lucky to find a small block of butter and a few ounces of flour.

When the festival began, the shops were packed with fresh produce. Three weeks of delicacies, exotic meats, and vegetables filled every table in the city. Romanians hadn't eaten so well since before the war had started.

"I saw boxes of dates in the state grocery!" Mihai exclaimed. "And there are chocolates wrapped in gold paper too!"

Sabina let Mihai eat the choicest foods because she knew it wouldn't last. When the festival ended, months of food shortage ensued. Only this time the famine was even worse than before. Bucharest had squandered its reserves in hopes of deceiving foreign visitors into thinking Romanians ate like that every day. Nothing could have been further from the truth.

Honest families resorted to stealing food to keep their children alive. Factory workers went without pay for weeks. Bucharest returned to its usual resource depletion—a city full of lies and spies.

Even the pastors of the underground churches began to participate in criminal activities. After their arrests, the full responsibility of the movement fell on their wives. Like Sabina, dozens of women became self-taught ministers, acquiring as much theological training as possible to carry on the work of their husbands. Women even learned to preach and led worship services. From every part of Romania, wives of arrested pastors flocked to Bucharest to seek advice and what little pastoral training they could glean. Women smuggled Christian literature beneath their dresses. Then, when alone and out of sight, they memorized the content and often recited the sermons.

For Communism to fall, it would take every Christian soldier—man or woman. If there were no men to carry forth the torch of truth, their wives would have to carry it in their stead. The light of the gospel must always shine forth.

Every Christian knew the signal. A candle would appear in a nearby window. Then Christians would patter up the stairs, give the secret knock on the door, and enter the small spaces. In cellars

and musty attics, the underground church met for worship, singing, and preaching. Even the flames of lamps struggled to breathe
in the crawl spaces Christians were forced to worship in. No place,
however dark or detestable, was too uncomfortable. Jesus was the
Light of the World, and Sabina knew He could illuminate even the
darkest basements.

• • • •

The persecution of the church continued to dissolve barriers that
once divided denominations. Under the threat of torture, it didn't
matter what tradition you belonged to—Catholic, Orthodox,
Lutheran, or Methodist. God's people found bridges stronger than
the walls that once divided them. Under Communism, Romanian
Christianity reverted to the way the faith was once practiced in the
first few centuries after Christ.

When Sabina met Pastor Grecu, her tactics against the
Communists changed. Grecu belonged to the state-sponsored
Christian church, which the government approved and monitored.
The authorities gave him great license because they knew his secret
sin—he drank alcohol.

Priests who drank excessively became excellent examples of
Christianity's errors in the eyes of the Communists. Their pictures
were often displayed in public and in books distributed to schools.
What the Communists didn't know, however, is that Grecu consumed alcohol only to stay in their good graces. His vice was his

virtue, and he never stirred up suspicion of his real agenda: to help the underground church.

Pastor Grecu became Sabina's leading encouragement and support. His work transcended every limit imposed by the state. Grecu taught Sabina how to adopt Lenin's tactic of infiltrating rival organizations. The Communists had succeeded at infiltrating the seminaries and the priesthood, but now the roles were reversed. The church would infiltrate the infiltrators.

"Christ called the temple a den of robbers" (see Matt. 21:13), Pastor Grecu explained, "but the apostles deliberately worked there after His death and resurrection. Strange circumstances call for unusual actions."

Sabina was hesitant. "But many of our brothers and sisters are going to have moral scruples," she said. "If they join Communist organizations, they'll be asked to do so much that's wrong. People with church backgrounds are bound to give themselves away. They would be weeded out in a month."

The pastor nodded. "But some of them may be good actors. The younger people will find it much easier. No trouble getting them into the Communist Youth. And from there into the militia. And then into the secret police and the party."

Sabina saw the wisdom in his tactic and began enlisting members of the church to help. She mentally divided every eager volunteer into one of two categories. Most would not be able to play the spy. The deception was too great. The mission would prove too difficult.

Sabina could choose only a handful to infiltrate the system. They had to be trusted. Their mission could get them arrested and even killed. Should they accept the challenge, they must penetrate deep into enemy territory where the underground church couldn't protect them. Betrayal couldn't be allowed, since so many lives were on the line. Only one in a hundred members of the church knew about Sabina's covert mission.

In a conversation with Sabina one evening at her home, Pastor Grecu expressed his doubts that parents would consent to placing their children in such great danger.

But Sabina told him, "When I was at school, they used to tell us about King Stephen the Great. Once, he was wounded and came to the gates of his castle. His mother said, 'Who's there?' He said, 'It's your son, Stephen.' Then she replied, 'You can't be my son. He would not leave the field while his army was still there. He stays and fights. I know no other son.'"

Sabina knew many mothers who were willing to sacrifice even their own children for God's kingdom to march forth.

"They must be dedicated women," Grecu said in amazement.

"I know how they feel," Sabina replied. "If the Communists were to prove to me now that Richard had died in prison, I wouldn't simply be sad. I'd be proud too. This spirit is spreading day by day. If one can be proud of a son who dies for his country, how much more could one be proud of a son who was a martyr for Jesus Christ?"

Grecu was encouraged to hear her brave statements. "Dying is at least a quick process," he said. "There are other martyrdoms."

Janetta chimed in. "Yes, there are many. And it may be a higher thing to sacrifice one's integrity in the cause than it is to sacrifice liberty, or even perhaps life."

The pastor stood up to leave but took one last look at the two courageous women and said, "How curious it must be to live in a world where one is called on to give up none of these things."

48

One day Marietta's friend Trudi visited Sabina. A quiet and intelligent eighteen-year-old, Trudi had flowing black hair and appealing brown eyes that commanded the attention of everyone in the room.

"In prison," Sabina told Trudi, "the guard used to tell us before we got a beating, 'You wanted to be martyrs, so now suffer!' And we did. But even at the worst times, there was the joy of knowing that it was for Jesus, like the early Christians."

Trudi listened intently.

Sabina continued, "But now there's something that goes further. And you, Trudi, can help us here."

Trudi wasn't afraid of risking her life for God. She had a shapely figure with strong limbs, and the way she carried herself convinced Sabina the young woman wouldn't break easily. For years as the eldest daughter, she had nursed her large, sickly family and became known for her bold and compassionate spirit.

Sabina explained the underground church needed girls to join the Communist Youth. "Now something new has come up," she said. "It may be a wonderful opportunity."

Trudi's eyes lit up with excitement.

"A colonel named Shircanu who works for the secret police has been asking his sergeant if he knows a girl to help in the house. They have a big place in one of the best quarters of the city. His wife seems rather extravagant and silly but kind enough. If you were to apply for this job through their special employment office, you might find out a lot that would help us."

Trudi said nothing but listened with interest.

"They wouldn't suspect anything," Sabina said. "The sergeant has asked his wife to check with her friends, and one of them comes to our services. Nobody knows she's a Christian."

"What would I have to do?"

"Nothing at first. Get the feel of the house. Get to know every-one. I've noticed that people enjoy telling you their troubles. Old Mrs. Tomaziu was showing you her varicose veins just yesterday."

Trudi pondered the opportunity for a minute and then, with bold resolve, accepted the mission set before her.

• • • •

Trudi succeeded in infiltrating the home of Colonel Shircanu. Months had passed since her employment as a house servant, and Sabina was beginning to wonder about her safety. Then came an urgent message to Miss Landauer, a teacher, who passed the infor-mation on.

Trudi had learned that Shircanu mentioned the name of an informant pastor who often came to the meetings. *Did he betray us?* Sabina wondered. The pastor visited Sabina and explained how the authorities had threatened him with long imprisonment and how his failing health had forced him to cooperate with Shircanu. Ashamed, the pastor moved away from Bucharest, never to return again.

Trudi also provided the name of a female student who might be an informant. When Sabina questioned her, the girl denied the accusation. Then Sabina laid her hands on the girl's and said, "Please be truthful. We know the kind of pressure they must have used on you. Many people have told us before—of their own free will—how they're forced to inform. You owe it to your real friends to let them know what happened."

The student began to sob as she knelt down.

"I was just walking in the street," she explained, "when a car pulled up and two men said, 'We're police. Get in.' They didn't take me anywhere—just drove me around for hours. They kept telling me I had to report every week about everything that was said and done in your house and in the church. If I didn't, they said awful things would happen to my family."

She swore she hadn't reported anything that would damage the underground church, but Sabina had her doubts.

Trudi continued to provide credible and timely information, but her most spectacular act of resistance came unexpectedly when she converted the colonel's home into a refuge for the Christians that Shircanu had been hunting down.

Trudi relayed the information to Sabina that Shircanu had begun to enjoy the privileges of his new position in the Communist hierarchy and often traveled on holidays to the coast or the mountains. Before he left, he placed Trudi in charge of the house. Mrs. Shircanu even honored Trudi by calling her "my little treasure."

"Why not have a meeting here in the Shircanus' home?" Trudi wrote to Sabina. "They're away for several days, and it's a big house with several exits. No one will suspect."

Sabina could not have been any happier with the news. After all, who would suspect Christians of meeting in the house of the very man who sought their demise?

Sabina and a half-dozen leaders of the underground church nervously approached the door of the colonel's house. Trudi greeted her guests as though she owned the place. The special surroundings were unfamiliar to the Christian leaders, but the house served as a welcome change from the uncomfortable locations they were accustomed to meeting in.

Every time the Shircanus left for vacation, Trudi played the spy and hosted the grandest worship services in Bucharest in the home of her enemy.

49

Sabina treasured the Bible Richard had given her in 1938, the year of her conversion. Every other page was blank to encourage her to take notes, which she did for many years. On these pages she recorded her thoughts, prayers, comments, and experiences. It was a diary of sorts, a book commemorating the major milestones of her spiritual progress. She wrote her notes in a coded language to prevent the authorities from reading them if the Bible was ever discovered.

At prayer services, Sabina was often asked about the time she spent in prison. The memories were too horrific to recount at first, but Mihai helped his mother reflect on her experiences. She told him about how the guards had beaten her, forced her to eat grass and snakes, thrown her into the Danube River, and made her carry stones so heavy that her bones felt like forged lead.

"How could you bear all this without giving way and denying Christ?" Mihai asked.

Sabina answered by saying that in the Hebrew language, future events are often described in the perfect tense, which signifies that an action is already complete and perfected in the past. She explained how in Isaiah 53, the coming of the long-awaited Messiah was foretold in this way. The Messiah's torture was described in the past, not the future, even though Isaiah wrote the prophecy seven hundred years before Christ was even born. When Jesus read the prophecy during His public ministry, He would have noticed this verb tense. His suffering had already begun in the past, but it also still lay ahead of Him in the future.

"That's exactly how I felt in the midst of suffering," Sabina recalled. "Joy is the everlasting present of the Christian spirit. I was in a heavenly place from which no one could move me. Where was the affliction through which I passed? It belonged to the past. I had lived the suffering long ago, while the present reality was only a delight in the closeness of the Lord."

One day Sabina flipped nostalgically through each page of her Bible, reading the notes she had written about Richard. She could almost feel her husband's prayers and presence in the room. She imagined his tall frame leaning over her and kissing her and almost heard his encouraging words. For the rest of her life, Sabina would keep the sacred, tattered book in her possession, a tangible catalog of all God had taught her.

Bibles weren't common in the underground church. Members of the congregation flooded into Sabina's attic to hear her read from the sacred pages of Scripture. Because of Sabina's growing popularity, traveling to secret meetings became more dangerous. She rarely left the neighborhood without noticing a man watching and following her.

But Mihai didn't share his mother's popularity and could go quite easily to open or secret meetings. Many of these services were conducted under the guise of parties. Up to thirty young people would arrive at someone's flat, noisily greet one another before playing music records so loudly that anyone passing by wouldn't think twice about the nature of the party.

Then, after the dancing stopped, the music was shut off, and one of the young people would speak about the gospel. Prayers were offered for those in prison, then a few more blaring songs for the neighbors' benefit, and then more worship. These services continued for months, sometimes disguised as birthday parties, anniversary celebrations, or even picnics. The mobile record player could travel anywhere, even deep into the Romanian countryside for Sunday excursions and prayer meetings. Lookouts peppered the path and would give warnings.

Every detail of a worship service was planned—a precise meeting time, a specific location, and a secret password. Danger made the services more intense. The brave teenagers attended at their own risk. For many of them, it would be the last time they ever saw their families. The melody of each hymn was sung with immense conviction. The words of each sermon were weighty, for they came from a preacher who might not have the chance to preach again.

50

Months after Sabina's release, an official from the ministry of the interior visited her attic. He was a fat man with a deep, booming voice and parted what little black hair he had down the middle of his head. In his hand he carried a bloated briefcase that looked as if it would explode.

"Are you a mother?" the man asked.

"I am," Sabina replied.

"Then what kind of mother are you? Don't you care anything for your child? Don't you want to give him the best education so he can get the best-paying job?"

Of course Sabina did.

"Then why don't you change your name?" he asked. "How dare you call yourself a mother!"

The man ranted for several minutes, but Sabina sat silently. The less she said, the sooner he would get to his point.

"What possible use is it," he continued, "to remain tied to your husband? Richard is a counterrevolutionary, and you'll never see him again."

Sabina allowed the official to say what he had come to say and resisted the temptation to interrupt. He said that a young, intelligent woman like her could easily get a divorce from a political enemy of the state, and if she didn't do so immediately, she could certainly do it later.

"How long do you think you can stand up against the state in this blind, stupid disobedience?" he shouted. "What you need is a new husband and father for your children."

Sabina wanted to scream, "How dare you say this to me in my own home!" But restraint proved a far more potent defense.

"I didn't marry my husband only for happy times," Sabina calmly said. "We were united forever, and whatever may come, I will not divorce him."

For thirty more minutes, the man lambasted and cajoled Sabina until he finally gave up, threw his hands in the air, and retreated down the staircase.

"Sooner or later, you'll come to us," he said. "They all do, you know."

The man wasn't wrong. Sabina knew many wives who divorced their husbands under pressure. Communists had become skilled at tearing families apart, placing the greatest amount of stress on the deepest bond of love—the love of husband and wife. Interrogators knew the destructive toll news of divorce could take on their prisoners, how it often shattered the last bit of resistance they might muster. Countless confessions, betrayals, and arrests occurred in the wake of news that wives had abandoned their husbands.

Divorce also forced Christian wives to become involved in the Communist way of life. Women, hoping to forget their husbands, were vulnerable to indoctrination. Scores of women turned their backs on their husbands. Some even orphaned their children.

There was only one word needed to divorce your husband: *yes*. Once a wife said yes, the officials would handle all the paperwork, make all the arrangements, and provide immediate stipends to her family. A few days later, guards would inform the husband, "Your wife has decided to divorce you."

Who cares about me now? the prisoner would think. *I'm a fool not to give in and sign whatever nonsense they want and go free.*

But for those prisoners who did sign their confessions, release took years. By then their wives had already married Communist men and given birth to children raised in a Communist home. Sabina knew scores of families that had been destroyed this way.

In prison, Sabina heard women say, "How stupid I was, bickering with my husband over nothing. What a good, loving wife I'll be—if we ever get out!"

But after their release, their thinking often changed. *Why shouldn't I divorce him? He might stay in prison his entire life! How can I feed the children without ration cards? How can I get work?*

Many wives talked themselves into divorce. But Sabina had said yes once at her wedding, and she would not say it again.

• • • •

Sabina was now a forty-three-year-old woman, all alone and supporting an adolescent son who needed a father more than ever. Her health had improved significantly, and the beauty she once saw in the mirror had finally returned. Years had passed with no word from Richard. *Is he alive or dead?* The years were speeding by at a breakneck pace, and Sabina felt vulnerable to temptation.

Her vulnerability was tested with the arrival of a man named Paul. A Jewish Christian in his early forties, Paul was a bachelor of solid build and handsome frame who lived in a single room with his elderly parents. Kind and gentle, he could make Sabina laugh—just like Richard did. Mihai liked him very much, and sometimes Paul took him to the cinema and helped with his homework.

Here is someone a woman can love and trust, Sabina thought. She vanquished the thought many times, but when he grabbed her hand one day while they were talking, she couldn't help but gaze deeply into his eyes. A longing sprang up within her. Her past—with all its temptations and promiscuity—suddenly became alive again.

Pastor Grecu luckily saw the man's interest and spoke to Sabina about it.

"You know how much I love and appreciate you," he said. "And whatever happened, that couldn't change."

The pastor spoke with unusual emotion. "I've known both you and Richard for many years. And I hope you know that whether you sin or you don't, whether you lose faith or keep it, I'll still care for you because I know who you are, not what you do."

Sabina knew where the conversation was going.

"So forgive me if I ask," Grecu said, "but how is it between you and Paul?"

Sabina remained silent.

"Don't imagine that I haven't had such trials too," he said. "Please answer my question."

"He's in love with me," Sabina answered.

"And are you in love with him?"

"I don't know," she said. "Perhaps." She could feel her face turning red with shame.

The pastor paused and then said, "I remember something Richard used to say. 'No passion resists before the bar of reason.' If you delay, if you give yourself time to think, you'll see all the harm you could do to your spouse, and to Mihai too."

Sabina remembered the words.

Grecu concluded by saying, "I want you to make a hard decision—the hardest there is. Don't see this man again."

Sabina knew her pastor was right. She avoided seeing Paul for a few weeks until he abandoned his advances.

Later Sabina learned that Pastor Grecu had also spoken to Paul, reminding him Richard suffered in prison. Sabina knelt down in her room and prayed God would forgive her weakness.

Over the fourteen years of Richard's imprisonment, other temptations presented themselves. They helped Sabina empathize with the struggles Richard himself had faced during this time. Sabina came close to yielding to some of the men who fell in love with her as her immoral past swept over her and tempted her to return to her former way of life.

But she had said yes to Richard—till death parted them. And God would give her strength to say no to lesser men.

51

In June 1955, Richard received word he would be transferred to another jail. Room 4 had failed to claim his life, and other tuberculosis prisoners needed his bed to die in.

"You're not fit to move, but there's nothing we can do," Dr. Aldea told him. "Take care of yourself. And if you lay hands on any more streptomycin, don't give it away!"

Amid many tears, Richard said good-bye to Professor Popp. "We'll meet again," Richard promised. "I know it."

When the guard shouted Richard's name, he joined a group of prisoners outside—a bizarre company of men with bald heads and patched clothes. The weaker men couldn't walk and struggled to obey their marching orders to form a straight line. Then a blacksmith began to shackle their ankles with a long chain, one by one.

The prison officer stood over the blacksmith's shoulder, and when he arrived at Richard, he said, "Ah, Vasile Georgescu! Surely you have something to say about being put in irons?"

"Yes, lieutenant," Richard replied. "I can answer you in song."

The officer folded his hands behind his back and smiled. "Oh, please! I'm sure we'd all like to hear you."

Richard burst into melody, singing the opening lines of the republic's anthem. "Broken chains are left behind us …" The other prisoners, amazed at Richard's resilience, stared at the lieutenant, clearly wondering how he would react.

When the blacksmith had finished hammering the chain in place, Richard said to the officer, "You Communists claim that broken chains are left behind, but this regime has put more people in chains than any other."

The transport arrived before the officer could reply. Richard and the other prisoners were loaded onto a train, where they remained for hours before the wheels squealed into action.

The cool air of spring infiltrated the carriage through tiny holes in the train windows. Richard lay on his side, peeking at forests and mountains along the two-hundred-mile journey. Over the next two days, rumors began to spread among the prisoners. Where were they being taken?

When they glimpsed the walls of the infamous Craiova prison, all became clear. As the train came to a halt, the carriage doors swung open. The guards hammered off the prisoners' chains and herded them into small groups in the courtyard. Shouts emerged from a cell behind the prison walls. "There's no room here! We're suffocating already!"

A guard shoved Richard into a dimly lit room. Hands outstretched, he slipped against a half-naked prisoner as the door slammed behind him. Richard's eyes slowly adjusted as dozens of sweaty skeletons came into view. Many were crammed together in rows of bunk beds that lined the room's interior. Others sat on the floor, leaning against the walls and gasping for breath. Richard almost fainted from the stench but managed to tell them he was a pastor.

For two agonizing months, Richard remained in this cell. The guards allowed him to leave only to carry lavatory pails to the cesspool of sewage in the woods nearby. He shared a bunk with Nassim, a Muslim who had heard him speak at the Congress of the Cults in 1945.

"It's good that I knew your voice in the dark," Nassim said. "I wouldn't have recognized you by sight."

Nassim became an instant friend, and they spent the stuffy nights discussing religion and politics. Richard often encouraged his thin new colleague to consume every bite of the soup provided by the guards, despite the repulsive smell of rotten cabbage and festering garbage.

"How can you eat that?" Nassim asked.

Richard took a mouthful of the vile liquid, swallowed, and said, "I remember friends in America who are now eating grilled chicken, and I thank God with them as I take the first mouthful of soup. Next, I rejoice with friends in England who may be eating roast beef. And I get down another mouthful. So by way of many friendly countries, I rejoice with those who rejoice—and stay alive."

Inmates like Nassim came and went, but the stifling air inside the cell remained constant. Discussions of food could last all night. A new prisoner named General Calescu, the former head of military justice, spoke of delicious memories—fish drenched in rich saffron sauce, truffles, warm toast with fresh Normandy butter. He told stories of exotic Burgundy and Hock wines, endless champagne, and the best cigars in the world. Prisoners salivated every time he described such luxuries.

Calescu motioned to Richard. "You like duck, don't you, Pastor? Or some *coq au vin*?"

Richard did indeed. But a simpler spread would have satisfied his palate—chicken stuffed with bananas, potatoes, and strawberry jam. When the cell had become a nostalgic frenzy of remembered dishes, the guard would wheel the usual barrel of rotten soup into the room. Richard had never tasted "food" as unappetizing in his life.

The only exception to the soup took the prisoners by surprise. One day the guards brought a canister of onion soup accompanied by a stew of *real* meat, white mashed potatoes, and fresh carrots. Each man received two bread rolls and a basket of apples. Heaven itself burst into the hearts and mouths of every prisoner that day. Richard later learned that a delegation of Western democratic women from Britain, France, and the United States had come to tour the prison. The women went home to report how well fed the prisoners were at the Craiova prison.

• • • •

Communism, Richard knew, would either destroy the West or be destroyed by it. President Eisenhower's words brought him hope: "I have only to do up the last button on my uniform, and the captives of Eastern Europe will be free!"

A pressing question often surfaced in Richard's mind: *Are the Christians in the West even praying for their brothers and sisters in prison?* Richard believed they were.

One night he explained to Nassim, "If I start to knock a hole in a boat that we are sharing and say, 'Don't interfere; this is my side of the boat,' will you agree?"

Nassim shook his head.

"No! The hole in my side will end up drowning us all!" Richard said.

So it was with the global church. As the apostle Paul said, "If one member suffers, all suffer together; if one member is honored, all rejoice together" (1 Cor. 12:26). But Richard held hope that pastors, missionaries, and churches in the West were raising awareness of the suffering of saints under Communism's evil iron grip.

"I rejoice with those in the West," he said, "by thinking of their comfortable homes and the books they have, the holidays they can plan, the music they hear, and the love they have for their wives and children. And I remember the second part of the verse, from the epistle to the Romans: 'Weep with those who weep' [Rom. 12:15]. I am sure that in the West many thousands think of us and try to help us with their prayers."

Richard resolved to rejoice with the Western church with hopes they were suffering with and mourning for him.

• • • •

After Richard's release from the Craiova prison two months later, a network of trains transported him to a series of prisons throughout Romania. The journeys seemed endless—a blur of fifty-pound chains, stubble-chinned skeletons, and the occasional burst of light illuminating the hellish interior of the carriage. Occasionally the cries of a newly arrested prisoner brought Richard out of his daze, but most of the time he remained in a semiconscious nightmare, unable to distinguish one jail from another.

As the train approached the prison at Poarta Alba, a villainous bandit named Calapod slapped Richard on the back and shouted, "So this is the holy reverend who likes thieves and robbers!"

"Mr. Calapod," Richard said, "Jesus did not mind comparing Himself to a thief when He spoke about His return" (see Matt. 24:43–44).

Calapod grimaced with disgust.

"Just as those people you've robbed never knew you were coming," Richard said, "so one night Jesus will come for your soul, and you won't be ready."

The train passed by the remnants of the labor camp near the canal where Sabina had been forced to work. Richard knew she was safe, living somewhere in Bucharest, but he hadn't seen his wife in eight years. Not a single day passed without picturing her face.

Fifty prisoners were packed into the primitive huts at Poarta Alba. Derelict barracks and overgrown vegetable patches flanked its walls. Sabina would have seen these, Richard imagined. But his fleeting moments of melancholy, like the fading memories of his family, were stolen once again when the guards stowed Richard back on a train, to be transported to another prison.

Next came the dreaded Gherla prison, a hellhole located deep in the mountains of Transylvania. Because Richard's tuberculosis worsened by the day, the guards stashed him in a group of cells that some called "the hospital." His doctor, a tall, fragile woman named Marina, was fresh out of medical school. Gherla was her first post, and she struggled to bear the horrifying sight of her dying patients. Marina's training didn't prepare her for the holocaust of hunger and cruelty she saw.

"You need good food and plenty of fresh air," she said as she examined Richard.

He laughed, even as tears welled in her eyes. "But don't you know where we are, Dr. Marina?"

The doctor shifted uncomfortably. "That's what I learned at medical school."

A few days later she confronted the high-ranking officers outside the gallery. "Comrades," she said, "these men haven't been sentenced to death. The state pays me to keep them alive, just as it pays you to keep them safe. I ask only for conditions that will allow me to do my job."

"So you side with convicted outlaws!" one officer replied.

"They may be outlaws to you," Marina said, "but they are patients to me."

Within a few years the overworked young doctor caught rheumatic fever and died.

• • • •

In 1956 the guards marched Richard to a large hall, where he stood behind a table and awaited a visitor. He remembered the visit with Mihai years ago in a similar hall at Tirgul-Ocna. A multinational summit in Geneva, Switzerland, had pressured Romanian prisons to allow inmates to see their relatives. Many prisoners had no families to visit them.

Richard was nervous but increasingly excited, his face bursting into a wide smile at the sight in front of him.

Sabina. All the drugs in the pharmacy couldn't cure him like the sight of his wife. Twenty guards surrounded them, ready to monitor the conversation at the small wooden table.

Sabina's imprisonment had aged her beautifully. The youthful smile Richard remembered had ripened in a way he did not expect. She looked peaceful, her hands folded together.

"Are you well at home?" Richard said, gripping the table.

"Yes, we are all well," she said. "Thank God."

A guard interrupted Sabina. "You are not allowed to mention God here."

"My mother is still alive?" Richard asked.

Sabina nodded. "Praise God, she's living."

The guard shouted louder, "I have told you that you are not allowed to mention God!"

"How is your health?" she inquired.

Richard tried to conceal his usual cough. "I'm kept in the prison hospital—"

The commander interrupted, "You're not allowed to say where you are in prison."

"About my trial," Richard continued, "is there hope of an appeal?"

"You're not allowed to discuss your trial," the guard said.

After endless interruptions, Richard finally said, "Go home, Sabina, dear. They won't let us talk."

Sabina smiled and stood as the guards led Richard away. Looking over his shoulder, he caught one last glimpse of his wife—a memory that would sustain him for months to come.

52

In June 1956, Richard departed the Gherla prison, bound for Vacaresti and ultimately for the prison on the outskirts of Bucharest, where he was first arrested. Richard's tuberculosis, now worse than ever, plagued him with nights of cold sweats and coughing up blood. The weight loss and scars from eight and a half years of imprisonment had ravaged his body. He had been beaten, starved, whipped, kicked, and tortured relentlessly, but he hadn't betrayed his friends, his family, or his Savior.

Richard preached two sermons to the troubled inmates in the Bucharest prison. "Patience, patience, and more patience," he instructed them.

Overhearing this, the guards took Richard away to be interrogated.

"You're telling them to be patient and the Americans will come and deliver them!" the police said. "You are telling them the Communists will not continue to rule! These are counterrevolutionary lies!"

One week later the guard burst into Richard's cell and said, "Interrogation, at once! Move! Come on, come on! The car's waiting."

The car?

Richard scrambled through the familiar corridor into the prison yard. But there was no car, only a clerk who handed Richard a slip of paper. He took it in his hand and, after examining it, almost collapsed to the ground in disbelief. It was a court order detailing Richard's release.

"But I've only done eight and a half years," Richard blurted, "and my sentence is for twenty."

"You're to leave immediately. This order comes from the highest tribunal."

"But I've got nearly twelve years yet to serve," Richard said.

The guard grew frustrated. "Don't argue! Get out!"

"But look at me!" Richard pointed to his ragged gray shirt and patchwork pants. "The first policeman who sees me will arrest me."

"We don't have any clothes here for you!" the guard shouted. "Go away!"

The warm June skies stole Richard's attention, and he departed. The steel gates clasped shut behind him. Richard didn't want to abandon the other inmates, but *he was free.*

"God," he prayed loudly, "help me not to rejoice more because I'm free than because You were with me in prison."

The insects buzzed in his ears as he walked alone down the secluded streets and the long white road that stretched into green fields. Cows barely bothered to notice the walking skeleton passing by.

For three miles Richard lugged his weary body through deep grass, forests, and plant life. He stopped to admire the flowers sprouting up despite patches of thorns. *I like those flowers best.* Richard's garments, a sad collection of filth, stuck to his sweaty body. But he didn't resent his rags. They were precious to him—witnesses over the years of God's amazing grace and providence.

An elderly couple saw Richard and approached.

"You come from *there?*" the man asked.

Richard nodded as the man handed him a coin.

"Give me your address," Richard said, "so I can repay you."

"No, no, keep it," the man pleaded.

As Richard continued walking, a Christian woman stopped to talk to him. Richard explained he was a pastor, and the two sat on the side of the road to discuss the beauties of Christ. Then she reached into her pocket and withdrew a coin.

"For the tram fare," she said.

"But I've got a penny already," Richard said.

"Take it for our Lord's sake, then."

When Richard had reached the outskirts of Bucharest, people crowded around him, asking if he had information about their family members in prison. He insisted on paying for his tram ride, but the attendant refused. As Richard boarded the carriage as a free man, some passengers surrendered their seats.

Richard glimpsed a basket of strawberries in the lap of a woman beside him.

"Haven't you had any this year?" she asked.

"Not for eight years," Richard replied.

"Go on, take some!" The woman gave him a handful of the delicious fruit, and he ate the soft berries like a child, one after the next.

When the tram approached Richard's house, he exited and walked to the front door. It was a strange sensation to stand before a door without guards or interrogators pushing him from behind. *What will my family think of me, looking like this?* Richard took a deep breath, reached for the knob, and swung the door open for the first time in nearly a decade.

"Father!" a voice screamed. Mihai rushed forward into Richard's arms. He was seventeen years old and much stronger than Richard, who almost fell to the floor from the exuberant embrace.

Sabina joined them and wrapped her arms around Richard's neck. He had forgotten the feeling of her touch. Unmeasured bliss encircled the family as they celebrated their reunion.

"Before we kiss," Richard said, "I have to say something."

Sabina held him close.

"Don't think I've simply come from misery to happiness! I've come from the joy of being with Christ in prison to the joy of being with Him in my family. I'm not coming from strangers to my own people but from my own in prison to my own at home."

Sabina sobbed as Richard held her thin face in his hands.

"Now if you'd like to," he said with a smile, "you can kiss me."

• • • •

From all corners of Bucharest, Richard's congregation telephoned Sabina to hear the exciting news. Guests continually spilled into their tiny two-room attic. When Richard walked through the shops and streets outside, everyone he saw tried to help him. He and Sabina strolled by the bars and nightclubs they had once frequented, thanking God for intervening in their lives.

Richard's new doctors couldn't believe he had survived eight and a half years without adequate medical attention. His lungs showed signs of scars from his battles with tuberculosis. The doctors gave him the best beds in the hospital, a sunny respite with windows. To avoid attracting the secret police, Richard moved from hospital to hospital as his health steadily improved.

He didn't have any money to spend on Sabina for their twentieth wedding anniversary, so he wrote her love poems in an attractive notebook he obtained. It was enough for Sabina to have her husband once again in her arms.

"Father," Mihai once said, "you've gone through so much. I want to know what you've learned from all your sufferings."

Richard wrapped his arm around his son's shoulders and replied, "Mihai, I've nearly forgotten my Bible in all this time. But four things were always in my mind. First, that there is a God. Second, Christ is our Savior. Third, there is eternal life. And fourth, love is the best of ways."

"That was all I wanted," said Mihai.

During his parents' imprisonment, bitterness and isolation had become companions as Mihai struggled to survive. At the age of thirteen, he had borrowed money to visit his mother in the forced-labor camp on the canal. He told Richard about the visit, remembering his mother's dirty clothes and tear-stained face. Sabina had shouted to him through two sets of iron bars, "Mihai, believe in Jesus with all your heart!"

"Mother, if you can still believe in a place like this," Mihai shouted back, "then so must I."

Four months after Richard's release, Mihai joined a small theological seminary at Sibiu with hopes of becoming a missionary to India. He spent his days researching in the excellent library, learning from his professors, and writing a thesis on William Booth, the founder of The Salvation Army, and Charles Spurgeon, the most famous Baptist preacher in the Victorian world.

Richard retired to the wooden bed Sabina had borrowed from the neighbors. She kissed him good-night, spreading the clean, soft covers over his body. Richard longed for rest and quiet, but sleep always escaped him. The ex-prisoner stared blankly at the ceiling. The absence of pain was palpable. There were no screams from prisoners, no rotten carrot soup, no threats from interrogators, no torture. To Richard's amazement and amusement, he could switch the lightbulb on and off. Also, instead of resorting to the usual bucket in the corner of the room, he could now use a modern bathroom. In the basement, he could even wash his hands beneath streams of cold, refreshing water.

Unable to sleep, Richard opened a copy of the Bible—the *whole* Bible. The gospel of John had sustained him in prison, but now he yearned to refresh his memory with the Old Testament. Problem was, he had forgotten the order of the books. He stopped

searching for the book of Daniel and instead flipped to the third
epistle of John: "I have no greater joy than to hear that my children
are walking in the truth" (v. 4). Richard got out of bed and walked
to Mihai's room as he had dreamed of doing hundreds of times in
prison. But this time Mihai was really there.

• • • •

By 1956 signs of de-Stalinization brought hope to the country.
Stalin's successor, Nikita Khrushchev, denounced Stalin at the
Twentieth Congress of the Communist Party and greatly reduced
the presence of militia and secret police in Romania. He opened
trade deals with Western businesses and freed hundreds of political
prisoners like Richard. But the fear of being betrayed by followers
and false converts still existed. A trusted network of friends became
the best safeguard against abduction.

For two and a half years, Richard resumed his work in the
underground church, even though the police stripped him of
his preaching license. The consequences of ministering without
proper identification could be disastrous. If caught, the police
would throw Richard back into prison.

But Richard couldn't be dissuaded. God had called him to be
a pastor, with or without government approval. Richard leveraged
his newfound freedom, often leaving his home without telling
his family where he was going. That way, if the police kidnapped
Mihai or Sabina, they wouldn't have any information to hide.

Richard continued in these activities with the support of his wife in spite of constant danger and fear. Richard ministered secretively, often in attics, basements, and flats far from the city center. Hidden groups of Christians flocked to hear his testimony—one of bravery, courage, and resistance. Richard even revealed his scars as evidence of his stories and led his clandestine congregations in singing hymns. When neighbors grew suspicious and raised questions, he said they were celebrating a birthday. One particular family, with only three or four members, celebrated thirty-five "birthdays" in one year.

The worship services reminded Richard of those in the early church when Christians, suffering under the persecution of Nero, Diocletian, and other Roman emperors, descended deep into catacombs and caves to worship. Persecution bonded believers of all denominations together. Their enemy was greater than the differences that separated them. If the early church father Tertullian was right that the blood of the martyrs is the seed of the church, then Romania, like Rome, became a garden of newly converted Christians.

Since the church was often unable to meet indoors, Richard conducted worship services outside in the fields surrounding Bucharest. He loved preaching in the fresh open air. The sky became his cathedral, frequently resounding with birdsong. For incense Richard looked to the fragrance of flowers. For candles he pointed to the stars. After his services concluded, he vanished into obscurity like a ghost, relying on the protection of his friends.

Mihai affectionately called his father the Phantom Preacher.

53

Under Communism, Romanian students couldn't read the works of Christian authors, and books by Greek writers like Plato and Aristotle, philosophers like Immanuel Kant, and even the brilliant works of Albert Einstein could not be purchased. Many university students came to Richard with questions about how to advance in their education. One such theology student from the University of Cluj asked Richard's advice about a thesis he was writing.

"What's the subject?" Richard asked.

"The history of liturgical song in the Lutheran Church," the student replied.

Richard, a proud Lutheran himself, rebuked the young theology student for not preparing adequately for the persecution he would soon experience. "You should begin," he said, "by writing that we should not be filling young men's heads with historical trivialities when tomorrow they may face death for their faith."

"What should I be studying, then?" the young man asked.

"How to be ready for sacrifice and martyrdom." Richard showed the student his scars and told him stories about the horrific tragedies he had encountered behind bars. Pastors living under Communism should be prepared to die. Richard focused first on these important lessons before turning to the student's secondary research interests.

"Our theology teacher says that God gave three revelations," another student told Richard. "The first was to Moses. The second was to Christ. And the third was to Karl Marx."

Richard had heard this brainwashing before but now refused to hear any more nonsense. He agreed to travel to the University of Cluj and preach in its ancient cathedral. The students spread the word about the upcoming sermon but couldn't circulate Richard's publications because his writings were banned. Anyone caught reading the illegal material could be arrested.

• • • •

Many years earlier, Richard made a promise to a prisoner to support the members of the Army of the Lord, an Orthodox branch of Christians who were being harassed by the secret police. Richard decided to pay a visit to a high-ranking official he knew named Patriarch Justinian Marina, believing the man could help.

Marina carefully selected a public place to meet Richard, and the two men walked through the garden grounds of Marina's palace, far from microphones and out of earshot of clerks.

"You are a patriarch," Richard began. "Men come to you for places and pensions, and everywhere you must preach and sing. So I thought I should come and sing to you."

Richard could tell that Marina wasn't expecting this and said, "This is a song of the Army of the Lord, which I learned in prison." He then began to sing.

After finishing the melody, Richard pleaded for Marina to do something to help the members of the Army of the Lord, saying, "They shouldn't sit in prison forever, just because they belong to a certain sect."

Marina promised to try, but Richard sensed the patriarch had drifted far from God. Marina added that his hands were essentially tied. He couldn't do much with Iustin Moisescu, the metropolitan of Iasi, watching his every move. If Marina stepped out of line, Moisescu would become the new patriarch, which would greatly damage the church.

Richard later discovered that Marina's secretary had overhead their conversation and reported him.

"So Wurmbrand told you to come, did he?" Moisescu said to Marina. "It's time for him to be back in jail."

• • • •

Richard traveled to the University of Cluj to deliver his sermon, and news of his visit spread widely. It was immediately reported to the police with warnings that Richard intended to denounce Marxism and instigate an uprising among the students under the guise of a lecture on Christian philosophy. A Baptist minister approached Richard just before his sermon and proudly claimed to be the informer who had reported him to the authorities.

The news came as no shock to Richard, who had known many betrayers like him over the years. In Romania, there were four categories of ministers. First, there were those in prison, tortured into divulging names and addresses of Christians. Second, there were pastors who passively obeyed the police and surrendered information without imprisonment. The third category comprised ministers who actually acquired a taste for reporting other Christians and were often rewarded for their information. Finally, there existed those, like Richard, who refused to surrender, even after losing their licenses to preach and suffering torture.

The Baptist traitor had submitted Richard's name to a fanatical spy named Rugojanu, who acted immediately on the information. He prided himself on sniffing out counterrevolutionaries like Richard and sat near the front of the cathedral for the lecture.

Fifty students and several professors attended the evening event. Richard first drew their attention to the dilemma of Darwinian ethics. If Communist Romania rejected all Western ideas, why did the University of Cluj teach the evolutionary theories discovered by the Englishman?

Rugojanu leaned forward in his pew, following Richard's argument. "If you believe you were created by God, then you will try to become godlike; if you prefer to believe that you spring from a tribe of apes, you are in danger of turning into a beast."

Richard's Monday and Tuesday lectures at the cathedral saw an even greater turnout of students. By Friday, Richard stared into the faces of a thousand people—the entire university. He knew many of them were sympathetic to his faith, but they feared the consequences. He told them the story of a pastor who was martyred at the hands of the fascists. The pastor had said, "You give your body as a sacrifice to God when you give it to all who want to beat and mock you. Jesus, knowing His crucifixion was near, said, 'My time is at hand' (Matt. 26:18). We too should regard suffering as a charge given to us by God."

If a pin had dropped to the floor at that moment, every person in the cathedral would have heard it ring. Richard examined his congregation, especially Rugojanu, who was busy scribbling notes.

"Don't let suffering take you by surprise!" Richard continued. "Meditate on it often. Adopt the virtues of Christ and His saints in your life."

He then recounted the story of a Christian leader who suffered under Roman persecution in the early church. The starved Christian told his wife that he had found a priceless remedy for pain, saying, "I've discovered a tea that's good against all suffering and sorrow. It contains seven herbs, and I'll list them for you."

The congregation listened intently as Richard described the seven herbs.

"The first herb is called contentedness: be satisfied with what you have. I might shiver in my rags as I gnaw on a crust, but how much worse off I would be if the emperor had thrown me naked into a dungeon with nothing at all to eat!

"The second herb is common sense. Whether I rejoice or worry, I'll still be in prison, so why agonize?

"The third is remembrance of past sins: count them, and on the supposition that every sin deserves a day in prison, calculate how many lifetimes you would spend behind bars. You've been let off lightly!

"The fourth is the thought of the sorrows that Christ gladly bore for us. If the only man who could choose His fate on earth chose pain, what great value He must have seen in it! So we observe that, borne with serenity and joy, suffering redeems.

"The fifth herb is the knowledge that God has given us suffering as from a father, not to harm us but to cleanse and sanctify us. The suffering through which we pass has the purpose of purifying us and preparing us for heaven.

"The sixth is the knowledge that no suffering can harm a Christian life. If the pleasures of the flesh are all there are, then pain and prison bring an end to a man's aim in living. But if the core of life is truth, that is something no prison cell can change. Prison cannot stop me from loving; iron bars cannot exclude faith. If these ideals make up my life, I can be serene anywhere.

"The last herb in the recipe is hope. The wheel of life may put the emperor's physician in prison, but it goes on turning. It may put me back into the palace and even put me on the throne."

Richard hesitated for a brief moment, moving his eyes from his notes to his audience. Then he said, "I have drunk barrels of this tea since then and can recommend it to you all. It has proved good."

As Richard progressed toward the conclusion of his talk, Rugojanu stood to his feet and marched down the aisle of the cathedral without even a single backward glance. Richard stepped down from the pulpit as the crowd erupted in a cacophony of chatter. Scores of students applauded and pushed through the crowded pews to shake Richard's hand. After the service, Richard telephoned Sabina with the news of his sermon. She rejoiced but feared the inevitable repercussions.

• • • •

The next day the bishop summoned Richard to his chambers. Suddenly Rugojanu burst into the room, glaring at Richard. "Ah, you! What excuses are you going to make? A torrent of treason—I heard it!"

Richard asked what part of his sermon displeased the spy. Rugojanu had problems with *every* part, but especially the seven-fold remedy for suffering.

"But what was wrong with my poor tea?" Richard asked. "Which herb didn't you like?"

Heat rose in Rugojanu's cheeks. "You told them the wheel always turns," he snapped. "But in this counterrevolutionary outburst, you're mistaken. The wheel will not turn, my friend. Communism is here forever!"

"I didn't mention Communism," Richard replied. "I said simply that the wheel of life keeps turning."

"No, no, no! You meant Communism would fall, and they all knew what you meant. Don't think you've heard the last of this!"

Rugojanu unleashed further accusations that Richard poisoned the young students with concealed attacks against the government. Then, just before he stormed out the door, he turned to the bishop and raged, "You may be sure that he will never preach again. Wurmbrand is finished! Wurmbrand is finished! Wurmbrand is finished!"

As he exited the building, a passing car swerved onto the sidewalk to avoid hitting a dog and slammed into Rugojanu, crushing him against the wall. With hatred still seeping from his lips, Rugojanu died on the spot.

54

The story of Rugojanu's last words spread throughout Romania. Richard could no longer conceal his visibility, and in January 1959, a woman told Sabina that hundreds of Richard's sermons had been photocopied and circulated. The police raided the woman's home and confiscated the illegal literature.

Sabina anticipated the fresh wave of terror unleashed on the church. In July of the previous year, a series of laws had been passed, tougher than any before. Even minor offenses were punished by the death penalty. Thousands of juvenile delinquents and Christians were arrested and sent "to the reeds" to clear the marshes that flanked the Danube Delta. In his seven-year crusade to eradicate every vestige of superstition in Romania, Khrushchev ordered the police to close churches permanently or convert them into Communist clubs, museums, or grain houses.

Richard and Sabina's tiny attic had become ground zero for the underground church. Every evening before dinner, Richard prayed, "God, if You know some prisoner to whom I could be of use, send me back to jail."

Sabina offered a hesitant "Amen."

The Wurmbrands' prayers were answered days later on Wednesday, January 15.

At 1:00 a.m., the secret police broke down the Wurmbrands' door and flipped on the lights.

"You're Richard Wurmbrand? Get into the other room. And stay there!" Richard and Sabina watched as a dozen guards stormed through their cupboards and drawers, shuffling papers and seizing pages of documents. They confiscated the small notebook Richard had given his wife on their twentieth anniversary.

"Please don't take that," Sabina said. "It's a personal item, a present. It's not of any use to you."

Ignoring the request, the captain in charge of the raid separated Richard from his wife, handcuffed him, and took him into the other room.

"Aren't you ashamed to treat innocent people like this?" Richard asked him. He bolted for Sabina, but the police grabbed his arms and held him down. "I won't leave this house without a struggle, unless you allow me to hug my wife," he demanded.

"Let him go," the captain said.

Richard knelt on the floor with his wife and prayed as the police surrounded them. Then they began to sing, "The church's one foundation is Jesus Christ, her Lord ..."

After a while, the captain, moved to tears, gently placed his hand on Richard's shoulder and whispered, "We've got to get going. It's nearly five o'clock."

"Give all my love to Mihai and the pastor who denounced me," Richard said as the policemen led him down the staircase and outside, where they shoved him into a van.

"Richard! Richard!" Sabina screamed, chasing the van until the vehicle vanished around the corner. She collapsed on the icy street, breathless and heartbroken. "Lord," she prayed, "I give my husband into Your hands. I can't do anything, but You can pass through locked doors. You can put angels around him. You can bring him back!"

Five and a half years later, God would answer Sabina's prayer.

55

Alice waited for Mihai in the small park near the University of Sibiu. She knew he would be devastated to learn that his father had been arrested again. The news would jeopardize his studies and possibly lead to expulsion, if not worse. If that happened, it wouldn't be the first time. Mihai had been expelled and forced to change schools many times, finding it difficult to get an education. A shiver ran down Alice's spine as she waited in the bitter cold, hoping Mihai would pass by. At dusk he came and learned the sad news.

"I've been expecting it," he said. "Tell Mother I'll come home immediately. They may take her too."

"What about your studies?" Alice said. "You've worked for nearly three years—"

"What does it matter?" Mihai interrupted. "It's sometimes the pastors with degrees who betray and destroy what the real fishers of men have built. Better without a degree. I'll be thrown out soon anyway, when they feel like it."

When Alice and Mihai returned to Bucharest, they found Sabina heartbroken and in shock.

Days later they heard a knock. Sabina opened the door to see an exhausted clerk standing on the threshold. He handed her a piece of paper that read "Wurmbrand, R., born 1909 ... was sentenced to twenty-five years."

• • • •

Sabina closed the door and burst into tears. Two officials from the tax office showed up the next day to confiscate anything of value in the attic, leaving only the beds, table, and two chairs. For the next several years the officials would return, each time harassing Sabina for money she did not have or could not earn. She balanced her time between working with the underground church and hopping from one government building to the next, pleading with the uniformed men to drop the expensive fine Richard's imprisonment had generated. If Sabina couldn't pay the government, she would lose her home.

For income, Sabina found an old sewing machine that worked only half the time. The needles were brittle and often broke. With the socks and pullovers she offered on the black market, Sabina generated enough rent money to keep the government from confiscating her attic. It was illegal to produce and distribute unauthorized inventory, yet Sabina's friends sold the clothing at factory gates, flea markets, bus stations, and anywhere crowds gathered.

One day as she sat at her sewing machine, an ominous knock interrupted Sabina's work.

"Comrade Sabina Wurmbrand?"

Sabina opened the door to find a man in a dark raincoat.

"Yes, I'm Mrs. Wurmbrand," she replied

"Tomorrow morning at nine o'clock, you're to report to the ministry of the interior. You'll show this card to the guards and ask for the room indicated on it." He shot Sabina a cold stare and turned to leave.

Convinced that someone had betrayed her, Sabina packed a bag of toiletries and warm clothes and said good-bye to her family— knowing it might be the last time she would ever see them.

The next morning she walked into the cavernous office filled with attractive secretaries. Colorful carpet decorated the floor, and portraits of Lenin hung on the walls. Sabina approached a desk the size of a grand piano where a rotund man sat wearing civilian clothes. Sabina guessed that he was around forty years of age.

"Sit down, Comrade Wurmbrand," he said, gesturing toward an armchair. "We've asked you to come here because we're taking an interest in your case. Tell me about yourself and your family."

Sabina hesitated.

"Don't worry. Nothing will go beyond these walls." The man riffled through papers. "You have a son, Mihai? How are his studies proceeding?"

Sabina finally understood. She knew this was another attempt to persuade her to divorce Richard. Pressure had failed, so the Communists would try politeness. The man leaned back in his chair confidently.

"I love my husband," she said. "Whatever happens, I will stay married to him. We are united forever."

"Well now," he said, "let me make a little proposal. You want your child to complete his education. You want the right to work, to live your own life. You can have all this, very simply. Just leave your identity card with me. And in forty-eight hours, we'll send it to you endorsed in your own name. Forget about big words like *divorce*. This is just a simple formality the state asks of you. Isn't it the smart thing to do?"

Sabina budged not an inch.

Then he said, "Of course, if you don't cooperate, there are other ways. When we want something, we get it."

"Suppose one day *you* are in prison like so many other officials," Sabina blurted. "Would you want your wife to divorce you?"

He exploded. "Don't you know where you are and who I am? How dare you ask questions of me!"

He threw his pencil into the fireplace. "Now get out!" he screamed. "And don't forget what I've told you! Understand?"

Sabina grabbed her bag and left. She understood perfectly well, but she knew he also understood. Communist leaders were often as afraid of prison as Christians were. That was the last time Sabina would ever be pressured. Instead, she was told Richard had died.

• • • •

One night several haggardly dressed young men came to her door. They claimed to be ex-prisoners and looked the part. The provocateurs described Richard but couldn't look Sabina in the eye.

"Poor Pastor Wurmbrand," one of them said. "We don't know exactly what happened to him. He became very moody before the end. Wouldn't talk to anyone."

"What are you trying to tell me?" Sabina said. "That he committed suicide?"

"You can never be sure. But we know he was taken out of the Gherla prison feet first. And who could blame him if he did?"

Sabina saw through the lies. "Please go now," she said.

"Poor Pastor Wurmbrand," one of the men repeated. "A real saint, he was. Everyone said so. We want to say, Mrs. Wurmbrand, how sorry—"

"Please go," she insisted, cutting him off.

• • • •

As Mihai expected, the University of Sibiu expelled him for refusing to comply with Communist teachings. He discovered the faculty and his fellow students knew all about his work in the underground church. The faculty kept files on Christian students, and Mihai feared their church had been infiltrated with spies.

One day he said, "Mother, I hate to say it, but you're too softhearted."

Sabina looked confused.

"You let all these people come to the flat. They only have to say 'Praise the Lord!' and they're in. But we've got to be hard with these informers."

Sabina tried to argue, but Mihai quieted her. "I'm scared they'll arrest you again, Mother. And me. They know I'm up to my neck in your secret work." Mihai had the safety of other people in mind also. "I'm also thinking about the boys I used to know in Sibiu who were taken twice a week and beaten until they promised to inform. They're all in jail now, perhaps being beaten to death."

Sabina thought about Alice, so sweet and gentle. Alice had devoted her whole life to caring for children of political prisoners. Because of her connections in the underground church, the secret police targeted and arrested her. Interrogators attempted to extract information, but when they failed, the guards beat her unconscious, broke several of her bones, and kicked in her front teeth with their steel-framed boots. For the next eight years, Alice endured unspeakable tortures but never betrayed Sabina, Mihai, and the others she had protected.

Sabina imagined Alice's body stretched out of joint on a rack until screams came from her lips. The police were becoming more aggressive, breaking up several underground churches and arresting the leaders. Mihai was right. Informers must be resisted.

56

After being interrogated, Richard was loaded onto a truck. When the truck finally came to a halt, the doors swung open. Richard's heart sank when he saw the ramp. He knew it well, for it led to the dreaded Jilava prison.

"Get them out!" someone shouted. Several baton-swinging guards with breath stinking of alcohol beat the prisoners out of the truck. Then the guards threw gray uniforms at them before shaving their heads and beards. Half-naked and bloody, Richard entered a large cell and sat on the frozen floor.

"All priests outside," a guard shouted several hours later. Richard could hear giggles and snorts outside as he and the other pastors exited the room. The guards swung their batons full force at the prisoners as they walked, and Richard did his best to protect his head. The guards mercilessly kicked and spat on the prisoners who fell to the ground.

Thirty minutes later, guards again called all the priests out, but no one moved. Guards rushed into the cell, swinging their batons wildly at the men. Richard tried to comfort those suffering around him. One man, an Orthodox abbot named Miron Cristescu, crouched in the corner of the cell. Richard had met the man years earlier while waiting to see his superior, the Orthodox patriarch, and had shared his troubles with Cristescu.

"Brother," Cristescu had told him, placing his hands on Richard's shoulders, "Christ will come again—we hope for it." Cristescu had worked tirelessly to save the Orthodox Church from becoming a pawn of the state, but he hadn't succeeded.

Now blood flowed from Cristescu's lips. The guards had kicked his mouth with their heavy boots, and he wept violently, fingering the broken teeth repositioned in his gums. His badly swollen lip and shaved head rendered him nearly unrecognizable.

"Here I am like all the rest," Cristescu said. "I was mistaken to try. I should have resisted from the start."

Richard changed the subject. "Don't let those kinds of thoughts sadden you too much."

"Brother Wurmbrand," he said, "I know only one sadness, the sadness of failure."

If Cristescu had uttered those words during a sermon, they would have been beautiful, but as he sat in the cell, bloodied and toothless, they revealed the greatness of the man.

• • • •

Richard's second imprisonment was more severe than his first. Because the guards had banned preaching, prisoners who were caught received brutal beatings. Richard and a few other ministers accepted the price for a sermon; they would preach, and a pummeling would follow.

Often one of the brothers would begin preaching a sermon, and then halfway through, the guards would burst into the cell, haul the preacher to the "beating room," and bring him back bruised and bloodied. After a few minutes, he would collect himself, smooth out his gray uniform, and say, "Now, brethren, where did I leave off when I was interrupted?"

Richard heard about a Christian at the Gherla prison named Grecu who was nearly beaten to death for preaching. For weeks the guards slowly abused him, striking his feet with rubber clubs. A few minutes after, they hit him again. They beat his testicles, and then the doctor injected him with serum to revive him. Some hours later after his strength returned, a guard named Reck began beating him again and again until he eventually died.

Reck belonged to the Central Committee of the Communist Party. Just before Grecu died, he exclaimed, "You know, *I* am God. I have the power of life and death over you. The One who is in heaven cannot decide to keep you alive. Everything depends on *me*. If I wish, you live. If I wish, you are killed. *I am God!*"

With what little energy he could muster, Grecu said, "You haven't been created to be a torturer, a man who kills. You've been created to become like God, with the life of the Godhead in your heart."

Not long after Grecu died, Reck became a follower of Christ.

Richard contemplated the one great lesson—or benefit—that came from being beaten: *the spirit is master of the body.* His body felt the pain of torture, but his spirit experienced a transcendent peace that passed his understanding. Guards could damage his body, but they could never diminish his spirit.

• • • •

One slice of bread and spoiled soup—that's all the food Richard and the other prisoners ate over the course of a week. Yet even on those meager rations, they tithed one-tenth of the food to the weaker, more desperate prisoners.

Christian prisoners who were sentenced to be executed were allowed to see their wives one final time. "You have to know that I die loving those who kill me," they said in their own ways. "My last request of you is to love them too. Don't have bitterness in your heart because they killed your beloved one. We will see each other again in heaven."

The guards who witnessed these conversations often became Christians themselves.

Richard witnessed the martyrdom of dozens of brave pastors. Supernatural acts of courage became commonplace. The beauty of their few final minutes shined brightly against the gray cement walls and prison uniforms.

Before being imprisoned, Richard loved Christ with every beat of his heart. But during his second imprisonment, he fell in love with the underground church just as much.

• • • •

Several days later, Richard boarded a train for Gherla, the Transylvanian town where he had been imprisoned three years earlier. From the windows of the jail, Richard could see gallows where prisoners had been hanged in the eighteenth century. The Communists preferred a more efficient form of execution: one bullet lodged in the back of the head.

Ten thousand prisoners crowded into the barbaric accommodations that were designed to hold only two thousand men. During the previous summer, the guards nailed the window shutters closed. Without light and fresh air, a riot broke out. Prisoners barricaded themselves into a wing, but the wardens smashed down the doors. Militia were marshaled, and hundreds of prisoners were wounded and killed. The punishment for the riot was still in effect when Richard was transferred to Gherla. Rations were reduced to the point of starvation, and many prisoners, Richard included, would eventually be relocated to other jails.

When he first arrived at Gherla, Richard had been forced into a long, dimly lit barrack that contained only fifty bunks for one hundred men. Beds were shared, but sleep was elusive amid the snores. The smell from the overflowing lavatory buckets became nauseating.

Unexpected security visits interrupted what little rest Richard enjoyed. Whipped and kicked with studded boots, the prisoners were forced to lie down in rows to be counted. As the guard took roll, he walked on the hands and back of the man whose name he recorded.

A minimum of twenty-five lashes became the punishment for even the slightest breach of rules. Even with a doctor present, many men died. Every man in the prison knew the sting of being flogged, some enduring twenty-five lashes several times a week. After sampling a variety of torture instruments, Richard and his friends agreed that rods hurt more than sticks or batons. Each lash burned like a furnace against the ribs and spine. The nervous system often became overloaded, causing a prisoner to pass out from the pain. Torture also noticeably affected the guards. Intoxicated with a mixture of blood and power, they became caught up in a frenzy.

Every day Richard carried the lavatory buckets from the barrack to the one flushing toilet on the landing. He stood in long lines, waiting his turn to empty the contents down the drain. He tried to be as hygienic as possible, but the waste often stained his hands and clothes.

The prison graveyard of Rozsa Sandor occupied a prominent place in every prisoner's mind. The sight of the gray headstones through the window reminded Richard that he was growing older. He couldn't escape death, only postpone it. Many of the inmates lost track of time when serving decades of imprisonment. The clock at the main gate of the Gherla prison was stuck in place—its hands hadn't moved in six years. In the absence of mirrors, the prisoners remained the same age in their minds as they were on the day of their arrest. Many dreamed of wives the way they once were, never as the beleaguered women they met upon their release.

• • • •

Major Dorabantu was a fat, red-faced little man who served as the chief commandant for the Gherla prison. When ranting about one thing or another, Dorabantu often burrowed his hand into a bag to extract a garlic-sausage roll or apple.

Richard stood before the commandant, watching the man feast uncontrollably. The only two things Dorabantu didn't hate were food and the sound of his own voice.

"So, Wurmbrand!" he said, making a mouthful of cake disappear. "A monk, huh?"

"I'm a pastor," Richard replied.

"Pastors, priests, monks! All the same to me. Grinding the faces of the poor to feather your own nests. I know!" Dorabantu became animated as he told stories of his boyhood and how, when he strayed too close to a Romanian monastery, the monks whipped him brutally.

A spark flashed in the commandant's eye. "Ever seen a priest firing a double-barreled shotgun at a hungry child, Wurmbrand?"

In silence, Richard felt his heart rage within.

"It's a pretty holy picture!" Dorabantu said.

The commandant wasn't the only tough character Richard encountered. His cellmates were murderers, thieves, and criminals serving life sentences. Those who had massacred Jews were bitterly hostile to Richard and once even cornered him.

"We told you to shut up!" one of the leaders threatened.

Someone pushed Richard while another tripped him. He landed face-first on the floor and absorbed a violent kick in his ribs. Others were about to join in the assault when the guards rushed into the room. The aggressors scattered to their bunks.

Prowling the halls later, Dorabantu heard about the assault. One of the guards had recognized Richard as the tallest in the room, but in the half darkness, he couldn't identify the attackers.

"Wurmbrand, who did it?" Dorabantu demanded.

Richard refused to answer.

"Why not tell me?" the commandant asked.

Richard, nursing the cut on his bottom lip, said, "As a Christian, I love and forgive my enemies. I don't denounce them."

"Then you're an idiot!" Dorabantu shouted.

Richard agreed. "There you're right. Anyone who isn't a Christian with all his heart is an idiot."

"Are you calling me an idiot?"

"I didn't say that," Richard said. "I meant that *I* am not as good a Christian as I should be."

"Take him away," Dorabantu ordered. "Thirty strokes! Crazy monks."

Richard's mouth throbbed as the guards led him away to be flogged.

57

Florescu, a half-gypsy thief, pulled up a wooden stool and sat down to talk with Richard in the cell.

"I believe in what I can see, taste, and feel," Florescu said. "We're all matter, like this bit of wood I'm sitting on, and when you're dead, that's it."

Richard had to prove a point. He stood up and kicked the stool out from under Florescu. The stool shot across the floor and slammed into the wall. Florescu hit the floor with a hard thump.

"What was that for?" Florescu yelled, scrambling to his feet.

"But you said you were matter like the stool," Richard replied calmly. "I didn't hear the stool complain!"

Some of the other cellmates laughed.

"I'm sorry, Florescu," Richard said. "I just wanted to prove that since matter doesn't react with love or hate, it's different from us."

Florescu pouted for a few minutes and then said, "I might believe that if the dead ever came back to talk to us."

"I'm sure men have been in touch with the dead," Richard said. "Great scientists from Isaac Newton to Sir Oliver Lodge have believed in spiritualism. The Bible even describes the evocation of the dead prophet Samuel" (see 1 Sam. 28).

Others gathered around Richard as he preached about life after death. His words captured their attention and raised immediate interest.

"If God had made us for this life only," Richard said, "He would first have given us age with its wisdom and *then* youth with its vigor. It seems senseless to gather knowledge and understanding only to take it to the grave.

"Martin Luther compares our life on earth to the life of an unborn child," he continued. "He says that if the embryo could reason in the womb, it would wonder why it grew hands and feet, and it would surely come to the conclusion that there must be another world to come in which it would play and run and work. Just like the embryo is preparing for a future state, so are we."

Richard raised his voice so other prisoners lying in their bunks could hear. In the dimly lit barrack, all eyes were on the pastor.

"Suppose I argue that there is room in a pint bottle for ten pints of milk. You would say I'm insane. Yet I can have together in my head thoughts of an event like the flood, which happened thousands of years ago, of my wife and son in the room where I left them, of God and the Devil. How does it happen that within the narrow limits of my head there are encompassed the daily things of life, as well as the infinite and the eternal? When your unfettered spirit can go anywhere in time or space, do you believe that it can share the fate of this shell that's the body?"

During all the years Richard had pastored in Bucharest, he had never experienced the kind of silence that permeated the cell. There were no yawns, no fidgeting, no jokes. Richard looked around the darkening room as he continued preaching about Christ. He saw in his cellmates a congregation he had never known before. Their clothes were soiled, their jaws angled, their cheeks hollow, and their eyes—wide with anticipation—revealed their hunger for the truth Richard was feeding them.

• • • •

Four years into his second imprisonment, Richard again became terribly ill and was moved to the prison hospital. After he had been there one week, the guards ordered him and the patients around him to march into the courtyard. Some couldn't walk on their own, so Richard helped those he could. For an hour, the patients were forced to stand outside and watch a makeshift theatrical performance by the other prisoners. The actors mocked Christianity, drawing the applause of the commandant, who laughed as he ate.

One by one the prisoners were forced to take center stage and repeat blasphemous slogans against Christ. "We *have* to say these things until it's over," one of the prisoners said, clutching Richard with tears in his eyes.

When Alexandrescu, the new commandant, called on Richard to perform, hundreds of eyes fell on the pastor. "Will he praise Communism too?" they murmured to one another.

Richard remembered Sabina's words at the Congress of the Cults: "Wash this shame from the face of Christ!"

"Go on! Speak!" Alexandrescu ordered.

Richard began cautiously. "It's Sunday morning, and our wives and mothers and children are praying for us, in church or at home. We should have liked to pray for them too. Instead, we've watched this play."

Richard could see tears running down faces as he spoke about families. "Many here have spoken against Jesus," he continued, "but what is it that you actually have against Him? You talk about the proletariat, but wasn't Jesus a carpenter? You say that he who doesn't work shall not eat, but this was said long ago in Paul's second epistle to the Thessalonians [see 2 Thess. 3:10]. You speak against the wealthy, but Jesus drove the moneylenders from the temple with whips" (see John 2:14–15).

Alexandrescu scowled but listened, apparently hoping Richard would say enough to warrant his execution. "You want Communism," Richard said, "but don't forget that the first Christians lived in a community, sharing all they had [see Acts 2:44]. You wish to raise up the poor, but the Magnificat, Mary's song at Jesus's birth, says that God will exalt the poor above the rich [see Luke 1:52–53]. Anything that is good in Communism comes from the Christians!"

Richard then quoted Karl Marx, who said in his introduction to *Das Kapital* that Christianity is the most fitting form of religion. He looked at the guards and asked, "Is there anybody, even a Communist, who is without sin?"

Richard began to preach openly about Jesus Christ, what He had accomplished on the cross and how much He loved even the Communists—*especially* the Communists. Examinations were part of life, he explained. From the university student to the factory worker, being scrutinized was a necessary part of living.

Richard turned toward the commandant and said, "You'll be judged too, Major Alexandrescu." The inmates exchanged fearful glances. Richard could have been minutes from his death, but he continued the sermon, telling the entire prison that Jesus gave eternal life to anyone who repented.

Before Richard could even finish his sermon, the prison erupted in cheers. Prisoners of all ranks burst into applause, clapping and hollering without caring about the repercussions. When Richard returned to his place, one of the prisoners, Miron, said, "You've undone all their work."

Gaston whispered, "Did you hear the cheers?"

Richard answered, "They were cheering what they had found in their own hearts, not me."

Richard's speech cost him his place in the prison hospital. The guards transported him back to the "priests' room."

Days later a lieutenant named Konya brought Richard two pieces of news. He said Sabina was in prison and also that he would be flogged at ten o'clock that evening for the repeated defiance in his speech. The beatings he had assumed, but the news about Sabina came as a terrible shock.

Waiting to be beaten could drive a man insane. But knowing his wife faced beatings was far worse. Richard waited by the cell door, occasionally hearing footsteps come and go. A prisoner screamed somewhere down the corridor, but nobody came for Richard.

Over the next six days, Richard was threatened again and again. Finally, after nearly a week, the guards took him and landed so many blows on his shoulders and back that he didn't think he would survive. Each scourge burned like fire.

After the guards stopped, Lieutenant Konya commanded, "Give him some more! Ten more!"

Two guards had to carry Richard back to his cell. Loudspeakers blared in the room: "Christianity is stupid. Christianity is stupid. Christianity is stupid. Why not give it up? Why not give it up? Why not give it up?"

Richard couldn't give up because Jesus hadn't given up. When faced with torture, Jesus could have summoned angels to rescue Him, but He endured the pain because of His love for the enemies crucifying Him.

The beatings intensified over the next few weeks. Richard and the other pastors were often ordered to drop their trousers for the blows. "Lie on your bellies!" the guards shouted. Others demanded, "Turn over on your back and hold your feet up!"

When the guards became bored, they isolated a couple of prisoners and said to one, "Slap your friend in the face!" If he refused, they said, "You've lost your chance." Then the second man was ordered to hit the first. "Now hit him back!" they said, roaring with laughter. Prisoners often beat each other until their faces hung loosely, swollen and purple.

Torture had proved useless on Richard. He had developed such a joy in his suffering for Christ that Lieutenant Konya had to try other tactics. He entered Richard's cell and demanded he gather his things.

Konya led Richard across the yard and into a building that contained a white-walled cell. Richard had never seen a cell like this before. Lamps adorned the corners, filling the room with splendid light. Just then, the loudspeaker came on, blaring, "Nobody believes in Christ now. Nobody believes in Christ now. Nobody believes in Christ now. No one goes to church. Give it up. Give it up. Give it up. Nobody believes in Christ now …"

Richard wanted to plug his ears and strained against the cuffs securing his hands behind his back.

When Konya came into the room the next morning, he removed the handcuffs and asked Richard to follow him down the corridor. The new cell that awaited Richard nearly stole his breath away. Fresh clothes were laid across the clean-sheeted bed. There was a table covered in a cloth and topped with fresh flowers in a vase. The sight overtook Richard, and he sat down on the bed and wept. Konya was pleased.

Richard flipped through the newspaper on the table—the first he had seen in all his years in prison. He slowly turned the pages, soaking up as much information as he could. Had the United States' Sixth Fleet entered the Black Sea yet? No word on that front, but there was an article about a Communist dictator in Cuba who was defying America on its very doorstep.

Commandant Alexandrescu entered the luxurious room. He acted impressed with the living conditions and promised to give Richard this cell permanently. Then he turned to Richard and attacked religion, claiming that Jesus Christ was a fantasy the apostles invented to give slaves false hope in a better life.

Richard handed him the newspaper and said, "This is printed on the party presses. It shows the date July 1963. That means 1,963 years since the birth of someone who—according to you—never existed. You don't believe in Christ, but you accept Him as the founder of our civilization."

"It means nothing," Alexandrescu said with a shrug. "It's customary to count that way."

"But if Christ never came to earth, how did the custom arise?"

"Some liars started it."

"Suppose you tell me that the Russians have landed on Mars," Richard proposed. "I don't need to believe you. But if I turn on the radio and hear New York and the Americans congratulate them, then I know it must be true. In the same way, we must accept Christ's existence as a historical fact when His worst enemies, the Pharisees, recognized it in the Talmud and also gave the names of His mother and some of His apostles. And again, we have to be impressed when the Pharisees attributed miracles to Christ while protesting that black magic conjured them. Many heathen writers also recognized Jesus. Only Communists deny this plain fact of history, simply because it doesn't suit their theory."

Alexandrescu did not launch into his usual rant. Instead, he sent Richard a book to read—*The Atheist's Handbook*, essential reading for anyone seeking a career in Communist countries. It was a beautiful book with tightly bound pages and colorful illustrations. Richard read every word, from the history of religions like Hinduism, Buddhism, Confucianism, and Islam to the history of Christianity. He was pleased to read that while Catholicism was besmirched, Lutheranism fared much better, since Luther had defied the pope. Nevertheless, science had proved that all Christian traditions were fraudulent and based on false assumptions. Richard read with interest the section about how Christian rites emerged from heathen folklore. The final chapter's title brought the book's thesis to a head: "Forms of Atheist Propaganda." After reading it, he closed the cover, thankful to hold a book in his hand. Then he slipped between the clean sheets.

• • • •

Richard knew that the Catholic Church had appealed for reconciliation between the "separated brethren" in the East and West. Was Christian unity possible? Richard debated the question in his mind, knowing that those who truly loved Christ must love one another. He imagined Jesus telling all His children throughout the world, "I have made you whole in different ways. Now you shouldn't fight but rejoice!"

Richard remembered a line from the famous German poet Goethe: "Color is the pain of light." He marveled at the thought. When light passes through a prism, it's torn to pieces as colorful shards scatter in every direction. Every beam is made up of the same light as the others, but they differ in appearance and direction.

In the same way, Christians in the West differed from Christians in the East. Their cultures were different; their traditions and customs were different. Even their national flags differed in color. Yet all of God's children around the world, purchased by the blood of Christ, received the same rays from the sun. God never intended sameness; He intended oneness—unity in the Son of God who made all things new.

Richard fell asleep knowing that division was the painful quest for truth from different perspectives. The words of Jesus served as a lullaby as he drifted off to sleep: "I am the way, and the truth, and the life. No one comes to the Father except through me" (John 14:6).

58

"Alice is home!" Marietta shrieked.

Sabina tried to believe the good news, but she hadn't seen Alice in four years. Snatching her coat, Sabina left with Mihai and Marietta for the tram.

Alice had aged significantly. She stood in patched clothes, and her thin hair covered deep wrinkles that the horrors of Communist torture had carved. But she was smiling, as always.

"Tomorrow we'll bring you some things," Sabina promised.

"But I know you don't have anything yourself," Alice said. She was right.

"Oh, but we live in the lap of luxury," Mihai said, smirking. "You should see our penthouse flat."

"Carpets on the walls," Marietta chimed in. "On the windows too! Running water straight through the ceiling!"

They deposited Alice at a flat belonging to Sabina's cousin and went home. Sabina tried to sleep that night, but every time she closed her eyes, she imagined seeing Richard again.

At every Communist festival in Bucharest, the police announced the names of political prisoners who would soon be released from custody. Sabina attended every celebration, listening for Richard's name.

Then on a warm day in the summer of 1964, Sabina arrived home to discover a daily newspaper waiting for her. A family friend had brought it by on his way to work. Sabina trembled as she read the big bold letters on the front page: *AMNESTY*.

• • • •

Sabina didn't know *who* would receive amnesty, but she prayed with all her heart it would be political prisoners like Richard. She read the article over and over and then hurried to her friend's room, where a few women were already discussing the headline.

"Oh, it'll be like last year," Miss Landauer lamented. "Criminals only!"

"No, no!" Sabina said. "Haven't I told you over and over? Let's pray and thank God, and you'll see."

Only five minutes after Sabina returned home, a neighbor came rushing through the door with news that his friend had been released from Gherla.

Gherla? Sabina's eyes widened as the neighbor continued. "He says your husband was on the list for today. He saw him waiting in the yard. He's coming!"

Sabina tried to peel potatoes that evening, but her heart almost exploded in her chest with excitement, and she had to sit down. A few hours later, someone else knocked on the door.

It was Mr. Ionescu from the floor below. He clutched Sabina's hand and said, "Someone's calling you from out of town." Sabina hurried after him and grabbed the telephone receiver in his flat.

It was Richard's voice! Sabina felt herself falling but couldn't prevent the collapse. She awoke to find anxious faces staring down at her.

"She's all right!" someone shouted.

"You fainted!" another said.

Mihai was laughing and chatting into the telephone. He smiled at his mother and told her that Richard was staying with friends in Cluj. Richard assured them he was well—and free—and would be coming home as soon as possible. He'd have to catch a train, but it would have to wait until the next day.

Later that night, after visiting with dozens of friends, Sabina received a telegram. She tore open the paper and shared the good news.

"Richard says he's coming on the overnight train!" she blurted. "He'll be here at 8:30 tomorrow morning!"

Sabina didn't even try to sleep that night. She rejoiced with other wives who celebrated the release of their husbands, some who hadn't seen their spouses in fifteen years. It was as if the grave was returning the dead into the arms of the living.

Flowers arrived almost every hour from those who couldn't come to Sabina's attic to celebrate. But the flat was already packed with people giddy over Richard's release.

• • • •

The next morning came quickly. The sun popped above the horizon with newfound speed, promising to shed light on a very good day.

As the noisy train approached, crowds of eager families watched its engine slip by, pulling carriages crammed with prisoners. Prayers for fathers, husbands, brothers, and sons filled the platform, but many prayers went unanswered.

Sabina searched the carriage windows as they passed, until her eyes landed on a familiar face. Richard was leaning out the window. His head was roughly shaved above his thin, pale face.

God has given him back to me, Sabina thought, rushing to embrace him.

Sabina saw Richard's laceless boots—far too large for his feet—and matched their pace until his frail limbs enveloped her tiny torso. Mihai joined in the embrace as the entire train station burst into shouts and greetings. Everyone wanted to congratulate him and find out information about the other prisoners. A cameraman pulled Richard and his family aside and snapped a photograph.

"Don't speak," Richard said to his family tenderly. "Let me just look at you."

• • • •

If Commandant Alexandrescu had told all the Gherla prisoners a few days earlier, "Tomorrow you will all be shot," the entire main hall would have broken into cheers. *Freedom at last!* But instead, the commandant had come into the hall and announced that the government had granted amnesty to political prisoners. The next day they would be released.

Blank faces all around. Was this another trick?

Richard belonged to one of the last groups to leave the prison. The guards who had once shown cruelty to Richard now handed him fresh clothes, which he donned gratefully.

"Brother Wurmbrand!" A man came up to the pastor and said he lived in Sibiu. "I've heard so much about you from your son. We shared a cell together."

"My son in prison?" Richard said. "No, no. You're mistaken!"

The man gave a sympathetic gesture and said, "You mean you didn't know? He's been in jail six years now."

Richard turned his back, as he had done a thousand times after receiving twenty-five lashes. But this news burned deeper. Mihai's health had deteriorated. There was no way he could survive years in prison.

Richard was still in shock when Alexandrescu approached.

"Well, Wurmbrand," the commandant said, "where will you go now that you're free?"

Richard thought for a moment. "I don't know. I've been told officially that my wife is in prison, and now I hear my only son is too. I have nobody else."

"The boy too!" said Alexandrescu with a grin. "How do you feel having a jailbird for a son?"

Richard answered, "I'm sure he's not in jail for theft or any other crime, and if he's there for Christ's sake, then I'm proud of him."

"What?" Alexandrescu shouted. "We spend all this money keeping you for years, and you think it's something to be proud of to have a family member in prison!"

Richard left the prison in another man's clothes. He had felt freedom like this once before, but with the news that his wife and son were imprisoned, he dragged himself along the street, heartbroken and forlorn.

But the streets did dazzle beneath the cars that zoomed by. A woman's colorful coat caught Richard's attention, a burst of flowers in a window, a radio playing music. The city was textured with beauty. The breeze carried clean, fresh air into his lungs.

Richard traveled by bus to the neighboring town of Cluj, where he once had friends. They had moved several times, and he would have to roam from house to house to find them. As the bus curved around the street corners, he remembered the woman who had offered him strawberries after his previous release from prison. What he wouldn't give for some berries to combat the sweltering midsummer heat.

When Richard found his friends, they gave him some fruit and cake, but what he really wanted to eat was the beautiful brown onion on the table. The tasteless prison food had produced in him a yearning for intense flavor.

After rehydrating, Richard picked up the telephone and dialed his neighbor's number in Bucharest. Within minutes he heard Sabina's voice.

"It's Richard!" he exclaimed. "I thought you were in prison!"

A loud thud came through the phone, followed by a cacophony of voices. Then Richard heard Mihai's voice. "Mother's fainted. Hold on!" More muffled sounds, and then he returned to the phone. "She's all right. We thought you were dead!"

Mihai hadn't been imprisoned after all. The commandant had orchestrated the false news to test Richard's reactions to the brainwashing.

Richard boarded a train for Bucharest, where a crowd of men, women, and children waited. Flowers filled their hands. *Who's the lucky person?* Leaning out the carriage window, Richard scanned the crowd until his eyes fixed on Sabina. As he stepped off the train, it seemed as if his entire congregation had come to the station to welcome him home. He forced his way through the crowd to embrace Sabina and Mihai.

• • • •

In the days that followed, Richard reflected on his imprisonment—fourteen years total. During that time, he had forgotten how to write, and because of his starvation and drugging, he had even forgotten much of the Scripture he had memorized. But he did remember one passage that offered sweet comfort: "So Jacob served seven years for Rachel, and they seemed to him but a few days because of the love he had for her" (Gen. 29:20). A new life of poverty awaited Richard and Sabina, but that mattered little. They had each other and would live in freedom together.

59

Every day and night, Sabina hosted guests in her attic. It seemed as if the whole country wanted to visit Richard. Everyone had words of gratitude and encouragement for him. Not even the secret police dared to control the enormous crowds flocking to the Wurmbrands' flat. They only hid in the streets, scribbling notes while admiring the pastor's magnetic popularity. Even the hospitals, which Richard visited occasionally, swarmed with visitors.

When hospitals could not ensure his protection, Richard traveled to the sanatorium in the village of Sinaia. A royal palace had been constructed on the edge of the mountain, but even so, pastors and congregations from other churches discovered Richard's secret whereabouts and traveled by bus, motorcycle, and even bicycle to meet him.

It would take years for Richard to regain his health. Thin as a twig, the pastor weighed ninety pounds. So many years of beatings and brainwashing had weakened his tall frame. Gaping holes peppered his back, but he still retained the ice-blue eyes Sabina first fell in love with. She saw Richard's true self through those windows to his soul.

· · · ·

In the same year Richard was released from prison, the government released tens of thousands of prisoners, many of whom had known Richard behind bars. Bucharest struggled to cope with the sudden surge of prisoners who needed jobs to provide for their families. Employment was competitive, and tragedies unfolded every day for those who had already suffered so much.

The police were occupied with the chaos in the city and didn't have time to prevent Richard from seizing opportunities to preach in any church that invited him. He even managed to restore his preaching license. He didn't need the government to authorize his vocation, but having a license opened doors.

Sabina and Richard were experiencing the busiest season of their lives. They often gathered in secret to bring hundreds of souls to Christ. Richard never felt he was doing enough. While in prison, he had once dreamed about how he would spend his freedom.

"What will you do now?" Sabina asked.

"Ideally," Richard said, "I'd like to be a recluse, retire to a desert like the hermits of old, and spend the rest of my life contemplating God and meditating on His Word."

Sabina agreed that rest sounded nice. In their former lives, they had pursued wealth, fame, and pleasure, but God had used their years of imprisonment and poverty to transform the couple into contemplatives satisfied with little more than the presence of Christ.

The gray walls of Richard's cell had not bound God. The Holy Spirit transformed those walls into displays of astonishing beauty. Like unrefined coal being crushed beneath the earth, Richard and Sabina came out of prison as diamonds. And for the rest of their lives, they committed themselves to casting light and life against the darkness.

For Richard, solitary confinement deepened his capacity to enjoy the Savior. He became meditative, having mastered the storms and hatred in his heart. No longer did he need to fight anyone. Love became more powerful than violence, for it could subdue the heart of even the most ruthless interrogator. Quiet years of peace lay ahead, but Richard wasn't going to waste them. He would construct temples to Christ through writing, speaking, and preaching the Word of God.

He comforted pastors who, with tremendous sorrow, had to confess to their congregations that they had worked as informers for the secret police against their own flocks. Fear of churches being closed swept through Romania, and many pastors betrayed the sheep they were called to shepherd.

Lenin once wrote, "Every religious idea, every idea of God, even flirting with the idea of God, is unutterable vileness … of the most dangerous kind, 'contagion' of the most abominable kind. Millions of sins, filthy deeds, acts of violence and physical contagion … are far less dangerous than the subtle, spiritual idea of a God."[1]

The Communist Party of the Soviet Union upheld Lenin's view. Religion, to them, was worse than cancer, tuberculosis, and syphilis combined. It threatened the very fabric of their national identity and had to be exterminated as efficiently as possible.

In Bucharest, the Communists shut down youth meetings and children's Sunday school. The rising generation couldn't be infected with the Christian gospel. Richard saw this anew after his release from prison, and though he had always loved Communists, he developed a fresh revulsion for Communism and vowed to resist it. One billion men, women, and children were still caught in its iron grip. Richard swore to spend the rest of his life freeing them from the tyranny of terror.

Seclusion must only be for a season, Richard knew. He remembered Saint Anthony, who had retreated into the desert of Egypt for decades. He spent his time praying, fasting, and gaining mastery over temptation and sin. But when he learned about the fight between Athanasius and Arius over Christ's divinity, he abandoned the quiet of the desert and traveled to Alexandria to help combat the heresy.

Romania had no shortage of evil to combat. Professors and intellectuals were forced to betray their own convictions and teach atheism. The Communist Youth Movement reprimanded and threatened teenage girls for even kissing a Christian; the government even told them which young men they were allowed to date. Richard also met the warriors of the under-ground church—seasoned comrades from years past who had resisted torture and evaded abduction after their release from prison. Richard joined them in the fight, attending their secret meetings and conspiring against the government. They even sang the hymns Richard had composed in prison and later published.

God had changed Richard's plans as a young man. Now that he was older, he knew God might do it again. The thought of retiring to a life of tranquillity gradually left Richard's mind and was replaced with another: to take up the fight for Christ. God had once sent ten plagues on Egypt to free His slaves, culminating in the death of the firstborn child. Richard knew God was unleashing a great weapon on Romania—the death of His own Son. Only the resurrected Christ could bring new life to the death that had devastated the land.

Other preachers criticized Richard for preaching against the corruption of the government. They encouraged him to preach a "pure gospel." But wasn't the preaching of John the Baptist pure? John didn't only say, "Repent, for the kingdom of heaven is at hand" (Matt. 3:2). He also rebuked King Herod "for all the evil things that Herod had done" (Luke 3:19). Jesus called John the greatest man who had ever lived and even sent words of encouragement to him during his imprisonment (see Matt. 11:2–6, 11).

Jesus too preached against the evils of His day. One day He preached the Sermon on the Mount, but on another, He confronted the church leaders, saying, "Woe to you, scribes and Pharisees, hypocrites!" (Matt. 23:27).

For Richard, Communism was sin, and as a pastor of hundreds, even thousands, throughout the land, he had a responsibility to protect his people. He knew that Socialism always failed as a template for community when governments unleashed it on their populations. Involuntary Socialism inevitably led to corruption at the top and marginalization at the bottom.

• • • •

After the government relaxed the ban on pastors, Richard took a church in the town of Orsova. The Communist Ministry of Cults said he could have thirty-five members, but not a single member more. They also demanded Richard work as an agent, spying on every member and keeping young people away from the church. Communists had learned this was a far more strategic weapon than trying to eradicate the churches that kept sprouting up.

Richard feared his sermons would bring hundreds of Christians to his church. So instead of working for the official church, he ministered to the underground church, sharing his story and showing his scars. God had worked wonderfully during the Nazi and Communist eras. He hadn't forgotten His enslaved, chosen people but had heard their cries, and so had the Americans who prayed for Richard.

One afternoon Richard heard words that warmed his soul: "Brothers from abroad have come." Western Christians had organized secret and dangerous ministries to provide relief for families of Christian martyrs. They broke the law by smuggling Christian literature across Romanian borders, along with other supplies.

Six of these Western Christians soon came to Bucharest in search of the famous pastor who had spent fourteen years in prison.

"I'm that man," Richard told them.

They were startled. "But we expected to meet someone in the throes of depression. Instead, we find a happy man. You can't be the person we're looking for, because you're full of joy."

Richard showed the men his scars and expressed his gratitude for their prayers. Lively and brilliant in his wit, he made the guests comfortable enough to laugh and exchange stories of pleasant memories. One of those visitors was Rev. W. Stuart Harris, who visited Richard in November of 1964. Entering the Wurmbrands' home very late one night, after having taken many precautionary measures, he brought them words of love and comfort from Christians in the West. Richard would never forget those meetings that were so meaningful to him.

The network of friendships that followed increased the accessibility of Bibles, sermons, and Christian literature for the underground church. For years Richard had prayed for the Christians in the West. To know they were also praying for him brought tears to his eyes. The years of brainwashing hadn't succeeded in convincing Richard that "Nobody loves you anymore," as the recordings had blared into his ears. American and English believers loved him deeply and even risked their lives to support him. They were angels sent to comfort Richard and his family. In return, Richard helped Western Christians gain greater access to Romania. He developed a covert system of communication so they could pass undetected beneath the noses of the secret police.

Richard's expanding friendships with the Western world made him more vulnerable than ever to another arrest. Two Christian organizations, the Norwegian Mission to the Jews and the Hebrew Christian Alliance, would not allow that to happen. They paid the Communist government a ransom of ten thousand dollars for Richard's life—five times the usual price for a political prisoner.

Jesus Christ had ransomed Richard with His death on the cross. Now the body of Christ on earth—the church—ransomed him as well. Richard told Sabina the good news. After so many years of uncertainty, torture, and interrogation, the time had come for them to leave Romania.

60

Word came quickly from the government that the ten thousand dollars had been paid for the Wurmbrands' exit visas. The secret police demanded one last meeting with Richard.

"Now you can leave," an official said. "Preach all you like abroad. But speak against us, and you'll be silenced."

The next morning was December 6, 1965. Richard, Sabina, and Mihai departed for the airport. The runway stretched into the distance and disappeared behind the mist in the air.

The future was as clouded as the horizon, but the Wurmbrands approached the DC-7 aircraft with sixty others who had been ransomed, mostly Jews. The airport authorities tried to prevent people from gathering at the airport, but their efforts were futile. A crowd soon joined the Wurmbrands to see them off. The guards shot jealous glances at the West-bound prisoners and helped them board the plane.

The wheels of the accelerating aircraft soon lifted off the gray asphalt. Many shouted for joy, but others struggled to cope with bittersweet emotions. They were grateful for their freedom but saddened to think of those still suffering beyond the window.

A couple of hours later, the plane landed in Rome. After a visit there, the Wurmbrands departed for Oslo, Norway. Richard had hoped to stop in Geneva, Switzerland, to give a report on the widespread persecutions in Romania, but the secretary of the Lutheran World Federation pleaded with him not to visit for fear that the Russians would find out.

Members of the Israel Mission greeted the Wurmbrands in Norway. Sabina embraced Anutza, the woman who had worked tirelessly for more than fifteen years to free their family. Richard also met the head of the Swedish Israel Mission, Pastor Gote Hedenquist, who had prayed ceaselessly over the years for Richard's release. Members of the Hebrew Christian Alliance, which had paid part of the ten-thousand-dollar ransom, came to the airport with immediate necessities.

From Norway, the Wurmbrands traveled to Britain and were greeted by their friend Stuart Harris, who arranged opportunities for Richard to speak at universities and preach in countless churches. At long last, the British could hear accurate accounts of the tragedies and triumphs of the underground church. English churches weren't aware of the persecution in Romania, and with grace and kindness, Richard unburdened them of their ignorance.

Richard and Sabina basked in the angelic hospitality of their new British friends. An alliance formed that would in time organize a new mission devoted to reaching the Communist world. But Richard knew he needed the support of the Americans.

61

With the Wurmbrands settled in the United States, the Romanian secret police soon ordered their assassination. Though he had been warned to keep quiet, Richard refused to be silenced and spoke out against Communism at every opportunity. The hand of God protected his family each step of the way.

Richard testified before committees of the United States Senate in Washington, DC, and then before Congress. He walked up to the platform and looked out over the sea of senators and representatives, newspaper reporters, and staff from radio stations. Television crews aimed their cameras as Richard began to speak about the suffering of the underground church.

"One-third of the world is entitled to one-third of your prayers, of your concern, of your gifts. In prison I saw men with fifty-pound chains at their feet praying for America. But in America you seldom hear in a church a prayer for those in chains in Communist prisons."

A senator asked Richard if he bore any marks of torture. The gangly pastor removed his jacket and shirt, revealing eighteen mutilations on his emaciated body.

"I don't boast of these scars," he said. "I show the tortured body of my church and my country. I speak for the heroes and saints who cannot speak for themselves: Protestants, Catholics, Orthodox, and Jews who died under torture for their religion."

Sabina couldn't suppress her tears any longer. She joined the majority of the Senate and wept openly, thinking of the farm women, nuns, and many young girls still enslaved in Romania. The faces of those who had died on the canal came into view.

Richard watched his wife as he continued to speak. He later told Sabina, "Your tears made a greater impression than all my words. Tears undermine the strongest walls."

• • • •

Throughout his life, Richard knew the pen was mightier than the sword. With memories of his imprisonment fresh in his mind, he dictated a book titled *Today's Martyred Church: Tortured for Christ* while in Britain. Sabina sat on the sofa and listened to him recount story after story. As he excavated from his memory forgotten names and painful interrogations, sobs punctuated his sentences.

Richard wrote his book with pen and tears as he recalled his suffering and the suffering of many martyrs. This was *their* story too, and he made sure to incarnate them on paper for posterity.

Tortured for Christ, as it was renamed, became an unexpected bestseller in the West. It was translated into dozens of languages and opened opportunities for Richard and Sabina to travel to different countries and continents and share the power of the gospel as demonstrated through the courageous witness of persecuted Christians. Nineteen mission efforts were founded throughout Europe and Asia, in Australia and America. These missions worked in cooperation to raise awareness of the underground church and provide Christian literature and relief for the families of martyrs.

More books, one after the other, flowed from Richard's pen. He preached tirelessly around the world and founded an organization capable of working secretly behind enemy lines. Some people questioned his methods, but Richard paid no attention to their criticism. He hadn't come back from the dead to squander his energy on critics. His eyes were locked on a greater, darker Enemy.

Wherever they went, the Wurmbrands sought Christian unity. They came to know Australian, Indian, and Maori Christians. They held meetings under apartheid in South Africa as Christians of all skin colors intermingled to listen to Richard bring words of healing and truth. An African newspaper reported, "We were hit by a hurricane called Richard."

"Hate Communism," Richard always declared, "but love and win the Communists for Christ."

Millions of Christians followed his instruction, knowing that humans cannot demonstrate radical love on their own. But with God, all things are possible, even forgiveness.

Sabina's approach may have been softer than her husband's, but she was a strong, vivacious woman who wouldn't back down when it came to the gospel and her relationships. Together the Wurmbrands were a mighty voice for persecuted Christians. They challenged the West with inspiring stories of courageous faith in the face of torture, imprisonment, and death, inspiring listeners in their commitment to Christ and sharing His good news.

Richard and Sabina complemented each other in every way, organizing the affairs of the missions that infiltrated Communist countries. Members of those organizations needed training to know how to acquire information without being arrested. Others would step into this role as they heard the Wurmbrands' testimony and were inspired to do something. Bibles needed to be transported, along with literature, tapes, and money. There were also guests to host. Sabina treated all clergy members and visitors as if they were Christ Himself.

Richard had been accustomed to neglect, humiliation, and mockery in prison. Now he was greeted with praise and adoration. Lesser men might have swelled at the adulation, but Sabina never detected a trace of pride in her husband's heart. Richard had descended into the scorching fires of the furnace to dwell with Christ, as the three men in the book of Daniel had done (see Dan. 3). There was no room for arrogance in a body that had been stripped, starved, and scarred for Christ. Richard confronted fame in the same way he confronted shame—with humility.

The Wurmbrands had experienced abject poverty in Romania, but now a new threat confronted the couple. Sabina feared the accumulation of wealth they might experience in the United States. As damaging as poverty, possessions had a way of possessing the possessor. Richard and Sabina knew this and never owned a house, a car, or even a bicycle.

When Sabina first married Richard, she wanted to be wealthy. Once upon a time, she desired a comfortable life, but now she felt that these luxuries could damage and distract their witness for Christ. Every bite of delicious food brought to mind hundreds of faces who had no food in prison. Richard never forgot the taste of rotten carrot soup. Every time he opened the refrigerator, he told Sabina, he remembered the feeling of being thrown into the freezers by the guards.

"I'm happy to hear that you despise money," Sabina told Richard. "Be sure not to stop when you've made the first million."

Richard and Sabina experienced many joys and anxieties. The threat of imprisonment, even in America, never went away. Sabina comforted herself, knowing if God's work was dangerous to do, it was even more dangerous to leave undone.

She often encouraged children that one doesn't have to be old to change the world for Christ. She told the story of the boy who stood on the shore waving at a large ship disappearing into the distance.

"Don't be silly," a man said to the boy. "The steamer won't change its course because you wave."

But the ship did return to dock by the shore. The boy dashed up the bridge and shouted to the man, "The captain is my father!"

EPILOGUE

According to Jewish tradition, when the Egyptians drowned in the Red Sea, the angels sang with the Israelites who had been delivered. But God rebuked the angels, saying, "The Jews are men and can rejoice about their escape. But from you I expect more understanding. Aren't the Egyptians also My creatures? Don't I love them too?"[1]

The darkness of fourteen years in prison brightened Richard's eyes to a glowing truth: God loved Communists as much as He loved the Christians they tortured. No one is beyond the redeeming grasp of God. Actually, He has a long history of turning rebels into soul winners, misfits into missionaries, and criminals into the finest Christians in history.

Richard was once asked what he would say to the Communists. He looked into the camera and said, "I love you with all my heart, and all Christians love you. Jesus wishes you to be in heaven more than you want to go there. He wishes to forgive you more than you wish to be forgiven. He wishes to save you more than you wish to be saved." Like Joseph, who told his brothers who sold him into slavery, "You meant evil against me, but God meant it for good" (Gen. 50:20), Richard also saw the hand of God working in the shadows to deliver His people.

The story of Richard and Sabina is a reminder that God can use anyone to bring hope and healing everywhere. Richard, the once-committed atheist, became a leading voice against an atheistic system that persecuted members of Christ's body. When asked how he learned to forgive his enemies, he said, "We cannot always *feel* compassion for men, but we must *show* compassion until we feel it." After his release from prison, he had a choice to make: "You can choose to forgive and love, or hate."

Richard came to discover the ultimate reason God allowed him to be tortured for fourteen years: *his torture rescued his torturers from an eternity of torture.* It was in prison where he found the hope of salvation for the Communists. It was there he developed a sense of responsibility toward them. It was in being tortured by them that he learned to love them.

Many of his guards and interrogators became followers of Jesus Christ, and some even became pastors. Ironically, God used Richard's interrogations to extract confessions from the interrogators. Even the iron-clad hearts of the Communists opened like flowers when touched by the holy hands pierced with the iron nails of the cross.

While Richard emphasized forgiveness and loving our enemies, Sabina emphasized the fellowship of believers, particularly with our persecuted brothers and sisters in Christ. She too had an eternal perspective on suffering: "Suffering inflicted on us by the will of God does not contradict love. It is one of its methods."

• • • •

Until Jesus's return, persecution will exist. In every generation, terrorism and the persecution of our brothers and sisters in Christ have occurred. Christians continue to suffer at the hands of Communist and other dictators, as well as Islamic and Hindu extremists throughout the world. Today Christians sit alone in prisons, hungry and hurting. Yet they endure torture, beatings, and humiliation because they love God more than they fear death.

Richard said, "After more than twenty years in the underground church—first under the Nazis and afterward under the Communists—I have learned not to fear man. I don't fear that [anyone] will kill my body."

In the Muslim world, many new converts to Christ are forced to flee from their families, who disown them for turning their backs on Islam. Others die in North Korean labor camps, accused of nothing more than worshipping God. The vast majority will never have books written about them. They are nameless and faceless, known only by the God who helps them forgive their captors.

While they need our help, love, encouragement, and prayers, we need their testimonies of courage, love, and hope in the face of beatings, imprisonment, and death (see Heb. 12:1–2). We need them to challenge us to a deeper commitment to Christ and the Great Commission that He has called us to fulfill—no matter the cost (see Matt. 28:18–20).

Richard Wurmbrand wrote, "Jesus has said, 'Go and teach all the nations!' He has never said, 'Go and teach all the nations until the Iron or Bamboo Curtain and there stop!' The first Christians risked their lives preaching the gospel where it was forbidden. We have to follow their example."

The example of our persecuted brothers and sisters inspires us to do likewise. Their faith in Christ and their obedience to His Great Commission have cost them everything. What will it cost you?

NOTES

Chapter 5

1. Karl Marx and Friedrich Engels, *On Religion* (Mineola, NY: Dover, 2008), 42.

Chapter 6

1. Mahatma Gandhi, quoted in Bill Wilson, *Christianity in the Crosshairs: Real Life Solutions Discovered in the Line of Fire* (Shippensburg, PA: Destiny Image, 2004), 74.

Chapter 8

1. The Iron Guard was a fascist organization in Romania that exercised social and political influence in the country. It began in the late 1920s and ended in 1941. The group was anti-Semitic and placed a strong emphasis on nationalism. See *Encyclopedia Britannica Online*, s.v. "Iron Guard," accessed September 20, 2017, www.britannica.com/topic/Iron-Guard.

2. The source spells the country "Rumania."

3. Joseph M. Siracusa, "The Night Stalin and Churchill Divided Europe: The View from Washington," *Review of Politics* 43, no. 3 (July 1981): 381.

Chapter 9

1. "Even before Romania fell into the orbit of Nazi Germany, Romanian authorities pursued a policy of harsh, persecutory antisemitism—particularly

against Jews living in eastern borderlands, who were falsely associated with Soviet communism, and those living in Transylvania, who were identified with past Hungarian rule." "Romania," *Holocaust Encyclopedia*, United States Holocaust Memorial Museum, accessed August 15, 2017, www.ushmm.org/wlc/en/article.php?ModuleId=10005472.

Chapter 17

1. Bianca Adler's account appears in her book *Serving God in Hostile Territory* (Penrith, Australia: Stephanus, 2003).

Chapter 19

1. "A Girl Who Hated Cream Puffs," *Time*, September 20, 1948.

2. "Raining in Moscow," *Time*, June 9, 1952.

Chapter 29

1. This information on reeducation is from Stéphane Courtois et al., *The Black Book of Communism: Crimes, Terror, Repression*, trans. Jonathan Murphy and Mark Kramer (Cambridge, MA: Harvard University Press, 1999), 420–21.

Chapter 38

1. A pneumothorax is a collapsed lung caused by a collection of leaked air between the lung and the chest wall. The air pushes against the lung, causing it to collapse. See "Pneumothorax," Mayo Clinic, August 4, 2017, www.mayoclinic.org/diseases-conditions/pneumothorax/home/ovc-20179880.

Chapter 42

1. Svetlana Alliluyeva, *Twenty Letters to a Friend: A Memoir*, trans. Priscilla Johnson McMillan (New York: Harper Perennial, 2016), 10.

Chapter 59

1. Vladimir Lenin, quoted in Peter Watson, *The Age of Atheists: How We Have Sought to Live since the Death of God* (New York: Simon & Schuster, 2014), 216.

Epilogue

1. "Sanhedrin 39b," Babylonian Talmud: Tractate Sanhedrin, accessed September 27, 2017, www.halakhah.com/sanhedrin/sanhedrin_39.html#PARTb.

About The Voice of the Martyrs

The Voice of the Martyrs (VOM) is a nonprofit, interdenominational Christian missions organization dedicated to serving our persecuted family worldwide through practical and spiritual assistance and leading other members of the body of Christ into fellowship with them. VOM was founded in 1967 by Pastor Richard Wurmbrand, who was imprisoned fourteen years in Communist Romania for his faith in Christ. His wife, Sabina, was imprisoned for three years. In 1965 Richard and his family were ransomed out of Romania and established a global network of missions dedicated to assisting persecuted Christians.

Be inspired by the courageous faith of our persecuted brothers and sisters in Christ and learn ways to serve them by subscribing to VOM's free monthly newsletter. Visit us at persecution.com or call 1-800-747-0085.

Explore VOM's five main purposes and statement of faith at persecution.com/about.